I Guess I Just Wasn't Thinking
Part Four:
At the End of the Rainbow
W.K. "Jake" Wehrell

*This series is dedicated to my four savvy kids,
who in spite of my flagrant and prolonged absences,
have grown up to be loving and capable parents,
unremittingly supportive of each other, and exceptionally
successful professionals. I would have to say,
all credit to their great mom.*

Published by
AfterWit Books
afterwitbooks@gmail.com

This is a conceivable work of non-fiction. Names, characters, places, and incidents are the product of the author's imagination or his recollections. Any resemblance to actual persons, living or dead, events, or locales is possible.

ISBN: 978-0-9987632-6-2 (print)
ISBN: 978-0-9987632-7-9 (e-book)
Library of Congress Control Number: 2017936006

TABLE OF CONTENTS

Continued on next page

TABLE OF CONTENTS *Continued*

ABOUT THE SERIES

This compelling Series recounts the consequences of a rarely spoken of condition. It is essential that one understands its origin and maturation, and Roger's fruitless battle. If this is your first purchase of the Series, in lieu of just reading the brief synopses below, please consider putting the book down and availing yourself of the first three parts!

I GUESS I JUST WASN'T THINKING is a four-part series that rides the rails of high adventure—written as if it were a first-person memoir. You will be at Roger Yahnke's side in five continents while he struggles to accomplish (or even survive) a diverse assortment of challenges; in the jungle and in the desert; in the cockpit and in the bedroom. While primarily aviation-oriented, there are ample engaging but questionable exploits on terra firma. Above all it is a compelling tale of one man's battle with a personal shortcoming; an honest and revealing account of his uniquely driven life. His head-shaking array of adult activities include a proud beginning as a Marine Corps carrier-based pilot, being hired by the CIA, flying covert missions for foreign governments and other improvident deeds. These activities result in him appearing in TV documentaries, having his photo in weekly newsmagazines, and residences worldwide; including everything from a bougainvillea-draped cottage on the French Riviera to a bamboo cage in Laos.

All this transpires in the midst of frequent (and always fruitless) feminine involvements. Every contemplated activity—besides its actual merit, is heavily weighted as to its likelihood of being graced by a responsive female partner. The tale then cannot avoid the resultant plight—the skewed perceptions, flawed decisions and zealous undertakings it evokes. Roger's life is consumed by the search for that one woman—the one with the right chemistry; the one who will unlock his manhood. The impact of the series is not so much in the action, intriguing venues or colorful characters, as in its keel beam: *the torment of an unremitting incapability!* It is a frank and intimate narrative of this condition's all-embracing mastery of its host; the crushing embarrassment when once again seeing the perplexed disillusionment of another female partner. To the dismissal of all else he remains hopelessly fettered to the quest to find that one woman. Wives and girlfriends who have blamed themselves for a failed union may be greatly comforted by this surprising explanation for their husband's or boyfriend's apparent womanizing.

I GUESS I JUST WASN'T THINKING

Part One: Instead of Skipping Stones is a harmless and unlikely prelude to his future duplicitous global adventures. It is a collection of innocent and endearing admissions; a fresh and confidentially narrated pre-teen to adult memoir. The reader will be caught up in a succession of delicate, weighty, and progressively more thought-provoking scenarios. As the reader you will be unable to resist the bonding, as it is obvious Roger trusts you, is willing to confide in you and share with you his innermost hopes and fears; in fact—even ask your opinion and seek your approval. You will find yourself smiling or wincing at Roger's adolescent doubts, conclusions, and best guess responses; up to and including his almost happenstance

I Guess I Just Wasn't Thinking

Part One:
Instead of Skipping Stones

W.K. "Jake" Wehrell

choice of a life's work. The last page of each chapter will find you shaking your head, with a knowing smile or tear in your eye.

Part Two: The French Riviera, Leo, June, and Big Trouble
We join Roger some years later—cruising the Mediterranean aboard a

I Guess I Just Wasn't Thinking

Part Two:
The French Riviera, Leo, June,
and Big Trouble

W.K. "Jake" Wehrell

US Super Carrier. You will be in the cockpit with him, jaws tight and hands clamped on the armrests, during harrowing airborne operations and icy night shipboard landings. You will witness his desperate search for that one woman (convinced she must be somewhere in Europe). You'll be with him as he traipses the Continent, cavorts with rogues and royalty, and blunders into barely credible scenarios, about which much doubt should ensue. You'll spend the night with Roger in an Istanbul jail cell with a famous German actor and a storied Middle East princess, and travel with him and his new friend Leo when they journey to Bulgaria to meet with the KGB.

The cover photo is the English dancer June, who you will meet and forever admire. You may wince and condemn him, or find yourself unable not to be on his side—earnestly pulling for him in each new inscrutable endeavor. In this part, the hurt generated by his disability can be seen as the likely reason for his future risky undertakings.

Part Three: The CIA Secret Airline and Eureka, She Exists! You
will find this way more than an exposé of covert foreign operations. Diverse
and widely separated genres abound. You will
turn no page without excitement and concern.
It begins in Southeast Asia where Roger is
witness to the defilement of humanity, seeing
firsthand, the results of flawed military policy,
and most importantly—the never understood
will of the Vietnamese "silent majority;" the
real reason the War was from the onset—
unwinnable. Back in the states, divorced but
dedicated to being the best provider for his
family, he finds himself pitifully out of touch
with all that surrounds him. After a series of
endeavors—including a nausea-provoking
"pyramid sales" scheme, he retreats to more
familiar activities. You will accompany him on single-pilot ten-hour
Atlantic crossings and all-night flights across the Sahara—the sole pilot in
small aircraft that were in no way designed for either.

I Guess I Just Wasn't Thinking
Part Three:
The CIA Secret Airline
and Eureka! She Exists!
W.K. "Jake" Wehrell

United States
of America

Have a cup of tea with Judy Garland; experience a UFO sighting over
the Caspian Sea, jungle crashes and Roger's capture, and his attempted
vision-saving surgery at the Clinica Barraquer in Barcelona (where he
happens upon a private dinner with John and Yoko)! Sadly, these exploits
do not mask the deficiency that has subjugated his being. Struggling in an
ill-fitting world, he continues to seek that one historically fated-to-failure
union. Ashamed and embarrassed he sincerely and apologetically strives to
explain his life-altering condition and his otherwise inexplicable behavior.
*Readers will be surprised and gratified; unable not to leap to their feet
and applaud an entirely unexpected but spectacular turn of events at the
end of this part.*

PROLOGUE

Part Four: At the End of the Rainbow. The conclusion of Part Three found us overjoyed. After a lifelong search (replete with humiliating outcomes), Roger finally finds that one woman—who for reasons not to be understood, decisively unlocks his manhood. He is inexplicably gifted a gloriously successful sexual encounter with an intimidating and unapproachable French femme fatale.

He is now a changed being, emboldened and empowered; at last knowing the fulfillment all other men regularly experience. However, he is now faced with a daunting challenge—a dilemma for which there may be no solution: he has to find a way to construct a life with Mireille. Could it be in France? Not likely. The states? What and where? Or in spite of the life of bliss it forecasts, this is just not something Roger will be able to construct. After seeing the majestic snow-capped mountains and pastoral French countryside, and meeting her circle of well-positioned friends, he is humbled; fearful Mireille would not be able to abide hot, flat Florida and the bourgeois, geriatric Walmart throngs.

In spite of this concern, Roger investigates every possible stateside opportunity, and is hugely lucky (after his share of insufficiently respected employments) in attaining a position with a Fortune 500 company. Unfortunately, he is sabotaged by a jealous co-worker and we see him reeling in the disgrace of being "Outplaced for Management Convenience." (Fired.) This nomenclature is often a euphemism for an act so dastardly, it's better left unmentioned. It denies the bearer any chance for a respected position.

We cannot expect Roger to "change his spots" so we again find ourselves screaming instructions at him as he retreats to more familiar territory—engaging in a string of dangerous and sometimes illicit jobs (such as being hired to break an old friend out of a Colombian jail). The unfolding of momentous events in this part see Roger having the highest hopes, the gravest disappointments, and finally—to your amazement, all that one might expect, or all that one might never have expected.

Chapter One
JULY 74' VIVE LA FRANCE

Dakar to Paris

On the drive to the Dakar airport I was in the backseat between Mireille and her friend Solange; I think in shock—hardly able to believe what I was embarking upon. The effects of the last few days had eclipsed all else: my concern for my family, a possible flying job in the States; in fact any plausible future—*everything*. Since I had no "must be back" time (not yet being scheduled for another aircraft delivery) and with no idea what this stay in France would bring about, I did not make reservations for my flight back to the states. I knew of course this first trip would not be permanent. And frightfully, if I did come back to France—for good, I had no earthly idea how I would be able to provide for Mireille. Although I knew little about her domestic situation I was sure finances were not an issue. Still, knowing the crowd she travelled in; to be worthy of her; to continue to merit her love, I would have to attain some reasonably respected position, and this would be next to impossible in France. My resume showed no more than three little-sought-after skills: fighter pilot, bush pilot, and transatlantic aircraft delivery pilot; no technical specialty or business experience (not to mention not speaking the language)! Even if I could get a work visa, the chances of obtaining a respectable position was just about nil. Living and working in France was just about out of the question.

Glancing at Mireille's face afforded me momentary reassurance. Her eyes were not only still glued on me (as they had been for the last three days), they were filled with contentment that she had done the right thing and apparently, sure of it. Inside the terminal and awaiting our boarding call, I could barely keep myself from shaking my head in wonderment.

1

Mireille, her sister and her husband and her friend; they all *knew* what they were doing: *going home!* They were anxious and upbeat—nothing but smiles and idle conversation. Me? The boldest, riskiest thing I'd ever done, and with absolutely no plan. I had no idea how my accompanying her back to France would work out. The flight was called on time. We boarded and it was uneventful; without any revelations or detractions.

From Paris to a Country Village

We arrived in Paris about 3 pm, picked up our luggage, after a short search found Jacques car and were soon on A6, bound for the Lyon airport (where Mireille had left her car when she flew to Paris to join the group). I was sure Jacques must have had a death wish. For the last 45 minutes the speedometer was locked on 160 km an hour, and *our front bumper was just two meters behind the rear bumper of the car in front of us!* Luckily that car's driver never felt it necessary to tap his brakes. It was a four-hour drive and my day was just about done before we got there. Upon arrival, while retrieving our luggage, warm and robust goodbyes were exchanged (me included). In a matter of minutes Mireille and I were in her sleek BMW, out of the parking area, and on our way. My nervousness was a bit lessened from that which I felt when in the larger group. It was an interesting drive, winding our way through tiny villages with streets of uneven pavers, and so narrow they all but excluded two-way traffic. We were passing by century-old facades just a yard or two away on each side. Their parched stucco, brightly painted casement windows, shutters and flower boxes were the thing of postcards. In the declining light, everything I was taking in—on all sides, was strangely appealing. Through the last town and fifteen more minutes on a deserted unlit road, we came upon a scattering of small, interesting looking residences. As best I could translate Mireille was telling me we'd arrived; her town: St-Martin-du-lac. While she was motioning and speaking I heard the French words *maison, mere,* and *mes enfants* (all of which having been in my first few French lessons, were part of my limited vocabulary) and I concluded correctly that instead of going directly to her house, we were going to her parent's home, where likely her children were being cared for by her parents. Up till now, other than knowing she was now single, the nature of her previous marital status had not been explored, and I of course was very interested. All in good time I suspected.

A Welcomed Evening

We arrived in a remarkably preserved and maintained downtown area of the village. She pulled up in front of what appeared to be a small "mom and pop" hardware store, and pointed above it to a second floor with a balcony. I was sure she was indicating that was where her parents lived. I later learned they owned the building and the hardware store. I don't know what kind of parents' domicile I was anticipating but this was not what I would have expected. Her parents must have heard the car and before we had a chance to ring they were coming out the back door with open arms and great enthusiasm. (Their welcoming of me caused me to conclude my arriving was not a surprise.) Inside the store in improved light I was surprised to see her father's eyebrows were located and shaped just like Mireille's—that same sweeping high outward arc (that the cover models seek to have tattooed on). Even with constant concentration I was only able to translate perhaps a third of the greeting conversation. First off, the reason we were here was affirmed: Mireille's parents had been baby-sitting her two young children—who were now asleep. We were stopping here first to pick them up.

I could see it would not be a quick stop. Upstairs, in confirmation of the most appetite-inspiring aromas from the kitchen, and a well-set table boasting two bottles of Cote du Rhone, a likely delicious dinner (I could certainly use) was going to be had. Correct again, and what a late night *repas*. Mireille's mother had prepared the ultimate French beef treat of *Chateau Briande*. It was absolutely delicious, melting in my mouth; at least those few morsels that weren't washed down with the Cote du Rhone. While I still understood only a short phrase from time to time, I was gratified that when her parents appeared to be referring to me it was audibly complimentary and accompanied by an approving smile. (And I can tell you—about now this reassurance was sorely needed.) This was the best I had felt since Dakar. To this day I can visualize the candle-lit table in a warm corner of the room, the softness, the special ambiance of the occasion. Once again I was far from anyone I knew, and at a location unknown to anyone; poised as I had been many times before (like arriving at the airport in Sofia, Bulgaria) unaware of what lay ahead. I was on the brink of something that could hold a new and exciting future; complete happiness or—I had to admit, possibly a sad, brutally disappointing outcome. The meal finished and ready to leave, a sincere discussion ensued between Mireille and her parents. They were offering something she seemed reluctant to accept, but finally did: they were suggesting she return to her house with me—just the two of us, and return in the morning to pick up the kids.

Home at Mireille's

We exited the small town center, through a sparsely populated area, and then onto what would have to be called a little-used country road; paved but unlit and deserted. The drive was pretty much without conversation, which was just as good. We both were tired and it probably would have been fraught with frustrating translation efforts and errors. After about fifteen minutes Mireille evidently spied some landmark. She turned the car sharply left into a mostly hidden, narrow break in the foliage bordering the road. I assumed we had just entered a private entrance to her property. We wound our way steadily uphill—quite a distance, low brush on both sides at first, and then—best I could tell (which was pretty good under a full moon) to the left, on the other side of a well-maintained white fence, an apparently open meadow stretching for as far as I could see. We topped a final rise—now in an open flat area. Ahead and to the left I spied two large stone pillars with a decorative wrought iron gate between them. Mireille touched a button on the dash panel and the gate swung open. What I will try to describe now, was in fact—from what little exposure I had to Mireille, exactly what I would have imagined. Some distance inside the gate was what appeared to be a faux thatch-roofed Shakespearean era stone cottage; a *large* stone cottage!

She parked alongside it and opened the trunk. I leapt out and grabbed our baggage, ready to follow her into what I had no idea about. As I got closer to the home I was further impressed by a two-foot thick straw roof and the exterior walls which I could now see were not concrete or stucco. They had obviously been built by a talented stone mason, being comprised of large, odd shaped rocks—carefully fit together and mortared. Inside, after passing through an old farm-style kitchen, I was surprised to see a contrasting ultra-modern interior décor. Most walls held large and brightly-colored works of abstract art. Some walls (shockingly—the bathroom walls) were see-through, made of only slightly tinted thick acrylic. It was obvious I was in a uniquely designed, one-of-a-kind domicile.

After stowing the luggage we (for some reason) returned to the kitchen. There, standing in the middle of the room, Mireille turned to me full face, moved up against me and slid her arms around my waist. Because of a kitchen skylight, her face was well illuminated by the moonlight flooding down through it. She was looking up into my eyes with the most loving and contented look I was ever gifted to receive, and said *"Je pense qu'on devrait se marier, "* which after about a minute or two of labored translating I was startled to realize was: *I think we should get married!* While I had dared to consider this eventuality, I had not dared to imagine *she* might have also considered it. My knees went weak and my heart was racing as I digested these now-spoken words. When I had my breath I exclaimed (in the best French I could) *"What will your parents think? "* Never breaking her smile or loving look at me, she replied in French *"I already told them. "* I was speechless (and thoughtless). *She already told them!? And before she told me.* I was stunned but also grateful for her seemingly entirely confident, doubtless position on the subject. I hoped she had considered all the obstacles, but was afraid she had not. I now realized Mireille was a dichotomy; an unsure but hopeful little girl living inside that outwardly dominating and assured exterior.

As long a day as we had endured; as much that we had encountered, and the doubt and lack of any certainty I felt, we still made love—I'm sure what would be described as ultimately passionate love. Even before Mireille's warm naked body was next to me, I was once again immediately aroused and in possession of a force and capability never experienced before my first night with her; and what transpired was another in an unbroken row of tearful "bests." I was taken aback, humbled, and hugely gratified at Mireille's physicality; unrestrained expressions of pleasure and satisfaction, gasps, cries, and for some time afterward—her emotional, thankful and tearfully loving utterances. I was at a loss to understand how I—me, could possibly be responsible for her bliss-filled reactions.

Chapter Two
ALONE TOGETHER

The First Day

The morning met us with a golden sun flooding into the kitchen, where Mireille was apparently pleasantly occupied making our breakfast. As you might imagine, it was delicious (even though I never eat my eggs "sunny side up.") For a meat she had a kind of dried or smoked ham she referred to as "prosciutto," and it was very flavorful. Once again I was dismayed that even in these private one-on-one associations, she seemed to never stop looking at me with a deep affection. I can even say "gratefulness;" a seemingly demonstrative appreciation for my being with her. I was reassured—honored. Although we had few conversations relating to our life views, what comments she did make about her social engagements and business experiences, were very surprising to me. They always portrayed a striking lack of confidence and a feeling of vulnerability; in every case containing fearful premonitions of hurtful outcomes. This frightful mindset was in striking contrast to her commanding presence and caused me to feel a want—even a need, to be protective of her; provide her assurance at that moment and henceforth.

After breakfast she took me outside the house where we sat on a wood bench atop a flagstone patio, observing the whole downward sloping, grassy meadow to the west of her house. It was beautiful, going several hundred yards, with a small trickling stream in the center. And not only that, though it wasn't made clear whose they were, there were at least a dozen large and healthy cows wandering on the meadow. Behind the house, when arriving I'd seen a thick tree line marking the edge of a likely rarely entered woodland.

The Village and Her Kids

Shortly before noon we made the drive to her parent's house, which included a tour of the town in daylight. It was a seventeenth century village, immaculately preserved; most buildings at least 200 years old, and not a broken window in one of them! She made a point of taking me to the city hall, which was fully functional, every room occupied and busy with people streaming in and out. I soon understood why she had brought me there when she pointed at the four large numbers etched in the stone over the front entrance: 1592! (I remember it exactly—being precisely one hundred years after the date of Columbus's discovery of America). The town was immaculate, not a single item of trash anywhere. One could not help feeling a respect for a population that would in such a practical way honor their heritage. Arriving at her parent's house, after a very warm exchange of pleasantries we picked up her two children—both boys: Paul and Pierre. They greeted me dutifully and with no suspicion that I could discern. I don't know what Mireille had told her parents before introducing me, but once again they seemed to regard me with approval, and even affection. (Perhaps they had not yet considered I might be leaving France with their daughter!) Back at Mireille's I began attempting to make some points with her by tussling with the kids—fake wrestling and then traipsing ape-like around the room on all fours carrying them on my back—both at once. They seemed to be enjoying the activity. I wondered if they had sampled this effort by other gentlemen callers, or might I be the first.

Me and My Big Mouth

During the afternoon the kids took a nap, and it was as good a time as any for Mireille and I to try to exchange information. Sadly on my part I was at a loss for what I could say about myself and my position, and be truthful. I had already made a big mistake in Dakar: in speaking with Jacques I admitted I was a pilot, but… and here I went again, instead of owning up to flying small, puddle-jumper aircraft, when asked I said a *"sept-deux-sept."* A 727! He likely told Mireille I was an airline captain. What's worse, not only was I not an airline pilot, at the moment I didn't even have a steady job. And in addition to living paycheck to paycheck (and not knowing when the next one was coming) I was legally separated from a wife, and had four kids. I was really in trouble. I managed to—as best I could, massage or minimize each of those missspokes, harboring hopes (but no real ideas) of correcting one if not all of them. You can be assured I felt artificial and deceptive throughout, and well I should have.

Our Activities

We spent the next few days carrying out mostly the same routine, including taking at least one sight-seeing trip a day to some local natural attraction. One day—because of some not-clear business she had to take care of, we drove back down to Lyon. Mireille was dressed to the nines. She was wearing a wide-brimmed hat tipped low over her face that made her presence even more striking (and intimidating). It turned out that her business would be conducted not only in the city hall, but with the mayor himself! As soon as we entered his office he was up from behind his desk, around it, and giving Mireille an enthusiastic embrace while proclaiming his pleasure in seeing her again. This meeting resulted in the mayor inviting us to lunch—which was a two-hour (not comfortable) affair. While in Lyon, knowing my first sojourn in France could not last indefinitely and might be best to not be too long, I did it: I made reservations for my flight back to the States.

One day Mireille drove around her town introducing me to some of her lady friends, one of whom offered me a piece of peach pie. Thinking we were only passing through—stopping there momentarily, when the host asked me if I would like her to wrap it for me, I replied in French—as best I could, that doing so would be just fine. In the car Mireille let me know that in France it's very rude not to eat an offering of food when it is made—there in the house; never take it home. That incident was the sole occurrence the whole visit in which Mireille showed any disappointment with me (and of course you can imagine I hated myself for it). Our nights continued beyond my wildest dreams, and even our days (me having left a knee-abraded blood smudge on her living room rug).

One Thing I Guess I'll Have to Get Used To

Something happened more than once while walking the streets in Lyon: a tall and handsome, obviously well-placed guy would pass us on the street, and after he passed, if I snuck a look back, in every case he was turned round, his eyes fixed on Mireille. I recognized this was something I would likely have to be prepared for, as unsettling as it was.

At Last, Hearing About Mireille

In the days that followed (while asking for about one word each sentence to be repeated and quick references to my pocket dictionary) I finally learned about Mireille and her husband. I just assumed she must have been very attractive since she was a kid, surprisingly she said she was not at all popular growing up, and that her schooling was not memorable or rewarding. And then she said—as best I could translate it: *It wasn't until I met my husband did my life begin.* Of course hearing such a touching and loving comment by her I was wondering why she was no longer married to him, and where he was now. She went on as I labored to interpret her sincere efforts to explain it to me in French: He had been from the southeast of France; from a family of Italian lineage. She went to a cabinet and retuned with a photo of her husband. I was surprised to see he was not at all handsome and shorter than Mireille by several inches. Her respect for him was obvious and deep-seated. He was college-educated and skilled as both an engineer and a businessman, and became a Vice President at Peugeot (one of the largest car manufacturers in France). As best I could translate—several times asking her to speak even more slowly, she told me her husband was diagnosed with brain cancer about a year and a half ago. And six months ago—while descending that steep and winding road above Monte Carlo, had gone off it and over a cliff, *and was killed in the crash!* The insurance company couldn't prove whether it was because he knew he was terminal and had committed suicide, or if it was because he had a seizure and lost control of the vehicle. Along with Peugeot, Mireille was the recipient of a very large settlement (though I could not accurately translate the amount of Francs). Not sure if this was their house together, or she used some of the death insurance money to build it.

Taking Stock of Our Situation

It was the night before my departure. All had gone as well, or maybe even better than I could have anticipated. Unfortunately—or probably as could have been expected, no definitive plans were made for our future (not that they weren't on both our minds). I assured her I would be back soon; as soon as I had taken care of a few things in the States. (*What* few things I had no idea.) I had not yet come out and asked her if she would consider leaving France to live with me in the States. Based on what I had seen here: the beautiful countryside, her historic town, her home, her closeness to her parents, her circle of affluent and sophisticated friends, I didn't have the nerve to even suggest it. And even if so, the chances of me getting a good flying job in Florida (or anywhere stateside) were not great. If I was lucky enough to secure one and she agreed to come to Florida, the absence of any elevation (even the slightest mountainous area), certainly no historic villages, and the aging population of Florida residents (nothing but silver and blue-hairs and aluminum walkers everywhere) she would undoubtedly undergo a cultural shock that could be fatal to our relationship. I could not envision her feeling at all comfortable with that lifestyle, and the tropical climate—either hot or sweltering hot. That night, my mind tired, in fact worn raw from considering "what ifs" I escorted Mireille to the bedroom, and yes, in spite of all my worries, it was another soul-altering experience.

Leaving France

The flight would depart from Lyon at 1 p.m. and the drive was only about thirty minutes, so we weren't in a rush and had a family breakfast outdoors—on a picnic table on that same flagstone patio. No matter where in France you take the morning meal, the coffee and bread—any kind of bread, is the best in the world. Mireille had bought croissants that we ate, warmed and with cold butter and black cherry preserves. (I learned a new word for jam—*confiture.)* We were in the car about 11, dropped the boys off at her parents, and were on the regretful last leg of the visit, with little or no conversation.

In the terminal we found a small table, ordered two coffees, and prepared to have our last closeness for who knew how long. Holding hands across the table, a warm and loving, peaceful conversation ensued. With only 15 minutes before my flight would be called, somehow—from one of us, the subject of a permanent union came up: our marriage. Still looking at me with those loving eyes, she said what I worked out to be, *"Roger, there is something I must tell you."* I was not anticipating the discussion to suddenly change to one of caution or confession. What could it be? I at least knew it was going to be something she thought was very important, as she was looking at me with an expression I had not yet observed. I was worried—soon to be justifiably worried. I cannot adequately express my state after hearing the next words to come out of Mireille's mouth, which ended with *"avec un seul homme."* Best I could translate she had just told me *that she didn't think she could live with just one man!* I could not have been more wounded if I had taken a spear through my heart. In just two seconds my mood plummeted to a sickening deflation, and cruelly, at last—an understanding of Mireille's unbridled pleasure during sex. It *wasn't* me, or "us." I had no choice but to conclude I had stumbled upon a female afflicted with nymphomania. It was a satisfaction she needed, and now I think she was telling me, she needed to be *with varied partners*. It seemed clear to me she was giving me advance warning that for her, it would be an "open" marriage. I may never have been so ill.

My Retreat, an Escape

I have no recollection of the remarks that followed; hers or mine. Nor can I remember the boarding call, my path to the gate or passing through the jet way. The first thing I remember is being in the seat, head back, eyes closed, numb to the core—all but dead. Never in my life had I ever been more happy and then more critically let down; more devastated and saddled with a dire necessity to discard, forget, never ever to reflect on something again. I had to blanch my mind of the many beautiful expectations that had elevated my being for the last two weeks. My memory bank then being erased (assuming that would be possible), I would have to embark on a radically different future path than the one I had been imagining up till an hour ago. This was going to involve a change in attitude and objectives like none other before. I had been living in a now obliterated dream.

Chapter Three
BACK IN THE STATES AND FACING REALITY

The First Couple Weeks

The flight to Florida was via New York. No matter how I tried to think of something—anything else, for ten hours those last words in the Paris airport haunted me. Even as I disembarked in Fort Myer, I could think of nothing else. Mechanically I hailed a cab and was on my way to the safety of my parent's home. The last year's aviation jobs having had me out of the state or even out of the country half of each month, it made sense (and saved money) to not get an apartment; just live with my folks until I secured a permanent position—wherever that would be. My current plan was to hide out here in Fort Myers until my heart had healed (if that would ever occur) and until I got a better picture of employment opportunities in the country. This location would also enable me to just drive across the state to visit the kids, which I did the first week—for the whole week (once again staying in a local motel). The times we had together were better than I could have hoped for (as long as I kept my thoughts on this side of the Atlantic). I learned all about their recent activities, new friends and hobbies—mostly surfing, but also another dozen pastimes. There were no cell phones in 1974 and Mireille didn't have my folks' address or phone number, so I didn't have to worry about her contacting me—she couldn't (whether or not she'd even try). And I knew that if I didn't want to someday be hurt very very badly, I must realize and accept that it was over; just dismiss any temptation to contact her. (I did have her phone number.) Although I had experienced a first and life-changing experience with her, I was now so wounded, I was unsure if I would ever try again. So now, to the task at hand: try to forget Mireille and devote all my thoughts and efforts to finding work!

At Last, a Mature and Practical Thought

Finally—instead of as usual just thinking two weeks or a month ahead, I at last looked far enough ahead to realize, irrespective of how much money I had made (processed) I had—now, no savings, and what's worse: *no retirement coming*! My best chance for a retirement income was to add another ten years to my Marine Corps service; *thus achieving the required twenty years to be eligible for a government retirement.* But what government service could I now become a part of? With only an aviation background I concluded my best opportunities would be with the Federal Aviation Agency. I inquired and received a packet (a *big* packet) of forms to fill out to apply for a pilot's job with the FAA. I was floored as I leafed through at least ten almost absurdly detailed forms to fill out. Usually when applying for a flying job, they want to know three things: what *types* of airplanes have you flown, how many total *hours* do you have, and, what *kind* of flying have you done. However, these forms were ridiculous! I couldn't imagine any applicant after looking at them, not just throwing them in the trash; deciding no job was worth so much trouble.

I decided that being the case, if I did labor through the process I'd probably be one of very few to do so—thus increasing my chances to be hired. The information they wanted was so nonsensically detailed that it took real motivation to fill it all in. Many of the figures they wanted, *no one* would have kept records for! (Meaning for at least a third of the blanks I had to just make an educated guess.) As a starter, they not only wanted to know how much flight time you had, but how much flight time you had in single-engine aircraft, how much flight time you had in two-engine aircraft, how much flight time you had in multi-engine aircraft, how much of this flight time was in nose-wheel aircraft, how much of this flight time was in tailwheel aircraft, and then, and get this, of all those listed hours in each of those type aircraft, how much of it was flown during the day, how much was flown at night, how much was flown under *actual* "instrument" conditions, and how much was flown under *simulated* "instrument" conditions. For every airplane! It took me a week, but I completed the forms and mailed them in. I was surprised a week later to actually get a response from them, indicating they had received my application.

Too-Dangerous Work Again

On my present job search: a break! Several weeks later while sitting in the doldrums of no leads or even ideas, I received a phone call from Jim

I GUESS I JUST WASN'T THINKING

Ryan, the one-legged guy that was my boss at Air America in Laos. (I had no idea how he knew I was staying with my folks.) He was offering me a temporary job: remember that turbo prop aircraft with the 900-round-per-minute Gatling gun—the Helio Stallion? The one I had flown in Cambodia with LJ Broussard? Well he wanted to know if I would be interested in picking up two of them in Montreal to deliver to Angola on the southwest coast of Africa. (I had to check a map to find its exact location—nestled between The Democratic Republic of the Congo to the north and Nambia to the south). The agency must have picked me because of my previous experience in this tricky aircraft, and because of my many transatlantic aircraft deliveries. Recently, reflecting on the danger of those transatlantic flights in single-engine aircraft, and being a little smarter, I finally admitted it was stupid—more than that, to engage in this type work; an engine failure anywhere on crossing would be certain death—you would *never* be found! I was thusly reluctant to put myself in that position again. However, two trips would net me four months' worth of alimony and child support payments.

Jim gave me a week to come to a decision. And knowing me—as you might expect, seven days later when he called—though I'd thought about it day and night, *I still had not come to a decision!* It was only on the phone call, and only when he asked the direct question, that I said "yes" (though I don't know how or why). The next week, the contract was signed, the advance payment wired, and some amplifying information received: *Angola was in the throes of a revolution!* Our CIA was training and arming the National Union for the Total Independence of Angola (UNITA), who were waging a fierce guerilla war against the Soviet-supported, People's Movement for the Liberation of Angola (MPLA), and these two aircraft would be the start of UNITA's air force! I packed all my maps and survival gear, which after the latest news included my Walther 9mm PPK, and took a commercial flight to Montreal. (Hard to believe now, but back then you could board an airline while packing a piece!) There I met my contact who filled me in on a few more details: Unfortunately, the airplanes were not fitted with auxiliary fuel tanks, and there was no way to deliver an airplane of this limited fuel capacity directly to southwest Africa. It was going to be necessary to take my old northern Atlantic route from Gander to Shannon, Ireland, and then turn south. (I guess they knew that since the planes were stationed here in Canada.) From Europe it would be south across the Med and then about 3,000 miles through multiple African countries, to Luanda, Angola, where I would deliver the aircraft.

As I had done on previous crossings, I took off from Gander at about 4 in the morning; an hour later being blinded by the rising sun reflecting off the ocean and piercing the arc of my prop. Nine more hours, and I don't think I stopped praying or uncrossed my fingers until I was within engine-out gliding distance of Shannon—which occurred about 6 p.m. Ireland time. Of course the Gatling gun had been removed and was being flown over on a Southern Air C-130 as part of an associated clandestine cargo trip out of Miami. In fact I didn't know why they weren't doing the same thing with the whole airplane. (I was pretty sure with the wings and tail surfaces removed it could fit in a C-130.) In any case, from Shannon it would be six more flights (days) to my destination; first to Nice, France, then markedly substandard airfields in Morocco, Mauritania, The Ivory Coast, Cameroon, and finally Angola. Each landing and refueling presented its own hardships (similar to when I delivered those W.H.O. planes across the Sahara). Again I was repeatedly told there was no gas, or a special additional payment (and four-hour wait) to get the fuel I needed from some restricted area, and that they couldn't accept a credit card! And then to be sure there were no contaminants in that stored old fuel, I had to wait another hour and then drain and inspect at least a gallon out of the low-point sumps.

I also had my share of administrative obstacles getting through immigration and customs—in fact spent the entire night in jail in Mauritania. And of course there were the bribe payments to deal with— usually at least two if not three at each stop. In the Cameroon airport while outside on the curb waiting for a cab to town, I noticed some suspicious-looking characters observing me as possible prey once I'd cleared the airport property; so I walked back in the terminal and decided to just sleep in the airplane. A trip the length of the African continent is a real ordeal, especially since I had no government sponsorship. (No phoning up the embassy. I was completely on my own.) At least I was a US citizen—that helped once. Finally reached Luanda. While the country was at war my arrival went smoothly, minus the fact no one was in the tower, so there was no control of inbound aircraft. You always land into the wind, so I picked the proper runway (the one that was into the wind). On my first approach, just before touching down, looking towards the far end of the runway *I saw another plane landing (downwind—the wrong way) and heading right at me*. I added power, aborted my landing, flew right over top of him and

15

took it around for another try. Found the pilot on the ramp—a Cuban pilot who apologized to me in his best English. He was delivering a Russian YAK-52 to the "bad guys." (The Russians again.) Instead of my usual routine of faring for myself, here I was met by Agency guys who took me to their compound (where I met a guy I worked with in Laos).

Delivering the second aircraft was just more of the same. First as I churned my way nine hours across the deserted Atlantic, and then endured the grilling and impositions of transiting five third world countries, I finally swore to never do it again. And I found out why they hired me to ferry the planes to Angola (instead of shipping them aboard a C-130). After dropping off the second plane, the CIA station manager made a serious plea for me to stay and train some new Helio Stallion pilots. They had let me ferry the aircraft over to re-familiarize myself with the plane and expose me to the project, *in hopes they could talk me into joining it!*

Searching for a USA Flying Position

Back at my folks' house, only interrupted by weekend trips across the state to visit my kids, I kept my nose to the grindstone trying to locate a decent flying position. Unfortunately, at my age, with a one-eyed license, and no civilian jet time, I had zero chances to get on with the airlines. There were only two kinds of flying jobs (and not very respected) that I could get: (1) as an on-call pilot for some fledgling (shoestring) charter company still using propeller aircraft, or (2) better but not good—flying for some small corporation that also still used propeller aircraft to fly their executives back and forth between their out-of-state production sites. I had sent out over 30 résumés to this last type employer, but didn't receive a single response. One reason: it was January 1975—a recession was upon us and aviation activity had slowed to a standstill. Charter companies and the smaller corporations were selling their aircraft. I spent some time each week searching the classified section of the most popular aviation newsletter—Trade-A-Plane. One week I saw an ad from a small printing company in New York City. They were looking for a pilot to fly their executives back and forth from there to Philadelphia, Baltimore, and a couple other out-of-state locations. The aircraft was a two-engine propeller plane manufactured by Beechcraft, called the "Baron." It wasn't a jet and it was old but, it had been a sought-after prop plane in its day, with a not-too-scary safety record.

Got it! A Corporate Flying Job

I had mixed emotions when after one phone call I was hired. I had the job, but not sure I wanted it. Remember my previous embattled employment with Banner Flight up there in Newburgh, NY? After having lived on the Bahnhofstrasse in Zurich, I encountered a crushing cultural shock interfacing with the impoverished local Kmart-population. (As you may recall, only being able to escape when Banner went bankrupt.) I was having a hard time envisioning a permanent domicile back in the Northeast. Here in the New York metro area I'd not have a single friend and I'd experience the same impersonal rush- rush, two hour traffic jams, sleet, snow, and icy roads (not to mention being a thousand miles from my kids). But I needed an income. My folks weren't making me pay rent, but I had the support payments for Sara and the kids, plus an unexpected big expense on the Hobe Sound house (a roof repair, and it was tile—over $2,000). I packed a couple suitcases, said goodbye to my folks and left for the "Big Apple."

My New Company

After an hour of expected formalities I was driven out to the La Guardia airport and introduced to my new plane—the Baron. It was at least out of the weather, but parked in a metal building sorely in need of repair. Except for where the puddles of oil and hydraulic fluid were, the floor was coated with dust and grime—not a reassuring sight. When I asked they informed me there was no Chief Pilot—the guy who would have trained me in the Baron. (I had not confessed I had never been in a Baron—let alone flown one.) In fact there was no other pilot, not even a co-pilot. The Baron was certified to be flown by a single-pilot, although for safety reasons the FAA discouraged it. In any case none were here and I was the whole flight department. Normally—besides having two flight crews for each airplane, most if not all corporations have at least two certified mechanics for each aircraft. They are responsible for all the inspections and repairs on the aircraft. This company didn't have a single mechanic. They just contracted with some mechanic on the airport to stop in and take care of things. Not good. The flight department was not striking me as being properly organized or staffed, and I was already having a hard time viewing it as a place I could stay. Rather than even look for an apartment I got the cheapest monthly-rate motel room I could find within ten miles of La Guardia airport. It would have been cheaper in Jersey, but involve morning rushes over the George Washington Bridge or through the tunnels. I was a loner here in the Big Apple. Although I must admit I had never seen so many well made-up shapely young working women; couldn't help from time to time wondering if one of them could possibly be another Mireille. However with my deficiency and the always shameful finalities, I was afraid to think of even trying again.

My New Aircraft

Each aircraft has a Handbook of Maintenance Instructions that lists the periodic inspections that must be done on that aircraft. It also has a Maintenance Logbook in which are recorded the date and aircraft hours flown when those inspections were done, and the signature of the person doing them. After locating it I was surprised to see the last two inspections had never been done. I brought this to the attention of who I thought was my supervisor, and told him to call me when the missed inspections were accomplished (by whoever they called to do them). Not having ever flown the aircraft and not knowing any of the systems or procedures or critical airspeeds, I spent the first four days in the motel attempting to memorize the entire Baron Flight Manual. I went over all the critical airspeeds, every system and recited the emergency procedures out loud, until they were (hopefully) set in my mind.

When I was informed the inspections were completed, I used the required "Post-Inspection Test Flight" as my own "Initial-Training" flight; to see how much I had learned (without any passengers to notice my hesitancies). System malfunctions are often caused by the tinkering around inside during an inspection, so piloting an airplane after an inspection one must be very careful. Before even starting the engine I found six discrepancies. Getting Air Traffic Control approval of a local flight in the busy New York area is not easy, but I ultimately succeeded. Scared myself to death a half dozen times but think I mastered the aircraft. Minus the discrepancies I found on my preflight inspection, an imbalance between control forces required in flight, and one—perhaps two, falsely-reading engine instruments, I believed my Baron it was generally airworthy.

My First Scheduled Trip

They told me to be at La Guardia in the morning to take two salesmen to Philadelphia; takeoff scheduled for 7 a.m. I arrived at 6 (meaning a 5 o'clock get-up). I was understandably becoming a little antsy when no one had arrived by 9. Called the office and was told the passengers were on the way. They seemed like good guys but didn't arrive until 11. We arrived at a small airport south of Philly shortly after noon. They said they only had a couple hours work at the plant and should be back by four. For lunch I spied a small "greasy spoon" restaurant on the other side of the airport; walked all the way around to it (about a mile and a half) only to find it was closed for renovations. Returned to the aircraft, sat in one of the passenger seats, closed the door, and hoped I could doze for three hours. Four o'clock came and went; then five, six, seven, and eight o'clock—with no passengers. I had filed and then cancelled, three flight plans. I'd now been on the job for fifteen hours! (By FAA federal regulations, a pilot's duty day cannot exceed twelve hours.) They didn't arrive till after ten! I'm tired as hell and it's pitch black. It wasn't hard to tell they'd been drinking and didn't have a care in the world, while I was heading back into the most congested airspace in the world on my first night flight in the Baron. Got home at midnight; a nineteen hour day. I was to find this to be a normal day for a Hanover Publications pilot. (Maybe this was why the previous pilot quit.) This daily routine, me the only pilot, and no assigned maintenance personnel, caused me a couple months later, to give them a two week notice and return to Fort Myers.

Oh No

If you can believe this, after six months ago having spent a week filling out that absurd flying job application for the FAA, I received the packet of forms again, but this time updated; revised with even more information required. Discouraging as this was, I wasn't going to quit now. I spent another three or four days filling out the same seemingly unending list of blanks. (And this time it was even more difficult, because I had to try to remember the numbers I had just guessed at on the previous submission.)

At Last, an Employment Revelation

I realized (at last) two things: First: Although the job in New York was the pits, my best chance rested with an upgraded version of this type employment; *getting a larger, more financially stable, respected corporation to hire me.* Second: Any corporation as described above—that could afford

a well-staffed flight department, would be operating *jet aircraft*. My problem: with zero civilian jet experience (just military fighter planes that no one cared about), I would never be hired by any big corporation such as IBM, or Pepsi Cola, or any one of the other New York Stock Exchange corporations. They were operating jets; Lear Jets, Citations, Falcons, Gulf Streams, and other sleek corporate jets. Though I had never stopped to think about it, I still was qualified for schooling under the GI Bill. Perhaps I could use it to pay for some civilian jet training, and add a huge plus to my resume. I checked and discovered the type of jet most in use—by far, was the *Learjet*.

Chapter Four
GETTING A JET RATING, SOMEONE NEW, AND MOM

Upgrading My Aviation Resumé

I had concluded the one thing essential to getting a good corporate flying job was to get a jet rating. And since there were more Lear Jets flying than any other type of corporate jet, it probably should be a *Learjet* rating. To fly an airplane over 12,500 pounds, you don't just need to have a pilot's license, you need to have an FAA *"Type"* rating in that particular type aircraft. I located a Learjet training company in Grand Rapids, Michigan that accepted payment via the GI Bill. I accomplished the necessary paper work to get myself approved and enrolled. Everyone there was courteous and efficient and I was put on the training schedule. The training program consisted of just six flights (which surprised me). This was a transonic, complicated, difficult-to-handle jet. I was wondering how could anyone merit a "Type Rating" in it after just nine flight hours? At the end of my first training flight I was sweat-drenched, hair plastered to my forehead, calves shaking, and dumbfounded as to how I would ever master this rocket. On takeoff I was going through 2,000 feet before I knew it or had raised the landing gear! Wow. One good thing: the Lear they were using was an older (less expensive) model that did not have many updated systems now in later models. In fact the instructors told us if we could handle this old one, we would be able to handle any Lear. A week later, as mystified about it as anyone, I was presented with my Learjet Type Rating (which I personally did not think I came close to deserving).

My First Flight as a Crewmember

One of the reasons I chose the company in Grand Rapids was because they promised that after you got your rating—before you left the area, they would schedule you as copilot on an actual charter flight, so you could observe an experienced captain managing a flight. Two days later they told me to be on their ramp at the airport at 6 am, for a 07:00 takeoff—*my first flight as an actual crewmember!* I found the plane, but the captain had not yet arrived. It was still before sunrise, the ramp was dark and abandoned, minus one young kid sitting on a nearby curb. Twenty minutes later—still no captain. While I'm standing by the airplane the kid comes up to me and says, "Excuse me sir, I'm supposed to be the copilot on this flight, are you the captain? *Holy Shit! Me? I'm the captain?* Five minutes later, who arrives but our passenger, Mick Jagger, and I had no choice but to act like I knew what I was doing, and take him to Las Vegas!

Now, to Put My New Rating to Good Use

Once back in Florida I was musing about my new type-rating, but it was hard to imagine that a barely qualified neophyte Lear pilot like me could be considered for employment by a respected Fortune 500 company. Still, I sent out about 25 résumés to high-profile corporations, and personally visited a couple dozen corporate flight departments that stationed their Lears at Florida airports. After a few weeks and having not received a single affirmative response, I saw an advertisement by a woman who was a "head hunter" for companies that were looking to add a pilot to their flight department. What could I lose, may as well register with her. I made a trip to her New Orleans office, producing all my aviation records, relaying a complete history of my employment, taking a written test, and sitting through a one-hour interview. Wasn't at all sure, but hoped it would turn out to be worth it.

Was it?! Two weeks later—perhaps good news: she contacted me and wanted another interview. I flew back to New Orleans and sat with her again. This time she wanted to know if I felt comfortable and ready to go in the Lear, more about my Spanish and French language capabilities, and also more detailed information about my transoceanic flights. I think it went well, and I'd like to say she looked satisfied. A week later I get a call from her, informing me to call a gentleman named Cliff Ward at 316-479-0035. I couldn't pry any details out of her, just that I should make the call straightaway. Of course I did, and you could have knocked me over with a feather! Cliff was the Chief Pilot for Learjet in Wichita, Kansas; *the world's largest and most prominent manufacturer of corporate jets!* They had hired Ms. Harwood to search for a pilot with three qualifications: (1) A Learjet rating, (2) Both Spanish and French language capability, and (3) Experience delivering aircraft transoceanic. While I had very little of any of those capabilities (especially Lear time), evidently *I was the only guy who had all three!* I was sent tickets to Wichita and flew there for an interview. Cliff told me they were making lots of sales of their new Lear 35 model to countries and businesses in South America and Europe, and therefore needed someone with my specific qualifications. Can you believe that? My decision to get a Learjet rating, my years of studying Spanish and French before turning out the light, and that crazy time ferrying aircraft from Gander to Shannon. They all paid off! *Who'd a thunk it?* Cliff was an okay guy, but not a personable or warm and fuzzy type of guy, so at the end of our time together I wasn't sure how it went. It must've gone well. I was hired, rented a U-Haul trailer, loaded it, and drove to Wichita. This time actually believing I was possibly—for the first time in my life, going to have a permanent and respectable job as an esteemed "factory pilot." *(What would Mireille think now?)*

A Short Update on my Sex Life

Since returning to the states—post Mireille, with whom I had that inexplicable, dominating performance—finding myself with a capability the likes of which I had never come close to experiencing. I had been euphoric seeing her display the bodily actions and cry out claims of ecstatic joy. After my years of failed attempts, with so many other women, I had little hope of repeating it with another female candidate. Only in the last two years, with two or three women did I have the nerve to let the relationship develop to where I found myself in her bedroom (alas to no avail). As I feared (now confirmed) while Mireille had turned my life around by unlocking my manhood; *it was only with her!* She had not cured my disability; she had not made me universally capable; not by a long shot (as the couple women mentioned above would surely testify). I cannot describe the overwhelming humiliation I felt when each time I was unable to perform. After months of sleepless nights and pondering my dilemma, I was on the verge of resigning myself to the fact that a successful sexual encounter was something that was not destined to occur in my lifetime.

Elsa

One night—returning to my folks' home, I was travelling through a sparsely populated portion of a bordering town, and encountered a strange sight. I drove past a three-story brick building that looked like a rehab center or assisted living facility, or white-collar detention center; the grounds around it were surrounded by a high chain link fences and were brightly floodlit by lights mounted atop tall stanchions. There was only one entry/exit gate. On the steps just on this side of the gate, brightly illuminated by the spotlight above her, was a young woman apparently awaiting the arrival of someone. From the windows on the upper floors of the building, people were looking down at her and making remarks that I could not hear well enough to understand. It was sufficiently concerning to me that I circled the block and made another pass by; still the same. I felt a compassion for the woman waiting—a need to perhaps somehow assist her. Another circle of the block; this time doing a U-turn so as to pass by on the same side of the street as she was on. I slowed, stopped, and asked if she needed to be taken anywhere. At first she didn't answer; looked interested, but reluctant. Finally, after repeating my offer she stood up and came to the car. I told her I'd be glad to take her wherever she was going. Cautiously she got in the car and told me she needed to be taken to an address in Lehigh Acres, not too far from my destination.

The Drive to Her House

She explained a gentleman friend was supposed to pick her up, but something must have gone wrong. I asked her what kind of place that had been. She answered it was a *mental hospital.* Somewhat shocked by her direct answer and stumbling for an appropriate comment or next question, I foolishly asked, "And why were you there?" She put an index finger to her temple and said, "Cuckoo." I thought that was a pretty good answer, and may have shown she had a sense of humor, but also could have set me to more serious thoughts. Besides learning that she was divorced with two children (who were presently being watched by her parents in North Fort Myers) there was not much more conversation. When we arrived at her small house, and I was ready to let her off and pull away, she surprised me by asking if I wanted to come in for a while and see if we could find an "oldie but goody" film on TV. It wasn't until then that we introduced ourselves. Her name was Elsa. In accepting her offer to come in at this late hour, I was perhaps setting myself up for another humiliating sexual encounter.

Once Inside

Walking in, and able to study her preceding me, I noticed (unfortunately) that she was at least an inch or two taller than me; likely of Scandinavian descent—tall, blonde, and with a nice tan. On questioning her she said her mother was born in Sweden. We did find an "oldie but goody"—a depressing movie with Kirk Douglas. I was in an easy chair and she was lying on the couch. Before the movie was finished she fell asleep. I didn't know whether to disturb her, say goodnight and leave, or let her sleep and just slip out. Whilst mulling this over she wakes up and starts into her bedroom, *with nary a word to me.* I wasn't sure if she was just asleep on her feet, the night was finished, or the lack of a goodbye meant she was inviting me to follow her. About five minutes later she called out, "Are you going to kiss me goodnight?" Still unsure of the intended outcome I went into her bedroom (which appeared to originally have been the garage). I leaned over the bed and kissed her goodnight, which answered my question. It was such that I knew she expected more closeness.

With the highest of hopes (and the same morbid fear) I disrobed and joined her in bed. *A partial miracle occurred*: not at first, not like Mireille, but stroking her skin was unusually arousing. Her skin was especially smooth, in fact, silky. *Her skin had that chemistry!* For the first time in a too-long time I believed I might soon be ready and armed; certainly not like with Mireille, but at least with a potential capability. *Hallelujah!* I *was* successful and it appeared provided satisfaction for her. I was to some extent—for the first time since France, able to feel the satisfaction of having apparently, sufficiently-well, carried out what other men thought nothing of. As I was leaving she got out of bed, put on a robe and escorted me to the door and then to my car. I noticed that her mail box had been knocked over and was lying on its side, in need of a new post. Good guy that I am, I stooped over and put it in the trunk of my newer 69 Mustang, telling her that I'd bring it back when I had it fixed (thus unknowingly or otherwise, confirming a second meeting).

Two Days Later

Saturday morning about 9 am I returned with the repaired mail box. When I arrived I saw Elsa's oldest daughter—Iris (age 13) nicely dressed in a plaid skirt and white blouse, standing on the front stoop. She spied me and waved. I took out the fixed mail box, laid it by the curb and walked to the front door. As I got closer to Iris I could see she was excited—smiling from ear to ear and in a highly anticipatory mood. "Roger, Roger, my dad's coming today. He's going to take me shopping and then we're going to have lunch together, and then we're going to go to the Shell Factory!" I responded that was great, and made a mental note to see if Elsa would like to fill me in on Iris's dad—who I suspected was Elsa's first husband.

Elsa greeted me at the door but not with much fanfare (a little disappointing to me in view of our evening together and me having taken her mailbox to fix). Elsa said she had to go to her place of employment (she was an administrative assistant at the nearby headquarters of a large insurance company) and then do some grocery shopping. She asked me if I'd like to come along. *Well that's something*, and I agreed. On the way to Publix she asked if we might stop in McDonalds and have a small breakfast. Being a big spender I took her to Denny's. At our table, after ordering she took out an 11x18 legal pad with her shopping list. Down the left side of the pad she had written the next 30 evening meals she would make for the girls, and down the right side of the pad, a list (aisle by aisle) of all the foodstuffs she would need to buy to make the planned menus for the month. I was impressed and had to admire such planning. (She'd even brought a cooler along in which to put all the frozen stuff and perishables.)

After her errands were accomplished we drove to the beach and took a stroll on the boardwalk. We passed a pleasant afternoon, in which I learned a lot. Iris's father had been a one-time center-fielder on a New York Yankee farm team—a man's man at 6 feet 6, but with a fault of spending most nights with the guys at the local gin mill in their Long Island neighborhood. After his short baseball career, he never was able to get or hold a full time job. Sometime after Iris was born, they divorced. Her second child Marisa was born out of a second marriage—with a Puerto Rican guy, who Elsa said ran away to Brazil with his secretary when Marisa was 8, *and never contacted her or Marisa again!* Later in the afternoon we decided to stay at the beach and have a seafood dinner. Elsa phoned home and got the okay, and we spent another two hours together.

We returned home about 8 pm, and get this: Iris was still standing on the front stoop, *still waiting for her dad.* Her expression was crushing. And as you might imagine—my heart went out to her. Because of my huge respect for how Elsa was managing her life—owning her own tiny home, being steadily employed, managing her limited finances, and raising two girls, both of whose fathers had abandoned them personally and financially, out of respect for her I was slipping into a possibly more serious relationship;

too soon and likely ill-advised. I must admit, in addition to my respect for her, at this time in my life—I did have an 'at least passable' success in bed with her. The rarity (I should say—invariable absence) of this outcome strongly weighted my consideration. Who knows, it could well be—no matter how many times I tried, possibly be the last time it would occur, or even the last time I would be able to muster the courage to try.

A Bit about My Loving Parents and Especially Mom

I hope you remember my Mom from Part One. Remember? The disaster when I was in Woolworth's trying to buy her a birthday present—those sleek tan leather gloves; and then that tall woman sabotaged the whole thing. And boy was Mom smart! Everyone knew it. In high school she won a nation-wide competition in writing a thesis on George Washington, and then upon graduation receiving a scholarship to Vassar College (the most prestigious women's college in the country). Her first job was with the *Bergen Evening News*—north Jersey's most prestigious daily paper. In just a few years she was promoted to Editor-In-Chief! Later, General Mills hired her to be the actual voice behind their iconic "Betty Crocker" spokesperson image. I always was a bit befuddled as to how and why she ended up married to my father; a *mashed potatoes and gravy* high school dropout; maybe because he was so motivated and such a good worker. In 1933 he owned a 1931 open Ford roadster (that he had bought—cash)! Or maybe because he could play the harmonica and was always the life of the party. He was some guy; more on him later.

As adults, my brother and sister (Hank and Laura) both *serious* born-again Christians, felt it necessary to believe that—like them, Mom was a God-fearing, Bible-reading Christian. But I well remember as a tyke, how when tucking me in at night, she would whisper in my ear, "*God is just love and he lives in your heart.*" (And I never saw her reading the Bible.) Mom did have one problem, one big problem—her heart. She had her first heart attack when she was only 48! And sadly, as the years came she had another and then another. In spite of these later health problems, both my Mom and Dad were always there for us kids. *It was late in life that I recognized and could appreciate how lucky I was to be born of these parents.*

Once Dad retired they decided to leave the Jersey sleet and snow and move to Florida, choosing the town of Fort Myers on the west coast. They stayed in the work force for the next five or so years, managing a hotel on the prestigious Estero Blvd. Compared to other establishments on "Hotel Row" it was by far the least glamorous—just a small, homey, three-story, wood-sided building, catering to the same visitors each year. Mom was overly dedicated to keeping it 100% occupied every week—the whole season. Dad recognized this constant goal of hers and the work it took, was not good for her heart. She finally had another more serious attack. Dad of course again called 911, the EMT's came, used the paddles (breaking her collar bone), put her in the ambulance. She spent almost a week in bed getting her strength back, but not in that part of her heart muscle that was permanently damaged.

That was it, Dad put his foot down. They quit managing the hotel and bought a small one-story, pastel-colored, concrete-block home. There they spent each afternoon in their famous "Florida Room" (a glassed-in sun-drenched back porch). When I came back—even after short trips, they always appeared thrilled to see me. Their appreciation of my presence was humbling, and I berated myself for in the past few years—the infrequency of which I gave them this opportunity. No two ways about it, it was just a lack of consideration on my part; a sad but accurate realization of the extent of my preoccupation with my own life—discounting other worthy considerations, was deservedly embarrassing.

Chapter Five
1976 AND I GOT IT MADE (FINALLY)

Welcome to the Midwest

I had seen Wichita two years ago when picking up those training aircraft for the Iranian Air Force. But those stays were just one or two-days. Now it could be an indefinite domicile, perhaps even my permanent, final hometown. (Mixed emotions on that one—being a thousand miles from the kids.) Wichita was ground zero for our country's civilian aviation industry; not only Learjet, but the headquarters and factories for Beechcraft and Cessna as well. I was nervous but excited, almost having to "pinch myself" realizing at long last I really would have a respectable, in fact—prestigious, flying position. I rented an apartment easily; a lot of recently built and inexpensive ones were available. Coming from Florida, a 12-month-a-year outdoor activity state where most the population was lean, here in Wichita—with much of the year prohibiting outdoor activity, I noticed a large percentage of overweight people, particularly women. (And I never saw so many kids with both braces and glasses!)

A Possible Roommate

Believe it or not, Elsa and I had discussed her coming out to visit me, *or even the possibility of getting married*; the thought of which—based on my track record (and hers) was real scary. Moreover, although I didn't mention it, she had admitted to me that she was and had been for quite some time—suffering with an acute bipolar illness for which she was forced to take strong medication. Perhaps because of this and her track record, she had confessed—almost insisted, that she believed she was "un-marriable."

29

My Job

I met with Cliff and learned I was going to be assigned to the "Flight Demonstration Department" of which he was the Chief Pilot. There were about a dozen pilots assigned. I met them all and in general they appeared to be a normal, friendly and accepting group. The primary mission of the department was demonstrating the aircraft and its capabilities to prospective purchases—usually Fortune 500, New York Stock Exchange-listed companies. I would do some of that, although my primary assignment remained demonstrating Learjets to foreign-language speaking purchasers from South America and other countries. After they had purchased the plane and sent their pilots here, I would be the one to administer their training (in their language). Not only that, after they were trained I would return with them to their country and fly with them there for a couple weeks, or as long as it took to get them safe in their own theater of operations.

To get me up to speed, I attended a thorough ground school on the model I would be flying most—the new Lear 35. Then I underwent a couple weeks of flight training in it to gain competency and hopefully (necessarily) even an excellence in understanding and flying it. I'm happy to say, both of the above went better than I could have hoped for; especially my final check-ride with Cliff and two department pilots (who probably went along to add their personal evaluations of my aptitude). I was thrilled when after making my third "touch-and-go" (a landing and immediate takeoff without stopping) Cliff said—in an almost bored fashion, *"Well I've seen enough of this, let's go home."* A few days later I heard one of the other pilots say that the guys in Marketing were working on a sale to a company in Lyon, France. You might imagine hearing that provoked a skip of my heart and some shaking of my head, sadly remembering my nights with Mireille, just 30 miles north of Lyon. Although I thought about her often, my fear that Mireille's likely need for an assortment of men, she would someday break my heart, I had managed to avoid contacting her.

No foreign purchasers had yet sent their pilots here, so I was used on in-country demonstrations to stateside purchasers. I remember one particular flight demonstrating the aircraft to some executives from the Deere farm equipment company. They would have the need to operate out of runways that were not long, and asked me if I could demonstrate a "short-field landing." This is a landing that requires the pilot to come in at the slowest speed, cross the end of the runway as low as possible, touch down early, and then apply full brakes and reversers to stop in the least distance. I was asked this as we approached Tucson for landing. To myself I said, *"Whoa. Can't we try it another place."* The weather was not conducive to attempting a short-field landing. The wind was gusting about twenty knots, and based on the runway we were assigned to land on, it would be a quartering tail wind (which increases your ground speed and landing distance, rather than the normal headwind which slows you down). This would make any short-field landing, not so short. And the temperature was over 100 degrees and the resultant convective currents were causing strong updrafts. On short final they would loft me higher, make my touchdown late, resulting in a longer rollout. I tried my best, battling the elements, the aircraft bouncing around at a critical low speed, and so much that I was afraid to get too low, too soon. I crossed the runway at 121 knots—about five knots faster than I would have liked, and also at about fifteen feet of altitude—five feet higher than I would have liked. To get her down I had to completely cut the power, but just as I did, we encountered a downdraft and "the bottom dropped out." We hit with a resounding smack! Bounced and hit again. It was more than just a little embarrassing. Walking into the terminal the passengers asked me, *after they'd bought the aircraft, how would their pilots get trained?* I responded that all new buyers got a free week of training for their pilots. The company representative then asked, "Well who's going to train them?"

I said, "I will."

He stopped in his tracks turned to face me and said in wonderment: *"You* will?!"

At Last Doing What I Was Hired For

Finally the first group of foreign pilots arrived: pilots from a Chilean Air Force squadron. The squadron had been assigned to commence airborne mapping of their entire country and had received a Lear 35 to do it. The cadre of pilots included an older gentleman—a Colonel, the squadron commander, one major—I think the executive officer of the squadron, two captains and two lieutenants. Only two of them—the Colonel and the major (named Carlos Ottone) spoke passable English. If you noticed the Italian last name, that's because most of the indigenous Chileans had been run out after World War II, and thousands of immigrants from Italy, Britain, and Germany descended on the country. Shortly after I started the training, I noticed the younger they were (the junior lieutenants) the better pilots they were, but the least English they spoke.

I GUESS I JUST WASN'T THINKING

I started a three week training syllabus that went as well as I could expect, minus the progress I was *not* making with the Colonel. Once again he was the senior officer and squadron commander. I knew it was imperative that he succeed; that he do well enough to graduate from the syllabus. His *not* making it would be an unbearable "loss of face" for him and upset the morale of the whole squadron. To do this I was going to have my work cut out for me. I shared my concern with Carlos (who was a fine man—a real gentleman) and learned from him that the Colonel had never flown a jet before; *any jet!* He had only flown slow, propeller-driven aircraft, and according to Carlos, very rarely the last few years.

Every flight, after the preflight briefing and while walking to the aircraft, the Colonel's extreme nervousness was readily apparent. My heart went out to him. I knew he fully recognized his lack of ability and the potential consequences. Once in the cockpit, in the seat and his feet on the rudder pedals, doing the checklists, I could see his torso shivering and his legs shaking. With the other pilots I flew both day and night flights, teaching a wide variety of maneuvers, normal and emergency procedures (often with one or more aircraft systems purposely failed). With the Colonel—a week into the syllabus I was still working with him on the same basic profile; the most elementary one possible. It included only the five minimum maneuvers required on every flight: the takeoff, the climb, the level-off, the descent, and the landing. We did this same profile—nothing more, multiple times, on every training flight. I was much relieved when halfway through the second week, he was able to accomplish these five phases of flight, if not smoothly (or with any confidence)—at least safely. He could get it airborne, climb, level off, descend, and land! I was able to graduate him, and in so doing, I'm sure earned his eternal gratefulness. (One thing: I did make Carlos promise me that he would never schedule the Colonel for a flight without one of the two hot-shot lieutenants going with him).

On one flight I used up a year's worth of luck: A young lieutenant was practicing landings at a little-used runway some distance from Wichita. It was about 4:30 and the runway was pointed due west. On final approach the glaring late afternoon sun was blinding—straight into our eyes (glinting through a layer of dust). This made it almost impossible to keep the runway in sight as you circled towards it; just too hard to distinguish it from the surrounding sand acreage. The sky, the sand, the concrete runway: everything was the same shade of tan. To make these training flights more valuable I would take two other pilots (squeezed in the cockpit opening) to observe. On my student's third or fourth landing— while he was maneuvering the aircraft to set up for landing, I twisted around in my seat to make some pertinent comments to the two observing pilots, momentarily taking my eyes off the runway.

When I turned back around and directed my attention to the upcoming end of the runway, something looked different. Suddenly I discovered what! While I was faced rearward towards the two observing pilots, Antonio had lost sight of our intended runway—drifted past it, and was now lined up— in fact about to touch down, on an adjacent, parallel *abandoned drag strip!* We hit and I grabbed the controls. *Oh no!* Just ahead—down the center of the drag strip there was a row of 10-foot tall metal pillars, each with a stack of car tires piled on them! I jammed the left rudder pedal and stomped that brake to swerve around the left side of the first post. My right wing tip miraculously missed the tires by inches! Soon as I cleared it I stomped the right rudder to straighten us out before we went into the soft sand off the left side of the drag strip. The flying gods were with me, my outside wheel stayed on the pavement and I missed the rest of the posts. Stopped at the far end, shaking in our boots, we shutdown, got out and contemplated how we were going to get back in the air. I measured how many feet from the line of posts in the center, to the outer edge of the pavement. Since I had just made it down the left side, I should be able to takeoff back down that same side. After taking measurements, we discovered if on takeoff I just cleared the stanchions by just six inches, my outside tire would have six inches to spare before going off the raised crumbling edge and bogging down in the soft sand. I did. *Thank God for small favors.*

Not Sure Why, But Did It Again

I certainly had not (could not) forget my prowess and joy with Mireille, but knew having consummated it would have set me up for a one-day broken heart. Now an aging realist I was ready to believe my success with her was a one-time fluke. Even if I had the time and wherewithal (and energy) to again search for it, it was not likely to occur again. It was time to recognize that if I didn't want to live out my life alone I was going to have to give it another try; *settle for the type of partnership that probably most people were living.* With my deficiency for some reason (I think her tanned, silky skin) noticeably lessened, plus the fact that she was such a good woman, and showed her gratefulness for me having confidence in her, I—not assuredly let Elsa know that I was ready to think of us as a couple. She still wasn't sure she'd be up to it (but also recognizing that she might have to give it one more try) she agreed. We did some planning and not long after, I flew back to Florida and we had a small wedding in nearby Cape Coral. I moved out of my one bedroom apartment in Wichita and rented one side of a two-bedroom duplex. She sold her house and she and the girls joined me. And I must admit (me able to mostly dismiss the possibility of some unknown but more fulfilling future) I concentrated on my current professional and domestic situation, and things went just fine. We enrolled the girls in school, and they seemed happy to be in a family unit. There were few problems, although I had a slightly strained relationship with Marisa (whose father had abandoned her at eight—never phoning or even sending her a birthday card). I became very close to Iris— who at 14 was already smarter than I would ever be, but seemed to have a readily demonstrated affection and respect for me, which I did not see how I deserved. And she was beautiful.

Oh No, Not the FAA Again

You're not going to believe this: while there in Wichita I received another pack of forms from the FAA; another, revised multi-page questionnaire to fill out if I wanted to keep my job application current. Christ! Can't they use one of the last two sets I sent in; just use these new forms for new applicants. I spent another week devoted to that task. After what I'd already done I wasn't going to give up now. Plus I felt that most guys, if they hadn't already given up would now give up, receiving this last pack of forms. And if that were so—it would mathematically increase my chances. Finished, I put this third set of ridiculous flight information in the mail.

An Incident worth Recounting

When the training program with the Chilean pilots was over, I hosted a graduation party for them at my house. (Elsa prepared a superb spaghetti dinner). During the evening, Carlos and the others confronted me with a mystery they had not been able to solve—even after many referrals to their English dictionary and calls back to their friends in Santiago. They begged me to explain what one word meant. Of course I said sure, just tell me the word. Each of them took a try at it. It sounded like "*Toobouie.*" I told them I had never said that word, and in fact, had never even heard it. This answer caused them to look at each other with quizzical—even skeptical expressions. They insisted I had said it, and apparently didn't believe that I hadn't, nor that I never heard of it. Being gentlemen—one and all of them, in spite of my apparently incredulous answer, they were willing to let it go and get on with the evening. I said the course was finished. Well not quite. Actually there was one more flight for one more pilot. We launched the next day and during it a big mystery was solved: The training pilot did an excellent job on a simulated loss of engine landing, and when he had rolled out, I slapped him on the back and said, "*Attaboy!*" He and the two pilots observing were all but in my lap shaking their finger at me. That was the "*toobouie*" they had heard; an expression I evidently used frequently without being aware of it.

The Last Project and Goodbye

In order to use the plane for aerial photography it needed a camera installed. With everything we have going for us here in the States, it's a company in Zurich, Switzerland that makes these cameras and installs them in the aircraft. The Chilean pilots drew straws to see who would be my copilot and which other four would go along. Once again I did my famous transatlantic flight—Gander to Shannon, where we overnighted and then continued on to Zurich the next day. The installation took a week and a fine time was had by all. Several days after returning to Wichita— the training finished, we left on the flight back to their base in Santiago. To give them confidence and get a better evaluation of them, I rode in the right seat, just performing the copilot duties, assigning alternate Chilean pilots to fly the left seat and act as captain on each of the five legs. They sincerely appreciated this.

I stayed in Chile—flying with them daily for about ten days. One thing that impressed me about Chile was the teenagers. Almost every one of them I saw was carrying a half dozen school books. The country was an industrious country and obviously stressed education. When it came time to leave, it wasn't without some sadness. I had grown attached to these pilots—who to the man were the most polite and respectful individuals I think I ever met. I learned a lot from them and will always think highly of Chile because of them.

One Other Interesting Foreign Training Experience

Unlike the smooth running program I had with the Chileans, I had a tougher one with the Bolivians. As usual, after their Air Force purchased the Lear they sent three pilots to Wichita for me to train. Supposedly all three had received some jet training from our Air Force. Well as soon as I started the training I had reason to doubt that claim. However, they all must have seen "*Top Gun.*" Each one showed up for training in their olive drab U.S. flight suit, with the front zipper down to their navel, with nothing but bare skin showing. No tee shirt. Not only that (but the sign of a really "hot pilot") they never went anywhere without wearing their yellow leather, US flying gloves. And they had learned the trick of a "super-hot pilot": spend the time and effort necessary to start at the wrist opening, peel the gloves off forwards, until the wrist opening was stretched tight across the knuckles, *leaving half the hand ungloved!*

The Wichita basic training syllabus completed, I readied myself for the next phase: fly with them back to Bolivia, and then stay there a week or two to make sure they were comfortable in the aircraft and conducting operations in their country. The flight went okay down through Latin America, and crossing Colombia. But sitting there offering little help, and letting them make the decisions regarding altitude, power settings, and fuel usage, and hoping they would be okay, turned out to be a little premature. On the last leg, still 800 miles north of our destination—La Paz, according to my calculations, *we were not going to have enough fuel to make it.* (They had not climbed to a high enough altitude to make the plane more fuel efficient, and then on top of that they had selected wasteful power settings.) I hoped to use this pending "flameout" (running out of fuel) to them, as an educational drill. I asked the pilot flying what our fuel flow was. Checking the fuel-per-hour usage gauge, he read it, and answered: "1,250 pounds per hour."

I asked, "And what's our speed over the ground."

Another short delay while two of them used an E6B to work it out: "420 knots."

I then asked, "At that speed, how long is it going to take us to get to La Paz?"

This was the famous 64,000 dollar question, and resulted in a consultation of all three of them. After several minutes of heated discussion and obviously a variety of conclusions, they came up with "An hour and thirty minutes."

I then asked them, "Burning 1250 pounds an hour, how much fuel will it take us to do that hour and a half?"

Another meeting of the minds. In not too long they came up with the answer, "1,900 pounds." I just waited for the next conclusion. (The "Fuel

Remaining" gauge showed *1,600* pounds!) It wasn't too long before they became aware of this and were now looking at each other with a measure of panic in their eyes. They now—for the first time, realized they were going to run out of fuel a hundred miles from La Paz. We would have to land and refuel. And worse, we were now overhead Peru, which currently *had broken off diplomatic relations with Bolivia!* However we had no alternative but to land in Peru, and unannounced! While rolling out on landing, heavily armed military vehicles were speeding down the runway alongside us. As soon as we came to a stop we were surrounded by a circle of jeeps, all of which had ugly, hood-mounted machine guns trained on the cockpit! Miracle of miracles: Six months earlier the Peruvian Air Force had purchased two Learjets, *and the colonel approaching the aircraft with his weapon drawn was who I had trained to fly it.* It was only this prior association that allowed us to be refueled and take back off.

One Final, Really Big Deal

After finishing their in-country training in Bolivia, I returned to Wichita, but did not sleep well for many months (and still worry somewhat to this day). Every aircraft including the Learjet comes with a "Performance Manual." It stipulates the aircraft's capabilities and is the Bible. It contains charts for every airport elevation and temperature; and in these conditions, let a pilot know how much weight he can takeoff with—*whether or not he can even get airborne with the available runway!* Most manuals—including the Lear 35 manual, only have charts for operations at airfields up to 10,000 feet of elevation, and the airport at La Paz is *13,200 feet* above sea level! It took me an extra week, to go through the whole manual—using a plastic French curve and (fingers crossed) mental calculations to draw upward sloping lines on the charts, indicating what limitations these pilots would have to conform to when operating out of the La Paz airport. There was no way I could know if my projections would be accurate. I didn't tell my company I had supplied Bolivia with dozens of charts that were of my own making, and based on no flight testing!

Thankful for My Career at Learjet

A year and then two at Learjet. Everything was going smoothly—maybe more smoothly and satisfying than ever before. I had many exciting experience with crews from all over the world. Cliff retired (or the rumor was—he had early stages of Alzheimer's and was let go). Yours truly was promoted to his vacated position. I was now the Chief Pilot of the Learjet Demonstration Department. From time to time I flew for the Production and Test Department, which provided additional pay because at least half the flights were experimental in terms of aircraft capabilities and limitations. Most these flights required I wear a parachute.

I had no complaints. I saw no reason that this would not be a job I would keep until retirement. I was content and respected by management and all my coworkers—a good feeling (like I hadn't had since Air America). Even on the home front. Minus occasional bouts of depression, Elsa was a good woman, loving and with a big heart, and I think she was proud to have me as her husband. It took a long time, but I finally "had it made."

A Momentary Thought, of What Could be the First of Many Such Thoughts

Now, with an elevated position, my own office, a group of respectful subordinates, I couldn't help wondering, if: when I had met Mireille I would not have been unemployed; if I would have had a respectable aviation position like this, I might have felt more eligible, more worthy of her. Still that being so, the reason for me painfully realizing I could not consider a permanent relationship with her would still be there; a fear of one day being gravely hurt.

Chapter Six
BOB AND DON AGAIN

A Great Meeting with an old VMA 331 (Forrestal) Buddy

Hopefully you remember from Part Two (the carrier cruise) my affinity for and praise of one young lieutenant: Bob Harmon, the guy who could fly like a bird, was a great practical joker, and had more integrity than anyone I had yet met. Well (and it was the Marine Corps' loss) shortly after I did—Bob got out of the Corps and joined the airlines. He did so with another squadron pilot—Don Goft. They had enrolled in Marine Corps flight training together and were best buddies since high school. On the cruise it seemed you never saw one without the other. They were now living together in San Francisco and flying for TWA, which at that time was one of the largest and most respected global airlines. On a break from training Spanish-speaking pilots, I was on a demonstration flight for a big bank in San Francisco and had to overnight there. I thought of Bob and having his number gave him a call. He was thrilled to hear from me (while I was surprised to have been lucky enough to find him and Don at home). Bob insisted on picking me up at my hotel and taking me to dinner.

When he showed up, guess what? They were in the sporty Jaguar XKE coupe—the one he bought in Europe and had shipped to the states while on the Mediterranean carrier-cruise. His wife Giorgi was sitting on Don's lap in the front passenger seat. I squeezed into what would serve for a back seat, but not without performing some award-winning gymnastics. They took me to a really upscale downtown restaurant. During dinner I asked him how he and Don liked flying for the airlines and he said that they were still both First Officers (not yet Captains) so it entailed a lot of kowtowing when matched with an irritable old captain, plus, they were at the bottom of the "pecking-order" when it came to bidding for good schedules. But they did have a lot of time off and were using it to good advantage; making a fair amount of money on the side. Knowing these two guys, that didn't surprise me. They were buying up condemned houses in the Haight-Ashbury district, hiring contractors to do the necessary renovation, electric, and plumbing work to make the houses legal for occupancy. Once the houses were "okayed," Bob and Giorgi and Don would move in, do what interior sprucing up they could, put it on the market, and lived there until it was sold! The one they were in when I phoned was their third one.

Seeing the attention Giorgi was showing to Bob and the contented look in her eyes, I asked them how it was they met. This question caused them both to look at each other with the cutest smiles. Even Don flashed a knowing smile. Bob (with some enthusiastic and affirming comments from Giorgi) relayed a priceless story: After piloting a TWA flight to New York City and visiting a small bistro for a late-night snack, *he spied Giorgi and knew his "bachelor days" were over.* Although it was a brief encounter, he was smitten—sure he had met "the one." Having only intercepted her on her way out—in the minute he had to introduce himself, he did not write down her phone number. He could only remember she said she lived in White Plains, and her last name started with a "B." The next week and the week after that, on each flight back to JFK, with fingers crossed and eyes to the heavens he visited the same bistro—with no luck. She was never there. On the next flight—her again not appearing at the bistro, Bob remembered (with no idea how it had originally come up) that Giorgi had said the people living across the street from her *were named O'Reilly and had seven kids.*

A plan: With a page ripped from the Westchester County phone book, he was able to—on his fifth call, find the right O'Reillys—*the ones with seven kids.* Perhaps sensing Bob's urgency they gave him the name and number of the prominent Italian family across the street—the Biancinis.

He called it and got a baby-sitter, who said that Giorgi and her parents were out for the evening—at the Fairview Country Club, *at Giorgi's engagement celebration!* An event her parents had organized for the man they had chosen as her husband.

Bob found the address of the country club (just across the Connecticut state line) and at 11:10 pm—after a harrowing drive, arrived. No valet in sight and no time to waste finding a parking lot, he left the car blocking the walkway to the grand entrance. In desperation he strode hurriedly inside. Hearing music straight ahead he continued. Arriving on an elevated indoor terrace, he found himself looking down at the engagement celebration. The darkened dance floor was empty, minus one couple centered under a large chandelier light and swaying to a romantic ballad. His heart sank—*it was Giorgi and what must have been her fiancé.* The broadly-smiling crowd encircling the couple were undoubtedly approving friends and family members. *She spied Bob!* She stopped dancing, stepped back, caught her breath, faltered and stood frozen for a half minute. Bob said he made some kind of weak hand gesture, but there was no way she could miss the look in his eyes. She looked at her fiancé, looked to the crowd—to her probably startled mother and father, then lifted the hem of her gown and ran to Bob, who grasped her, spun around and hurried out to the car. That was the beginning and here they are now with two children!

Chapter Seven
A BIG CHANGE OF PLANS

An Unexpected Call

April 1978: At Learjet and things still going just fine. It was 8 p.m. and I was relaxing at home, *but not for long*. The phone rings and it's my son Mark, calling from Florida.

"Dad, dad. We have a huge problem!"

"What kind of problem? What do you mean?"

"Mom and that Air Force Major are going to get married." (Which was fine with me.)

"So?"

"He's being transferred to Okinawa and Mom's going with him, and she says we're going to have to go with them!"

"Yes..."

"We don't *want* to go! We have to stay here. We started high school here in Hobe Sound, and we want to graduate from high school here. We know everybody. Everybody knows us. Every one of us including the girls is on at least two sports teams. And we're getting good grades. Dad, we just have to stay. We need you to get a job here in Hobe Sound, so we can live with you and stay here and graduate from St. Michael's!"

Holy Christ. What am I going to do? Hobe Sound doesn't even have an airport and I'm not qualified for any other line of work. Geez, and when at last I am finally settled in my life; secure and happy, and qualifying for a retirement.

"Dad, dad are you there? Did you hear me? What are you going to do?"

"I'll call you back in a couple days Mark. Let me think."

Maybe There Is a God

When I hit the rack that night, and the following night, I still didn't have a glimmer of an idea. I'd spent every waking hour weighing the pros and cons of the possibilities, dreading the thought of trying to start all over again (for about the fifth time) and having to do it in a small beachside town (with no airport), all so my kids could continue the life they had created there. I did understand this was critically important to them at this time (especially since the alternative was to move to a small island in the South Pacific). About 10 the next morning the phone rang—striking terror in my heart; expecting it would be Mark. Reluctantly I answered it and breathed a sigh of relief when it wasn't Mark.

"Rog, Stu Carlton here, how you doing?" It was an old friend from Banner Flight. Remember? That short employment disaster in the end of 74, in upstate NY, when I was ready to quit after two months—dismayed at not being able to see how the company was making a profit, until thankfully, halfway through my third month the owner told us we were declaring bankruptcy and shutting down. I hadn't spoken to Stu in at least a year and was not sure where he was calling from. You must remember Stu. He was the guy who had informed me of my habit of pulling the elastic on my jockey shorts away from my leg, and wiggling my hips to let my balls hang free.

I answered him "Just great!" (At the moment a major untruth.)

But what I was about to hear represented a possible solution to my new dilemma. "Rog, I know you got your family there in the Jupiter area, and last I heard you were trying to get a flying job in Florida. Well listen to this: I fly for a big technology corporation—SSL Systems, and we keep our planes at the West Palm Beach airport—about 25 miles south of your house."

"And you're calling because…"

"We've requested a Lear 35 demonstration flight, I think for next Wednesday and Thursday. You may want to schedule yourself for the flight, because I know we're looking to add another pilot, and you may be interested."

Holy Shit. In view of my current quandary, this sounded like something that could be an answer. Of course I thanked him profusely and the next day when I checked the Pending Demos schedule, sure enough there it was—*"SSL Systems in West Palm Beach."* I wasted no time in putting myself on the flight, thinking I could possibly be the pilot they were looking for. Being able to hire a *factory* pilot is always a priority to new purchasers; what better way to learn all the ins and outs of operating the new aircraft. You might imagine the next day—as preoccupied as I was, it was hard to even function. I felt the comfort and security of walking around the now-familiar Learjet property; visiting the flight offices, the factory floor, the hangars and the ramps. This was my home now. I tried the best I could to get out a cheerful "Hi" when one of my pilots passed, *while contemplating a possible end to it all.*

The Demo

The demonstration called for two days of flying. I told my copilot to go sit in the back, and had the SSL Chief Pilot (Perry Dawson) ride in the right seat. He was a polite, tall and impressive-looking guy, but with a not-forthcoming personality. It was not easy to feel as if you were on the same frequency as he was; just a shade unnatural. Still—with him sitting next to me, it gave me the chance to try to (tactfully) impress him with my proficiency, and display a friendly, outgoing personality. The first day was from WPB to O'Hare airport in Chicago; a few hours there and then a longer leg to Los Angeles. We overnighted in LA and all ate dinner together. I used that occasion to act and make comments that would strike Perry as me being a team-player, not infused with self-importance, and be glad to carry out any instructions he issued. My efforts must have been successful. The next day, just before boarding the plane for the flight back to Wichita, he asked me if I would consider resigning at Learjet and hiring on with SSL. I told him I'd be honored to be a member of his flight department. (Thanks to Stu, an unthinkable dilemma may have just been avoided.)

The hiring-on was easy, as compared to telling Lindon Blue (the Vice President of Learjet) I was going to have to leave the company. I was shaking in my boots preparing to meet with him. I guess one of my many weak-points is an excessive feeling of responsibility, doing the right thing, and not letting people down—*in this case my managers at Learjet.* (Don't know how I could say that based on my carrying-on while married to Sara.) Lindon gave me all the time I needed to justify my need to leave. Of course I wasn't the first factory pilot to opt to go with a new purchaser's flight department. Lindon was more than gracious, at least feigning that he understood and wished me well in my new job. I explained the whole program to Elsa and the girls, and they took it surprisingly well. All along I knew that Iris was fond of my other kids and envious of their "Beach Boys" Hobe Sound lifestyle, and was eager to become part of it. We were ready to do it. Together we spent several days packing a bunch of boxes of lamps and small appliances and our breakable stuff, leaving the furniture and larger items for the movers when they would come.

This, You're Not Going to Believe

All four of us were standing in the street alongside the cars, ready to pull away, watching the movers make their final few trips in and out of the house. Both cars were packed with our preferred clothes, important papers and valuables. Just as the movers were closing up the truck and we were ready to climb into the cars, the mailman came—putting his last handful of our mail in the box. I strolled over, took it out, and perused the envelopes as I walked to the car. One was from the FAA. Oh no, *not another set of forms!* I handed the rest of the mail to Elsa and ripped open the one from the FAA. You could have knocked me over with a feather. *They were offering me a job as Chief Pilot for the US government National Park Service, to be stationed in Lake Mead, Nevada!* Well too late now. So much for qualifying for government retirement in ten more years of a federal job. We made it to Hobe Sound on the east coast of Florida okay; in three days, two nights in a motel.

Oh No, You Can't Be Serious

Of course, what I was banking on—inasmuch as Sara and her new husband would be leaving for Okinawa about a week after our arrival, *was to just move into the vacated home I had bought seven years ago and already owned.* When I mentioned this plan to Perry (the SSL chief pilot), I was surprised when he drew back his head, flashed a disapproving look, and then said: "Too far. Too long of a drive. All my pilots live in the West Palm Beach area." (I already knew that wasn't entirely true, because Stu lived in Jupiter—just ten minutes closer to the airport than Hobe Sound.) But it was useless. He was convinced if an unplanned trip suddenly came up, I would not be able to get to the airport quickly enough. Much as I tried, it was not going to happen. My only fall back plan was to live as close to Hobe Sound as Perry would let me, which would probably be Jupiter— since that was already approved in Stu's case

A New Home for All of Us

I was fortunate to find a new three-bedroom-two-bath home in a nice development in Jupiter. Fortunately, a month before leaving Learjet a prospective purchaser pulled me aside and asked me if I knew where he could get an 'almost' new Lear (and thus avoid the 18 month wait while a new one was built). Turns out I did. I airlined to its location, performed a series of flight tests, directed certain maintenance be done, and then after negotiating with the owner, was able to close the deal. In so doing I received a "finder's fee" of $14,000! Without this windfall money I wouldn't have been able to buy the house. When Sara and the major departed the area, Mark, Stacy and Kevin moved in with me, Elsa, Iris, and Marisa. I already knew that this mixed families thing—even with only one or two kids, was hard enough, but this would be like *The Brady Bunch*. (It was one less than it could have been since Donna—now 18, had moved in with her boyfriend.) I bought an old Buick station wagon like Chevy Chase drove in the family's trip to WallyWorld. Mark, Iris, Stacy, and Kevin climbed in it each morning for the commute north to St. Michael's High School in Hobe Sound, and I climbed into my car for the trip south to SSL in West Palm Beach. Marisa was okay with being enrolled in the nearby middle school here in Jupiter.

And What about That Other Hobe Sound House

Decided (stupidly) to sell it. Which I went on to discover—to get it ready for sale, damn near took a complete renovation. I couldn't complain too much about it because it was my house and I'd benefit financially from the eventual sale. As you might remember, at the time of our separation I promised Sara I would provide a home for her (this one) that she could live in—without a single expense, until she got married or died of old age. I confirmed I would continue to pay the monthly mortgage on it, the real estate taxes, the insurance, and all the maintenance costs as long as she was there. But! We agreed when she no longer needed it (got married or died) the house would belong to me (which since it was in my name only would not be a problem). However, getting it ready to sell was a real project. The laundry room had one of those old-fashioned green shag carpets in it, and the nap was alive with candy, pieces of food, and even moving creatures. When I moved the refrigerator I found things behind it that they had lost five years ago. I must have repaired a hundred holes in the wall, spackling and sanding them flat, and then doing a week of touch-up painting. Far as the outside was concerned, I rented a pressure cleaner, blasted it all and then did a week of exterior painting. Finally had it ready to sell.

My Kids Thought What? For How Long?

When the house was sold and the closing was held, with nothing else to do that day, Elsa accompanied me to the closing. For some reason the couple purchasing the house wanted her to sign the forms as well. I told them "This wife has nothing whatsoever to do with this house. She is not shown as even a part-owner and never lived in it." The couple appeared uncomfortable with that explanation and consulted with their lawyer. They then told me that for them to 'just be on the safe side' they wanted her signature. I again told them it was completely unnecessary and that this wife had no claim on the house. More discussions with their lawyer, and they said if my current wife didn't sign it, *they weren't going to go through with the closing.* Obviously at this point I had to give up and let Elsa sign her name (Elsa A. Yahnke) to it. And listen to this: I did not learn until 20 years later that Sara's husband (don't know where he got his info) had erroneously told my kids *that Elsa had forged Sara's name on the closing forms!* For 20 years all my kids thought this version was what really happened, and never approached me about it. I never knew or had any reason to suspect my kids were tolerating me *while believing I had cheated their mother out of "our" house.* Which I hadn't!

Chapter Eight
MY EMPLOYMENT WITH SSL SYSTEMS

My New Florida Job

I would be the newest member of a nine-pilot flight department. My checkout went smoothly and quickly. What training was deemed necessary was administered by the Assistant Chief Pilot—Dave, who shocked me by never missing a chance to bad-mouth Perry, who he quite frankly said more than once—*had no idea of what a chief pilot was supposed to do*. I was not only surprised that as a long-time member of the department he had this opinion of his boss, but moreover that he would risk sharing it with me—who he didn't know (and could have been an old friend of Perry's). The flight schedule for SSL wasn't difficult and remained the same throughout my time there. It usually consisted of one if not two of our aircraft being scheduled every weekday. (One plane—two pilots. Two planes—four pilots.) The flights were usually to transport three or four executives to one of the company's satellite locations (in Cleveland, Atlanta, St. Louis, or Long Beach, California). Often when visiting two or three of these locations, the flights kept us away from our home base for a couple days, overnighting in one or two cities before returning. Another common trip was bringing the CEO or Chairman of the board to DC for some high level lobbying. Most meetings were scheduled for 9 am, which (leaving from Florida) would require a 06:30 (or earlier) takeoff. For the pilot, this meant a 05:30 airport arrival (which required a 04:30 get up)! We didn't have much weekend work, maybe a single flight every other weekend.

My Domestic Situation

After two years I had to admit that moving here had been a good decision. Things had gone just fine. In fact, better than I deserved. The kids were thoroughly enjoying their time at high school, with many friends, on a variety of sports teams, and academically all but one on the Honor Roll—which may be not by accident. Not too many weeks after the kids had moved in I realized there was no "study area" in the house where they could do their homework. To correct this—with the help of another guy (who knew what he was doing) I knocked out part of the back wall, poured an extended slab, and tacked on a study room. Inside it, along one wall I installed an eight-foot long counter with three dividers positioned at even intervals, so four kids could study at one time, without being distracted by the kid next to them. This room had no TV or radio, and each kid knew upon arriving home from school, he or she had to spend one hour at the desk. If they said they already did their homework in study hall. I answered, "Then go in there and check out what you're going to be studying next week."

Every week I must have attended at least two school functions, a basketball game, an academic competition, or school play. And I have to admit Elsa was a good stepmother; joining in whole-heartedly on any activity my kids were involved in. In fact, one time (completely on her own) she bought and gave my Mark a pair of white, low-cut football cleats. Of course whenever I could, I tried to do the same for her kids. And it was obvious the kids were well-respected by all the students and teachers. During the first year I officially adopted Iris and her sister Marisa. Later in life after familiarizing myself with my father's family tree and the accomplished lives of his forbearers, I reflected on having given away his name—to kids I barely knew, *without ever consulting him about it.*

Some Hidden Thoughts

Although my sex life with Elsa continued, I guess—satisfactorily, from time to time I couldn't help reflecting on those long-ago nights with Mireille; the power she gifted me with, the euphoria I felt, and the satisfaction she demonstrated. I am embarrassed to admit I sometimes wondered: if I wouldn't have married Elsa—just looked a little longer, *could there have been another Mireille out there.*

Flying for SSL and the Chief Pilot

During the second year, Dave—the guy who had checked me out and badmouthed Perry the whole time, quit, and I was appointed the Assistant Chief Pilot to replace him. I was honored, but never felt I was on the same frequency as Perry. Bit by bit I began to share Dave's evaluation of Perry. I've been too embarrassed to mention it until now, but there was one activity unheard of in any other flight department: On our days off—when we weren't scheduled to fly, Perry insisted that we all come in; just wander around the hangar and see what was going on (which the pilots hated and referred to as "logging face-time"). To add insult to injury, there were two large patches of grass on each side of the hangar, and Perry would assign one pilot a week *to mow these two lawns!* Last Christmas he called us all in to make an announcement relative to the grass-cutting; that he assured us we would all appreciate. Of course we knew it would be the end of our landscaping duties, so we showed up in gleeful anticipation. Guess what the good deal was: the company was buying us a *riding* mower! Obviously, as good as the flying part was, things like this were not good for morale, and resulted in a constant undertone of resentment for Perry (and even for me, as I was the Assistant Chief Pilot) for not putting our foot down with management to relieve us from these non-standard pilot duties. This particular event caused my good friend Stu, to quit.

If the previous two activities weren't bad enough, at least they didn't impact flight safety. The worst of Perry's shortcomings involved the duty hours he set for our 5-man—permanently assigned, aircraft maintenance staff. According to FAA regulations, before a pilot can depart in an airplane, it must be "released" by a certified mechanic, and when an aircraft returns at the end of the day, a certified mechanic must meet it and correct any discrepancies that had popped up on that day's flight. To accomplish this industry-standard procedure, since we usually departed at 6:30 am and returned about 8 pm, it would have been necessary to split the maintenance shift: have some come in at 5 am and go home at 1 pm, and the others come in at 1 pm and go home at 9 pm. Instead of this, Perry (intimidated by the raw-boned Chief of Maintenance) allowed the maintenance department to stick with normal office hours: 8 am to 5 pm. This meant sometimes for four or five days straight, based on our early takeoffs and late returns, *no certified mechanic checked the airplane, either before a flight or after a flight.* This was a serious "Safety of Flight" omission and I continually harangued Perry to alter the maintenance department work-hours. I never succeeded.

All Thanks to Alex

You may remember the Tech Rep (Alex Weber) from Garret Engines (the smartest guy I ever met) who was assigned to Air America in Saigon (and whose job I tried to save). He was the first person to explain to me that by knowing how to compare the BTU's provided by the fuel entering the engine, the torque or thrust produced, and finally—the Interstage or Exhaust Gas Temperature, a pilot could recognize an engine that was losing efficiency, *and thereby identify an engine that was on the way to failing completely!* On every flight, there is a metal log book containing forms to record the details of that day's flights (primarily destinations, takeoff and landing times, and a list of the passengers). I designed a new form for the SSL flight department; one that added a preprinted column of blank "engine-monitoring" blocks. At least once a day, at an altitude of 41,000 feet (our most often used cruising altitude) and after setting a fuel flow of precisely 1250 pounds per hour, the pilot would record the readings of four key engine operating gauges. If a pilot noticed a reading out of the normal, he could flip back through previous log sheets to see if there was a trend; a slowly developing indication of the engine becoming less efficient. We began using my forms and started recording the engine parameters that would monitor the health of the engine. It was well received by the pilots and once understood—by upper management as well. When word of it got to The National Business Aviation Association, they published an article about the procedure, the SSL flight department, and me. *Thanks Alex.* (Sadly, I lost contact with him and hadn't heard from him for ten years.)

The Same Old Grind, But with a Couple Wrinkles

The next few years were more of the same; the same destinations, the same flights, the same vice presidents as passengers. I couldn't complain. It became "old hat." The only thing that was a problem: *my boss Perry Dawson.* I mentioned before about none of the maintenance staff staying late enough to meet us when we came in after five. (One time taxiing onto our ramp at about 4:55, I saw the last maintenance guy arm the alarm system and start running towards his car.) Perry's deference to whatever the Maintenance Chief said got worse. He told Perry that refueling a Lear and letting it sit all night with the weight of full wing tanks, was not good for the seams at the root of the wings; leaks could develop. Terry believed him and relieved the maintenance staff of fueling the planes in the afternoon or evening when we returned. Guess what this meant: when we pilots came in for their next day's 7 am takeoff (with no maintenance staff at work yet) we had to hook up a tug and pull the aircraft out of the hangar and to the gas pumps. Pulling a plane with one of those tugs—is not an easy job. Throughout the industry, we pilots are justifiably not trusted to tow aircraft. And then we had to fuel the aircraft ourselves, and wrestling those thick black rubber hoses around is a dirty job. Knowing this (*Thank you Perry*) he provided us with bibbed overalls and rubber gloves to don before commencing the refueling. This did keep your white shirt clean, but also resulted in it being soaked with sweat by the time you were done. Assigned this pre-launch manual labor, two pilots threatened to quit, and one did (joining Stu, who was now flying for a BB&T Banks in Charlotte).

Just Two of Many, Not-so-Uneventful Flights

We took off from West Palm Beach at 8 pm on a two and a half hour flight to Boston Logan airport. The weather was real bad in Boston, so I not only checked the latest aviation weather reports and forecasts, but had my copilot phone the weather station in Boston, personally asking an observer for the latest forecasts for our arrival time. Arriving in the Boston area we were directed to proceed 45 miles northeast (out over the Atlantic) to a holding point, descend to 19,000 feet and call entering the holding pattern. The airport weather was a 200-foot solid overcast, a half mile visibility, and blowing snow. Not good, but not so bad as to be "Below Minimums" (which means no landing approaches are allowed to be attempted). At present, while it would be a difficult instrument approach (solely on the gauges with no outside reference), at least you could legally try one. Each airplane arriving at the holding point is issued an "Approach Clearance time." That is the time that Air Traffic Control would (hopefully) clear you to commence your approach to landing. Aircraft are not cleared to make an approach until they are number one, having finally gotten down to 3,000 feet. At 19,000 feet I would have to wait until all 16 planes under me had descended to 3,000 feet and made their approach.

I had a pad strapped on my right thigh where I began writing down the time delays between aircraft at 3,000 feet receiving their approach clearances. Each time when that bottom one commenced its approach, I'd be able to cross it off and we'd all be able to descend another thousand feet lower. It was now averaging three minutes and fifteen seconds, so 15 aircraft times 3.25 minutes, means it would take 49 minutes for me to make my way down to 3,000 feet. My fuel flow was 980 pounds per hour. In 49 minutes I'd burn 800 pounds. I checked the Fuel Remaining gauge; it showed 1300 pounds. Based on how long it would take me to be number one, I should be able to land with about 500 pounds, which would be acceptable (but an absolute minimum). *Shit!* After about twenty minutes and down to 10,000 feet, *they stopped issuing approach clearances!* Aircraft waiting to takeoff were backed up, so they were closing the runway to landing aircraft, to allow for those departures. My wait for approach clearance would be extended for who knows how long, sabotaging my computed times and possible fuel reserve.

I was able to makes small adjustments in the aircraft attitude (nose position) and improve the lift/drag ratio of the wing. With this increased efficiency I got our fuel flow down from 980 pounds per hour, to just 925 pounds per hour. Seeing our approach times delayed and our fuel gauges going down, my copilot Jim began to panic. He was urging me to cancel our intentions to land here at Boston, and divert to Providence, Rhode Island, where he said the weather was a little better. I told him: first, the weather at Providence was very little better; second, the instrument approach at Providence was less precise; third, the lighting at Providence was terrible; fourth, the runway was not as wide. *Did he realize the approach there would be far more difficult than here?* Here at Boston, I knew we were at least going to live through the flight. I told Jim, "Even if our fuel gets so low that I have to declare an emergency to get priority landing, and no matter *how* bad the weather gets—*even ceiling zero, visibility zero*, I know I can land here at Logan. They've got great approach lights and the touchdown zone lights are blindingly bright. If we leave this holding pattern you're going to hear everyone above us say thank you." I convinced him. After only 9 minutes they opened the airport for landings. We got down to 3,000 feet and were issued our approach clearance. We landed with 550 pounds.

On another flight, I had to rush a "blue baby" (suffering from oxygen loss) to a special hospital in Atlanta. On these flights, instead of using your whole aircraft number, you use a call-sign of "Lifeguard" plus the last two digits of your aircraft number. I knew how long the flight would be and how much oxygen a person would use during that time. Before taxiing out I asked my copilot to check that the oxygen bottle the nurse had was full (at least 1,800 pounds of pressure). He checked and the nurse assured him it was almost 2,000 pounds. We taxied out and were airborne without delay—headed north. Fifteen minutes into the flight, I told my copilot to go back and check the amount of oxygen remaining in the bottle. A minute later he comes crashing up into the cockpit (panicky) and tells me that it's half gone—already down to only 900 pounds remaining! While the nurse was right: the bottle did have enough pressure, *it was the wrong sized bottle; too small.* We weren't going to make it to Atlanta. We'd be out of oxygen in another fifteen minutes! *Okay I can't make it to Atlanta. What can I do?* Jacksonville was about 40 miles in front of us. The crash crew there should have oxygen. But then, if I landed and something went wrong and the baby died, how culpable would I or SSL be? I contacted the JAX tower and had them connect me directly to the Crash Crew Chief. *Great.* He said they *did* have portable oxygen! And what's more (one of those good guys) he told me to check the fitting on the oxygen bottle, and let him know if it was "male" or "female" and give him the size; he might have to get a different connector. Checked and told him. He said he knew that one and had it. I landed and while still rolling out on the runway, the crash crew vehicle was right alongside us. The copilot opened the door before we had come to a stop and the crash crew guys came thudding inside and in thirty seconds had the new oxygen bottle hooked up. The baby appeared no worse for the wear and we were able to takeoff for Atlanta with sufficient oxygen. The copilot and I got an award from the local hospital, and a letter of commendation from the company.

Chapter Nine
THE WORLD IS A LESS GOOD PLACE

Mom and Dad

For my parents, quitting the hotel-managing adventure and moving into their new home had been a good idea. Mom was involved in things she could enjoy without putting a strain on her heart: gardening, book clubs and bridge groups. Dad was always fixing something at the house and got in all the fishing he wanted. The Caloosahatchee River was only a mile away, and in his development there were a dozen nearby canals to try his luck in. (In fact, Dad caught a 32-pound Snook in one of these canals.) They led a comfortable easy life, spending each late afternoon in their "Florida Room" (a glass-enclosed back porch). It was a perfect place to have a couple Manhattans, discuss nothing important and watch the sun sink over the gulf. But in spite of this, Mom's heart got weaker and weaker. She had two more attacks, resulting in the 911 calls, the EMT's crashing into the house, the hysteria, the ambulance ride to the Emergency Room, and then the battery of tests and invasive procedures.

Dad contacted each of us kids, and coordinated a weekend that all three of us could pay them a visit. This was a little unusual, but Dad didn't seem to converse in a manner that we felt we should ask why. Everything was just fine when we arrived, minus the fact that none of we kids could see the usual cheerful expression on Mom's face. The wear and tear of these repeated attacks had taken their toll. Nothing transpired during the afternoon, nor during a great pork loin roast that Mom and Laura prepared. But after supper, sitting around the living room, Dad brought up the subject that had prompted the meeting.

I GUESS I JUST WASN'T THINKING

"As you know, Mom's heart is so weak she can't stand more than about a minute before she starts getting light-headed. At Sunday's church service, Pastor Weldon lets me park right at the end of the front walk, so after the service Gay can sit in the car and talk to people—without having to stand. I think she's had a total of four cardiac events in the last ten years.

"Five," added Mom.

"Your mom made something known to me after her last siege. I told her no; no—that's not right. I can't do that. But she insisted, saying she just could not go through one more of the series of events that transpired with each attack. She told me, the next time she went down, and was unconscious, *not to call 911*. She just couldn't take it, probably wouldn't make it anyway. I told her I wasn't convinced, but if she truly, truly wanted that, *she* could tell you kids. So hon, you've got the floor."

"Thanks Kenny. Well kids, your dad just about said it all, and it *is* what I want. I won't know the difference, I'll just avoid ending up enduring all the undignified, invasive things I've been through so many times. And all just to barely make it to the next one. What dad says is true, and it's what I want, and I want each of you to know it, and know it *is* what I want."

Mostly what then transpired was no verbal communication; just glances, pursed lips, head shaking, and finally exchanging hugs. The next morning we all went to church together and afterwards Dad took us on a drive along the beach. Around four we stopped at an outdoor "Peel and Eat" shrimp place. In the evening we sat in the Florida room, enjoying our own company, and making no reference to the previous evening's discussion.

It wasn't a month later that each of us got a call from Dad. It had happened, and he had honored her wishes. We three kids packed a few things and left immediately to join him for as long as we had to stay. Seeing him I could tell he was in a painful state, but, knowing his constitution, I wasn't surprised to see how well he hid his loss. Although he was actively pursued by every widow within ten miles, he could muster no interest in any of them. I was proud of Dad.

Chapter Ten
AN OPERATIONAL AUDIT AND MORE

Whoaa, We're Going to Have One

All corporate flight departments are subject to operational audits; usually ordered by top management within the company. Their objective is to get an impartial, qualified evaluation of how well-managed, professional, and safe their flight department is. SSL contracted with one of the better organizations conducting these audits. (A company started by the renowned ex-chief pilot of IBM.) When the word came down that we were in line for this, I was worried. I don't think Perry was that worried, and I considered it my job to warn him about the likely results. We still had about six weeks—enough time to hopefully eliminate the procedures we shouldn't be doing, and implement the ones we should have been doing. Prime among our faults (brought about by an 8 to 5 work schedule that Perry had approved for our maintenance guys), was the fact that they were not there at 6 a.m. to sign the required "maintenance release" for the aircraft, or checking them clear of discrepancies after they had returned. This was an unforgivable situation; in violation of printed FAA regulations.

Flight duty time was another problem. Federal regulations stipulate how many flight hours and how many duty hours a pilot can have in any 24 hour period. Against my repeated complaint, Perry had continued to schedule pilots in excess of these limits. I presented him with a list of fourteen items (of which five were "Safety of Flight" items) that I deemed would have to be corrected before the audit, *or we would fail*. I was floored when he deemed my list just minor things that many flight departments were doing, and that they would not be a "federal case." It also included minor items such as our maintenance guys were inflating tires without putting them in a metal cage first (in case the tire exploded), and when Perry decided to paint the hangar floor, without regard for my insistence that we used a sand-infused, non-skid paint, he chose to do it in a high-gloss enamel. When it was wet, at least one mechanic a day found himself flat on his back

We had the audit, and we failed—miserably. Perry called me in and accused me of having given the examiners the list I had given him—since *eleven of my items were on the list of violations!* Of course I told him I certainly had not shared that list, and when interviewed had not even shared my thoughts concerning the items—in fact hoping like hell that they would miss at least some of them. The vice-president in charge of transportation gave no indication that Perry might be in trouble as a result of this audit, however, one of our pilots scanning the classified ads in *The Wall Street Journal,* spied one announcing that a high tech company in West Palm Beach was looking for a Chief Pilot. (We guessed senior management just thought there was no reason any of their pilots would ever pick up a *Wall Street Journal.)* Several weeks later the VP of transportation had the audacity to call a meeting of all the pilots and announce that Perry had personally decided he no longer wanted to be in a management position, and was going to revert back to just being one of the line pilots! *Can you believe the company did this with a straight face?* All the pilots assumed I would be promoted from Assistant Chief Pilot to Chief Pilot. This was not to be. The company had already hired Perry's replacement; a guy from Wisconsin named Jonathan Jeffrey Symington III (and that name should tell you something). Also, maybe a factor—his father was on the Board of Directors of Procter and Gamble. And I found out, Perry didn't go quietly. He informed every vice president who would listen, that we had failed the audit because I had sided with the examiners and revealed our shortcomings. (Not sure they believed him, but it didn't help.)

A New Boss

When the new chief pilot arrived, ten minutes after being introduced, I knew I was in big trouble. I could sense (and Elsa could see) he was worried about me, maybe jealous of my Learjet experience or my existing relationship with the pilot group. The first six weeks he was only in West Palm Beach a couple days a week; the company gave him time off to travel back to Houston and address personal problems. One of the pilots said Jonathan had confided in him that his son had joined a rock band

and was now in some kind of trouble with the police. He didn't go into detail regarding an even more unsettling problem with his daughter. I drew some consolation comparing this with how *my* kids were faring. In their junior and senior year, I had taken the oldest ones on many visits to the colleges and universities they were considering. They were now there, absent from the house, but definitely not in any kind of trouble. Donna was one semester from a four-year degree and Mark was at the University of Florida; an honor roll student and a 162-pound wide receiver for the "Gators." Iris had gotten a marine biology scholarship at the University of Miami. Stacy and Kevin were still living at home and still attending St. Michael's high school. Marisa was happy in her junior high school in Jupiter. With Jonathan's demonstrated lack of approval of me, this comparison of our offspring gave me some assurance of my own worth. At work it was still awkward; no indication of anything improving. When Jonathan was there, he never took me in his confidence, never asked any questions about existing flight department operating procedures (or if I had any suggestions). He *did* call long-lasting, entirely non-productive meetings, with frequent coffee breaks and smoking breaks, and lots of talk about current movies and popular sports teams. These meetings somehow avoided discussing any operational procedures, and as far as I could see accomplished nothing.

I Felt It in My Bones

I was worried, and I well should have been. He had only been our chief pilot for two months (and as I said, only in town a total of about three weeks) when he called me into his office and spoke: *"Roger, I just can't manage effectively with you staying on board, so I'm terminating you. You'll have to turn in your keys."* To say I was stunned would of course be an understatement. While I knew we'd never be confidants, this action was something I hadn't envisioned. *Turn in my keys? Is this a normal procedure?* Did they think I was going to come back at night and steal something? I was numb and had not yet responded. Jonathan spoke a second sentence, *"And it's of right now. You can empty your desk and leave."* Of course I asked why. What happened? I asked him what the heck had I done? He responded with a second sentence: *"I was hired 'carte blanche' with the approval to do whatever I want personnel-wise, and as I said, I just won't be able to manage effectively with you still here."* No reason, no latitude, a done deal. I stood up—shakily, and gave him my keys. He added one more thing: that I was to report to Bill Goodwin in Human Resources right away. I turned and exited the office; think I passed a couple of pilots in the hall, but they were a blur going by, couldn't even voice a *Hi*, just made a waving motion. Mentally staggering, I filled up one cardboard box with items from my desk and another one with plaques and certificates that had adorned my office walls.

I went directly to the HR offices, hoping I might be able to make some progress there. Maybe even get this thing turned around. But if you think I was surprised and stunned by Johnathon Jeffrey, it was nothing as compared to what I was shown and told at my meeting with Bill Goodwin. One thing that didn't help: Bill had only been with the company for one month. When he arrived Jonathan was already here and the supposedly established and respected chief pilot. And Bill knew nothing of my reputation—of my years of exemplary performance. Of course I started by pointing out I had no idea what I had done that could have prompted Jonathan to come to this decision. After saying that Bill looked up at me with a sarcastic expression on his face, opened a manila folder, and spread three 8x11 pink sheets across his desk. I looked at them unknowingly; not understanding what they were or signified. "Well Roger, I don't understand where the mystery is. Here are three filed reports of reprimands Jonathan gave you in the last month and a half!" *Three reprimands? In a month?* There *were* no reprimands, no meetings, not even any brief conversations that could have been interpreted to have been a meeting or reprimand. Bill went on: "And look, right here on this second one, he told you that one more occurrence and it would be grounds for termination." I was at a loss to speak and almost unable to remain standing. It wasn't that Jonathan had exaggerated a meeting we had. We didn't *have* any meetings. *None!* He had completely forged the three reprimand forms. There never was a single one. Not one meeting occurred!

I quickly pointed out one important, but soon to be discounted fact. Knowing Bill had been a personnel officer for 20 years, I urgently asked him, "Bill, with all your experience, have you ever seen an employee receive a final warning before being fired, *where the supervisor didn't have a witness to that final warning, or get a signature from the warned employee?* There's no witness, and you don't see my signature there; right there—in the block specifically designed to hold it." This of course was factual and *did* cause him pause—a fleeting moment of doubt he could not disguise. But evidently he knew it was a done deal and mumbled his way to finally informing me that I was being *"Outplaced for Management Convenience."* Corporate aviation is a family—a tight group. When a pilot is let go for reasons thought best to avoid mentioning (exactly what this "Outplaced for Management Convenience" usually implies) his chance of being hired by another corporation are nil! Being terminated in this fashion I was in very very big trouble, and weak with the inability to think of any solution. Whereas when high on the totem pole at Learjet, I had mused about at last being in a respected position and *what Mireille might think if she could have seen me then?* I shuddered in my present plight; being glad she couldn't see me in this situation. Of course, that was just a momentary reflection, while my actual situation was real and immutable!

Worth a Try

I asked each of the pilots if they would be kind enough to write a testimonial letter as to my flying skills, management techniques, and ability to carry on an amiable relationship with just about anyone. I was gratified and humbled by the sincere and convincing letters I received from each of them. Along with these letters I made up a chronology of my history with SSL, pointing out innumerable pluses, and delivered the packet to three vice presidents I knew reasonably well. (Two others I really knew well and who had high opinions of me, had unfortunately—just recently left the company!) The ones I did give it to, did me the favor of reading the materials carefully and confided in me that it sure looked like I was victim of one person's personal motives, *but in view of the new chief pilot's "carte blanche" I was screwed.* One thing that surprised me was a couple of them said, "Don't worry, this happens to senior managers all the time." In fact one VP said it happened to him twice.

I was able to get a meeting with the president of the company, who was sincerely sympathetic and said the company would offer me a reasonable settlement. But in spite of the pilots' letters and the many contributions of my past service, he could not overturn Johnathon's decree that I must go. *Seven years shot and back to no retirement again!* As I said earlier, the wording of my termination was often a euphemism for some other dastardly act that it was felt best not to mention. With this implied cause for termination it was highly unlikely (I'd say impossible) that I would ever secure another position with a respected corporate flight department. Now once again, in 1984—even later in my life, with less time remaining to recover, I was indeed at a loss, with no plan and little optimism or energy. (*Geez, just imagine if I was with Mireille now!*)

Chapter Eleven
TRYING MY HAND OUT OF AVIATION

A Note to You My Dear Reader

Please bear with me through this chapter of apparently mundane vocational activities (absent any affairs or even attempts thereat). Your patience will be rewarded in chapters to come, as action-packed exploits are undertaken, and new feminine interests evolve.

Finding the Lord, or at Least Looking for Him

The first week as an unemployed, not young (aging), one-eyed pilot (recently put on blood pressure medicine), with no solution whatsoever in mind, I was distraught. I could not clear my mind of destructive thoughts of an unknown and frightening future. I couldn't fall asleep at night and had a hard time getting out of bed in the morning. I was at this time, not a capable person. I guess—should I have gone to a doctor, he would have diagnosed deep depression. For something this unjust—this uncalled for, to have happened, made me—for the first time consider there may be some actual *master plan*, and I was just now carrying out my designated part in it. How else could this have happened? *Maybe there is a God.* My brother Hank (a serious born-again Christian) is always talking about that *"peace that passeth all understanding."* Maybe I can find it. If I try, maybe it will be the change in my life that might salvage me, I decided I would. I joined a small wooden-shingled Lutheran church just down the street— and did so with a vengeance. Within a month I was the Head Usher and the Director of the Youth Group. I was hoping for some answers, maybe a revelation, where I might be led, if I just "turn the other cheek."

Could I be an Entrepreneur?

At the church I met Nick; an especially energetic young Christian in the throes of starting a his own business in Contemporary Christian Music.

His plan was to make posters featuring the latest hit songs of popular CCM artists. Unknown to me, every city has a Christian radio station that plays CCM music all day long. There are even two well-subscribed-to monthly magazines featuring articles about popular young Christian Music artists. Nick claimed he was well on his way, having already secured the rights for one artist and done a poster of their latest song. However, Nick was penniless and was going no further until he secured capital. You guessed it: I was going to prove to the Lord that I was ready to join Him by providing the funding for this Christian project. After hours of discussion with an almost breathlessly excited Nick; asking him a ton of questions, drafting several business plans, and hours of praying, *I found a place for my recent financial settlement from SSL*. Before embarking on this project for redemption (of which I was a long way from being convinced), I'd sent out about 50 aviation resumés to respectable corporations, just in case.

I flew to Nashville, popped in unannounced at the studios of several well-known CCM artists: Sandi Patty, Amy Grant, and the new rage—a guy named Michaels. Surprisingly I was able to gain their enthusiastic support and an implied willingness to give us a try. (I would find out later it is much easier to get someone to say, "Wow—that's a great idea! Count me in," than to get them to write a check.) The lyrics of these CCM songs could be interpreted as having come from scripture. So on the poster— along with the artist's name in bold print, in smaller print we listed the chapter and verse Nick felt inspired the lyrics. This gained us the respect and admiration of pastors and especially—the youth group leaders, who knew their teenagers would be more receptive to Biblical study based on one of our colorful posters. (Unfortunately, pastors and youth group leaders are not at CCM concerts buying posters in the lobby.) We had two (flawed) marketing plans:

Plan "A": Get the touring schedule of the artists who we had done a poster on, and ship the posters of their new song to each stop on their tour. This was expensive *and a total bust!* No matter how many calls we made; no matter how much encouragement we gave to local kids, or how much commission we offered them, we never could get reliable sales persons at the venues. We would often end up with a box of a hundred posters lying around some auditorium in Peoria (that we couldn't easily retrieve). And the artists themselves sabotaged us! Lo and behold—just before starting their tour they recorded a new song that became a hit, *and they didn't even perform our poster's song at their concert!*

Plan "B": Christian bookstores are a big business. Every town has at least one. In my business plan I computed that if we got just two; only *two* bookstores in each state, that would be 100 sales outlets, and result in the business realizing a rewarding income. Perhaps you're familiar with poster display racks—those clear acrylic frames, mounted atop a tripod, that you turn like pages in a book, each one displaying a poster. *I had neglected to enter the cost of these necessary items in my business plan.* Even buying re-conditioned ones, the cheapest price I was able to get was $1,000 per unit. *My business plan had a $100,000 shortfall!* This of course sunk the project. The Lord had let me down, but then I guess I had let him down first, and often.

On Being a Real Estate Developer

Reeling from the disappointment of my first business venture (and the loss of my SSL settlement), I could not discount once again flying for one of those low-paying, "shoestring," "mom and pop" jet charter companies. They'd hire me because they don't care much about whatever "Outplaced for Management Convenience" means. They just want to know that wherever you're sent, whenever you're sent, you're going to get there— every time. (I was good at that.)

While debating whether or not to hook up with one of those 'bare-bones' Ft. Lauderdale charter companies, I was introduced to a local guy (coincidentally—because he too only had one eye). He was a real-estate developer, and told me about an oceanfront project he was working on. I volunteered my years-ago project with Ron, marketing that Spanish seaside resort (Playa Granada), and my work with him again in the states trying to develop a network of wholesalers for that nausea-provoking pyramid sales company (Bestline). He said my marketing and fund-raising skills might help him. He was investigating a variety of revenue-producing ideas for a beachfront lot in Hobe Sound that he (as the General Partner) and 25 other individuals (Limited Partners) owned. It was ideally located; only a quarter mile from the center of town and zoned commercial. He assured me if I could offer assistance, it would result in me receiving a share of the profits (and he indicated large numbers). To make ends meet while waiting for the final "big payment" Doug set me up for a monthly advance on the calculated profit we'd make. Thank God, it almost equaled my previous salary at SSL.

You might ask why would I be interested in something I wasn't qualified for, and that was somewhat of a gamble? An understandable question to which I don't have a good answer. Ever since my early morning paper routes, afternoons of stocking-shelves in the grocery store, nights spent cleaning the gym in college, and working a second job in Wichita, I had a hard time passing up the chance for more income and maybe even—this time, hitting the jackpot. We can speculate whether it's from my father's constant financial warnings or just in my DNA, *I had a hard time not finding myself in need of additional income* and thusly doing whatever I could, whenever I could, to guard against that eventuality.

The Project Begins

Doug scheduled me for a meeting with the other owners. I put on a button-down shirt, regimental-striped tie and my dark blue blazer, hoping to impress the group (inasmuch as he had been bragging to them about what a difference this pilot from West Palm Beach would make). At the meeting I discovered what the situation was: They owned the property and now wanted to develop it, *but what kind of developing?* I got their approval to hire a company that did "Best Use Studies" of commercial property, hoping they would come up with a good idea. It was 1984. A new type of real estate project was the rage: Time-Share Condominiums. At this point there was only one in Florida—the Marco Polo in Miami, and it was making money hand over fist. A "Time Share" is radically different than a normal condominium. It's a whole new concept. The purchaser buys a unit for a *specific week* during the year, and can only occupy it during *that* week, each year—forever. Thus a developer could sell a single unit to as many as 52 buyers! This significantly increases the revenue over a standard condominium sale.

I presented this option to the owners. They went for it big, but the other problem: *they had no money to start the construction of anything.* The current market value of the property was $280,000. I suggested a possible solution: This amount worked out to each of them having a current equity of $10,769. If we could find 26 more people to buy in at that amount—$10,769, the new owners would then have the same investment as the original owners, and we would have over a quarter million dollars cash to construct a small "Time-Share." They approved the idea and my first big (bigger than I thought) task was in front of me: commence an effort to recruit the new investors.

I GUESS I JUST WASN'T THINKING

Searching for Qualified New Investors

First, I needed some sales materials. I rented one of those elevating basket cranes and took a bunch of aerial shots of the property, printed a map showing its location relative to the center of town, made up several paragraphs boasting of the project's potential, and used this material to design a slick brochure for my sales efforts. Coming up with enticing advertisements was not difficult; finding people willing to part with the money *was!* I placed some ads and spent every day answering inquiries and setting up appointments. I found out quickly there was no sense in giving a pitch with one of the spouses absent; the one present would consistently claim that with the other spouse absent, they could not make a firm decision. Many people did inquire, and irrespective of their qualifications or lack thereof, I still gave a presentation. One night I had an appointment with the Smedleys. When I arrived at the house I almost didn't knock. It was in a lower class neighborhood and theirs was one of the less kept-up homes (with a beat up old Chevy in the driveway). Inside I met a slovenly dressed guy with a beer belly and a three-day beard. His wife was in a ragged bathrobe, no makeup and her hair in rollers. They had two snot-faced and poorly behaved kids. Not being in a position to walk out (but wanting to) I rushed through one of the worst presentations I ever made and quickly exited.

But every now and then I'd stumble on someone who obviously could afford to get one or more of the units, and who from our first meeting was excited about it. One such gentleman called me up after seeing the ad and asked a series of intelligent questions (even expressing an interest to be taken to the property as soon as possible)! He wanted me to give him a presentation right away and of course I was thrilled to schedule one for the next night. He lived in Jupiter. His address was an expensive gated community and when I arrived at his house it was one of the most impressive (and there were two BMW's in the driveway). Inside I had the privilege of meeting an established and handsome couple, who were both attorneys. I immediately sensed something was wrong. As soon as we made the proper introductions, the husband—sincerely apologetic, explained that when we scheduled the meeting he had forgotten tonight was his daughter's recital which started in an hour. He begged me, if we could delay it a day; tomorrow night for sure! I had no alternative but to understand. Not wanting to appear adverse, assured him I understood, wished his cute and well-dressed daughter good luck, and left.

You can be sure I was there as scheduled, at 7 pm sharp the following night. No cars in the driveway. When I got to the entrance, there—tacked eye-height on the carved teak door was a well printed note: SORRY!! HAD A MEETING COME UP. WILL CALL TOMORROW. *Shit!* But surprise, he *did* call! And we *did* get together. The meeting went well (with a glass of wine and some cheese and crackers provided by his wife). It may have been the best presentation I ever made! He asked about the possibility of someone buying *multiple* units. (*Whoaa!*) At the conclusion of the presentation he asked if on Saturday or Sunday I could bring him up to actually "stand on the property." Another great sign. A Saturday morning car trip was scheduled and accomplished. On the property the guy and his wife were like kids with a new puppy. *I was seeing dollar signs.* Monday he called me and asked if I could come over that night, he thought they were ready to make a move. *Holy Shit! Thank God!* Got there—right on time as you might imagine, nervous as hell, ready to pick up a check, and hoping like hell one for three or four units. *Oh no!* Eye-height on the teak door, another of the hand written signs begging my forgiveness and promising he'd be there tomorrow night, same time, come hell or high water! I was there, but he wasn't. I never did get another personal meeting. Never heard from him again. And you remember those first people I met, that down-on-their-luck, slovenly couple, with the rusted car and snot-nosed kids—the Smedleys (to whom I gave the worst presentation ever), a couple weeks later they called me *and bought five units!* Took me several months, but I found enough new investors to raise the equity-equaling $280,000 and we were ready to start construction on a small, two-story, 22-unit time-share.

The Oceanfront Hideaway and Selling the Unit-Weeks

I won't bother you with the long list of obstacles and frustrations we had building it. The time-share thing had just started, and was not well understood. The zoning board wouldn't approve the project *unless we added the word "motel" to the name!* Now, instead of finding investors my new job was to find buyers—people to actually *purchase* one or more of those new-fangled "unit-weeks." Keep in mind that twenty-two units times 52 weeks each, meant I had an inventory of 1,144 unit-weeks to sell. A bunch. Any evening I didn't have an appointment I spent it making calls, which was no fun. Each one included a difficult and extended sales pitch (that required me to generate and maintain a high level of enthusiasm). I was exhausted at the end of each call. During the days, I'd be walking the beach by ten in the morning and there till 4 in the afternoon—handing out brochures to every beachgoer who would take one (and this pastime was not uplifting). Some days I didn't go to the beach; instead I'd drive maybe 75 miles to visit one of Florida's big tourist attractions. There I'd spend the day in the parking lot slipping brochures under the windshield wipers, or better—sticking them down between the glass and the rubber strip at the bottom of the driver's-side window. (By the end of the day, even switching hands midday, this effort resulted in broken back nails and bloodied finger tips.)

After several more months, no matter what marketing innovations I tried, the sales finally ground to a halt. Although I had sold more than half of the 1,144 unit-weeks, 400 still remained unsold (partly because they were not in desirable vacation seasons). The guy who had hired me— Doug, the General Partner of the Limited Partnership found a marketing firm that had him real excited. They guaranteed him they would sell it out in six months. And they did! But guess how: *They doubled the price of the units, and gave all that extra money to the salesmen!* I could hardly believe after all the trouble I was having selling a particular unit-week at $1,200, these hard-nosed, manipulative (in fact—ruthless) "closers" were bringing in signed contracts at $2,400 per unit week! Once "sold out" I received a satisfactory amount that made my year and a half of effort (a mostly discouraging effort) almost worthwhile. I could take a breath.

Next: Becoming a Licensed Contractor

One would have thought when I finally was relieved of the harrowing responsibilities of the Oceanfront Hideaway Motel, I would not have had the energy to undertake another new occupation; just give up and take one of those lousy charter-flying jobs out of Fort Lauderdale. At least it was something I was familiar with and could do well. But no, with no respected corporate flying possibilities, and still concerned about no savings for my old age, I gave thought to what I might be able to do locally. There was one addition to residential dwellings that had always interested me: *skylights.* With little thought to what responsibilities I might be undertaking, I did some research on the subject and formed a Sub-Chapter C corporation called Modern Home Skylights. I was going to try my hand as a small business owner, *installing skylights!*

I chose my own house for the first installation. It had a tile roof, which at first I thought would be more difficult (until I encountered similar problems with shingled roofs). To figure out exactly where to install a skylight, one had to first determine where the roof joists were. You could do this by an interior examination of the ceiling; which if it was not up against the joists, often resulted in opening it up to visually locate the joists. The reason most residential skylights are made 24 inches wide, is because that's a common distance between joists. If someone wanted a wider skylight, this would involve cutting out a section of one joist so it would not interfere with the skylight opening. This required the installation of supporting cross members; not an easy job and a modification that some lawyer could later claim caused a roof failure (and me ending up being named in a law suit).

I didn't stick with this endeavor long. I think I did eleven before giving up. When home at night and hearing a torrential rain I said a little prayer: "Please God keep my skylights from leaking." One of the reason I gave up the business—*was* leaks. This was 1984, before the availability of space-age sealants such as silicone polymers that had a half-life of a hundred years. I had to use petroleum based products—tar! It was vulnerable to ultra violet rays from the sun as well as the hot Florida temperatures. I had many "call-backs" and was lucky in being able to stop the leaks (sometimes after several attempts). I was as glad to finish this avocation as I was to be done with the Oceanfront Hideaway Motel.

Chapter Twelve
A MOST EMBARRASSING OCCURRENCE

A Not Well Understood Decision

Whereas the past seven years had seen me actively involved with all the kids' high school activities, and with the older ones—helping them choose a college, it was less complicated now: only Marisa was home. Donna was away at college (working on her PhD). Mark had graduated from the University of Florida with a Masters in electrical engineering and was living in southern California. Stacy had done the one thing she had always talked about: she became a flight attendant and was living and working in Houston. Kevin had graduated (like his brother) from the University of Florida, with a degree from the College of Architecture, and was living and working in Atlanta. The house was empty except for Marisa, who would be graduating from Jupiter High School next year. My domestic life was suddenly different, and took a strange turn.

I would like to blame what I'm about to tell you on the work-life and stress I was under for the last couple years, but I don't think I can. It was just *me*. Ten years ago you may remember in Part Three, I wrote: *"Of all the selfish, inconsiderate things I've ever done"* referring to my divorce from Sara. *Well I did it again*. Elsa and I decided to go our separate ways. Being the person I am now—at this writing, many years later, and (thankfully but way too late) viewing situations and relationships much differently, and finally understanding more bad stuff about myself, if I had it do over again I would never have divorced Elsa. *"Dance with the one that 'brung' you." "You made your bed, now lie in it!"* Sure, my friends all sympathized with me, telling me they knew what a burden it must have been to be married to a bipolar person. Well maybe it was a burden, but not that much of a burden; not more situations than I could handle. And this woman was a faithful, loving wife. She had a good heart, good intentions, and often did special generous things (like I mentioned before: surprising my son Mark with a pair of low-cut football cleats). All in all, she did the best job any woman could have, managing a mixed household that started out with five kids from two families. We had few if any substantial disagreements. Well then, what was it?

It was me! A failed, flawed spouse and partner; one who had not yet been able to feel and show devotion. We're talking a *major* deficiency, but in my case, not a new one; one that had been present as far back as I can remember (and certainly and cruelly with Sara). Tragically, inside my soul, there was this irrepressible fright, that once married I was cornered, disqualified, shut off or excluded from some other, great situation (though God knows what that might have been). I cannot deny we did seem to grow apart, but I also cannot deny that it was my fault; my inability to hug her and reassure her. I was the one responsible for the changing complexion of our marriage. It would not have occurred if I would have just been a normal, 8 to 5, run-of-the-mill, loving husband. I was not. I think I would have liked to have been, but the unremitting restlessness, the "calling," turned me into a dissatisfied partner. This in turn filled Elsa with doubt, and resulted in her withdrawing, and understandably treating me in a similar manner, which I deserved, but which only contributed even more-so to the dissolution. I beg your forgiveness (as even now I am looking down and shaking my head). The fact that all the kids were gone, living on their own elsewhere, made it somewhat easier. The fact that I left Elsa the house, and all our cash holdings, helped somewhat to assuage my deserved guilt. Although not stipulated anywhere to do so, I would assist her financially for the rest of her life.

Chapter Thirteen
THE DEA. YOU CAN'T TELL THE PLAYERS
WITHOUT A PROGRAM

One of Those Kinds of Flying Jobs Again

Alone again, as I deserved to be; not a fitting partner. Embarking on my next revenue-producing activity displays as well as anything, my inability to consider possible consequences (in fact my inability to even consider *likely* consequences)! One of my Air America pilots—Colt Chance, who I hadn't heard from in years, phoned me. Far as I knew, he was retired and living in southern Georgia. After a few pleasantries he said he was going to be passing through West Palm Beach and suggested we have a beer together. *Great!* In Laos Colt and I had some real close calls together! The idea of reminiscing together sounded good—especially now. He arrived and we went to "T J Gators" where it turned into more than just a reunion. After some fish and chips and a couple cold beers, adjudging the time was right, he leaned closer and began to share something with me; something a little scary; something about which I was afraid I might become interested.

"Listen Rog, I don't know if you'd want to do it, but let me tell you about it. A friend of mine is a professor at Valdosta State College. He has a brother in the Keys who owns a small trailer park in Marathon and works for the DEA. The professor put me in touch with him and you should see what I'm doing now and the money I'm making"! I knew Colt was always ambitious and not averse to taking risks, so not sure I wanted to hear about it, but told him I was listening.

He said that after a couple meetings with the brother—Rich (who had his own single-engine Cherokee Six), Rich flew him back up to Valdosta

Regional Airport. There parked on the ramp of a small Fixed Base Operator, he showed Colt another Cherokee. (An "FBO" is usually a 'mom and pop' outfit, making their money parking and refueling airplanes.) The airplane was going to stay there and be *for Colt's personal use any time he wanted it!* But there was a catch. Rich had some ideas about just what that use would be: Colt was to start flying down to the small Homestead airport just south of Miami.

Colt went on: "And listen to this: After landing I was to taxi to Stewart Aviation—a small FBO seemingly on-the-verge of going out of business. Once parked on the ramp there I was to roam around until I found two guys. Rich gave me their names and a couple photos. Once I found them I was to strike up a conversation with them; make friends with them and get on their good side. I understood the directions, but of course asked him *why?* He just waved a hand and said they were both pilots who owned single-engine planes that they used primarily for pleasure trips to the Bahamas. They would be easy to find, because almost every day they were hanging around Stewart Aviation. Rich said I'd find them either on the ramp, in the hangar, or when not there, having a coffee inside in the rundown luncheonette."

Colt was not only able to find them, but being a renowned aviation story-teller (and knowing more risqué jokes than any standup comic) he was able to begin developing the relationship Rich had wanted him to achieve (though still not knowing why).

"After a couple weeks I had their confidence, and they began to be less guarded in their comments, and I understood why they didn't appear to have a job. They began to drop vague remarks that hinted as to their source of income: *smuggling!* Of course Rog, I was shocked when they admitted this to me; first—that these nice and normal guys were smuggling, and second—that after knowing me only a few weeks, they would let me know that they were doing it. That night I phoned Rich and asked him what the fuck was up? I told Rich that while the guys never outright admitted to it, I damned well thought they were smuggling pot or something. Rich said *he already knew that,* and while he didn't say it, he implied he was with the Drug Enforcement Agency *and he was counting on me to infiltrate their operation.* He said there was no way he could have told me that first, because if I knew it, those guys would have smelled it on me."

"What else did he tell you? What was the plan?"

Colt finally got to the heart of it, saying "My job was to keep the friendship going until I'd gained their complete confidence, and *they asked me (and my Cherokee) to join them on one of their runs to Colombia and back."*

"Christ Colt, he's asking you to actually take part in a smuggling mission?!"

"Yeah—exactly! Of course I questioned that too. Rich I guess was expecting this. He laughed and put his hand on my forearm, saying that he understood my worries and knew there were two big ones: first, they'd be caught—me among them, and I'd be thrown in jail while babbling my story about being an undercover DEA contractor, and second—and worse, the guys might find out I was a 'plant.' And if so, I'd leave on a trip and never come back. Rich said he was in a position to take care of at least the first concern. He also said that while he didn't know about Carl's generosity, suffice it to say he said I'd be extremely well paid for any trip I made, and that money did not have to be accounted for! And before the operation was wrapped up, I might have to make several trips. Evidently I was doing okay because one day Rich asked me if I knew anyone qualified who might be interested in working with me in the project to break up this ring, and I thought of you."

Can't Believe I Did It

The result was—after this discussion with Colt, though I don't know why I did it (maybe because of no job, no income, and still no retirement) though *very* unsure—I told him I would be willing to at least meet with Rich and hear it from the "horse's mouth." Colt set up a meeting with Rich in a high-rise in Fort Lauderdale. After listening to Rich I heard myself agreeing. I heard the words—not believing I had signaled my vocal cords to produce them. Don't know if it was because I didn't want to let Colt down, or appear like a wimp to Rich, but I responded by saying *I'd be willing to give it a try.* My commitment to come onboard resulted in Rich positioning another Cherokee Six on the ramp at West Palm Beach—for my use. The Cherokee Six was the "plane-of-choice" because it had a 300-horsepower engine that would be necessary when taking off and trying to climb in an overweight condition. Colt asked the two guys if after adding him to their operation, they'd ever thought about even one more plane. (Another plane. More cargo, more revenue!) The subject was brought up from time to time and finally Colt was able to convince the two guys (Carl and Daryl) that he knew a guy (me) with his own Cherokee Six. And that he had known me for years, that I could be trusted with anything, was a great bush pilot and had done things like this before. During the next two months, after many flights to Homestead, many bullshit sessions at Stewart Aviation as well as having my share of beers with them at the nearby Blue Boar Tavern. I was invited to be part of the operation.

Fearful as I was, the Day Arrived

And finally it was time for our first trip. Carl said it would be a round trip non-stop flight to Colombia and back. We would leave from the smaller Fort Lauderdale Executive airport at eight in the morning—for a couple reasons: there were a lot of departing aircraft at that time; it was a shift-change in the tower, and those that were arriving were busy opening up their egg and sausage McMuffins. And one other thing that Carl told us: if a DEA guy was in the tower and spied a plane taxiing out with no seats, they would suspect that was because they needed the cabin space for bales of pot on the way back. So to escape this detection, before positioning the plane to Fort Lauderdale for departure, we would take out the real seats and install throwaway Volkswagen seats (that someone had picked up from a junk yard). Surprisingly they fit on the seat tracks and were not dissimilar from the original seats. And here was the real risky part we couldn't avoid when taxiing out for takeoff: already plumbed into the engine fuel line would be a half full bladder of fuel laid the length of the cabin, stuffed between the two rows of seats. With the long-range fuel tank in the airplane, if we ever got stopped taxiing out, we would have to do some fast talking to explain why we needed the extra fuel.

Finding Out Where We Would Land on Our Return

Carl had Colt and I climb up into a huge, big-tired F550 truck (completely painted camouflage). He then took us to where in a few days we would be landing *at 3 in the morning.* We drove into the Everglades until we came upon a locked metal gate, with an official-looking sign above it that read "No Trespassing. By order of US Bureau of Land Reclamation." *Whoaa.* Carl motioned to Daryl to jump out and unlock the gate. No idea how Daryl got a key. (I later learned that these guy grew up here and had childhood friends working for just about every state and federal governmental organization). We went through, driving on a narrow path atop a raised dirt dike that split multiple canals. Carl stopped on a stretch of east-west dike, about five hundred feet long *that was going to be our runway.* Man! I could see why they wanted a bush pilot. It would be pitch black—no light except the moon. Although I had a lot of night flying experience, Carl said we would not be able to use our landing lights until we were only 50 feet above the ground! The dike was short and narrow. If you went off the end or over the side, the airplane was wrecked and you were marooned! Not only that, landing to the east (which based on the prevailing winds we would) we had to clear a tree line and then drop down quickly, to hit close enough to this end of the dike to leave enough distance remaining ahead to get it stopped. I could see why they picked this dike; at the left side of the far end was a fifty-foot wide flat area, so at the end of our landing roll there was enough space to park and unload. As things began falling in place—becoming more and more real, I was not feeling confident, or in the right place, or that I was doing the right thing.

Learning More—a Lot More, About Carl

Before dropping us off at the motel Carl said he'd buy us a beer at a local dive (that besides alcohol, mostly sold smelly bait). Surprisingly, once there and sort of "old hat," Carl seemed to shed his rough incommunicado disposition, and talk with us on a personal level. I was surprised when in our conversation Colt mentioned something about other operations bringing in not just pot but cocaine or heroin, and if Carl did, he could make ten times as much money each trip. Carl took on a look of indignation as if he'd been offended. He pulled his head back and said: "That shit's ruining the country. It's bad stuff. I promised myself I wouldn't touch it, and I won't!" Of course I was surprised to hear this opinion. We like to say "there's no honor among thieves," but *this* guy had staked out a position and was sticking with it. As Leo Lippe (the gun manufacturer in Italy) had told me in Part Two: *In life it doesn't so much matter where you draw the line, but if after having drawn it whether or not you can adhere to it.*

And that was only one surprise. Colt asked Carl how he got into smuggling. He answered that it wasn't too long ago, and he'd soon be out of the business. "My wife Shirley made me promise it would only be temporary. Our son was born with about the worst Talipes condition the doctors ever saw; not just a regular club foot, you know—turned down and inwards, but Chad's was at such an exaggerated angle, the front of the foot was rotated far enough inward, that it was permanently positioned a full 90 degrees sideways. To correct this requires at least two if not three surgeries—six to eight months apart. And only one doctor in the world does it and he's in Germany. The fix costs about $175,000, and as soon as I've got that, I'm through with this shit!" *Boy, what you don't know about people till you ask.* I was gaining a whole new perspective on Carl.

After finishing our beers and while walking to the truck, thinking about Carl's singular need for money, Colt asked him when he had saved almost enough for the surgery, why couldn't he just sell his airplane for the rest. "Shit Colt, where do you think I would have gotten the money to buy an airplane? It's not mine. The main guy—Sinclair, provided it for me. And Daryl's too. (We found out that Daryl was Shirley's brother. It was a family project.) On the ride back to the motel Carl asked if we had gloves; if not—buy some. He dropped us at the motel, and after a quick trip to a nearby ACE Hardware to pick up the gloves, we were back at the motel. Colt phoned Rich and told him (without any reference to the personal portion of the conversation we'd just had) that neither of us understood the big picture of what was happening here, and what precise role we were playing. Rich answered that he couldn't tell him everything yet, except: while they knew who *these* two guys were, they didn't know who was getting the stuff—who they were working for. And that was what they needed to know. Colt then remembered Carl having referred to the "main guy," Sinclair, and relayed this to Rich, which *did* get his attention.

"Is Sinclair his first name or his last?" Colt said he didn't know. Rich told him that was his next project: find out as soon as he could and let him know. At the end of the call he gave Colt a website that ended .gov, and told him to check it out (implying that Colt would read about the department that Rich was in). He did, and did find the department Rich referenced, but there was little information and of course, no names.

Final Preparations

The day before "D-day" Carl had us fly to a rural area west of Kendall Lakes; almost on the east edge of the glades. No residential developments nearby— just a barn or a warehouse every couple miles. Our designated landing area was a pasture next to a large barn. No other structures, just green fields stretching for miles. We landed and after bounding through the high grass to a stop, we were met by a guy we'd never seen before. He had us taxi *inside* the barn. A barn with a concrete floor that was completely empty except for what looked like a well-outfitted machine shop on one side. We wasted time while the unknown guy installed the big rubber bladder that would be our extra fuel tank. It was evidently not an easy modification, involving cutting metal, installing valves and connectors, and then hooking up hoses from the bladder to the fuel line that went to the engine. The only control for the pilot was a large "T" handle that when turned would both close the valve in the fuel line from the wing tanks, and at the same time open the valve to allow fuel from the bladder tank to flow to the engine. When finished we installed Volkswagen seats on the tracks on each side of the bladder. The guy who had led us in gave us some alcohol rags, told us to put on our gloves and wipe down the whole airplane, inside and out; anywhere and everywhere he or we might have touched.

The Trip Down

The next morning about 7 am I was parked on the ramp at Fort Lauderdale Executive; not far from Carl and Colt in their planes (no Daryl—just a three-plane flight). At 8 am sharp we called for taxi clearance and started out to the runway. I was nervous as hell and wishing I'd never got myself into this. I was just praying there was nobody in the tower with binoculars. *Afraid to even turn my head in that direction.* One by one we were cleared for takeoff. As my wheels came up I thought: *one* thing under our belts, we're airborne. As a pilot, once you break ground there's a feeling of satisfaction and well-being, but not this time. We headed southeast over Biscayne Bay, on our initial heading towards Haiti; 700 miles—about five hours. As we went "feet-wet" (over the Atlantic) all three of us checked in on our VHF frequency of 123.45. To ascertain radio contact we didn't speak; Carl clicked his mic button once, Colt clicked his twice, and I followed suit with three clicks. Rich said that if the DEA caught Carl and Daryl before his sting was completed, they'd never find out where and to who the stuff was going, and get the big guy; and that was what they wanted. We might have to keep it going (not get caught) a couple more trips, to get Carl to mention Sinclair's real name. That being the case I spent the first thirty minutes scanning the sky, searching for a King Air or Cessna Citation that Rich told us his other operation was flying.

After an hour I was more relaxed; thinking the DEA wouldn't be flying this far offshore. Though I couldn't relish it today, I must say, the turquoise and emerald green water surrounding the Caribbean islands is mesmerizing. About 1:30 we approached the open water between the east end of Cuba and the west end of Haiti. Once there, we made our turn due south between the two islands—toward Colombia: 540 miles and another four hours. Not another plane. Not a sound on the radio. Four hours and twenty minutes later, Carl made a slight heading adjustment; I'm assuming a more direct route to wherever our landing site was. Ten minutes later I had Barranquilla in sight. Shortly thereafter, even in the now limited daylight I had what must be our destination in sight: a dirt strip carved out of the jungle; not a wide or long strip, but not as bad as the ones I landed at in Laos. Carl made a transmission: "Get in a thirty second trail and follow me in. Don't waste any time in the air. Don't circle overhead, just land straight in." Colt adjusted his position and I reduced power to slow down and get spacing behind him. We all three landed no sweat (except for teeth jarring bumps) and taxied back to what would be the loading area.

Somewhere About 25 Miles Outside Barranquilla

On the ground, I didn't know what to expect—probably chaos. Instead it was pretty well organized. None of the people there looked friendly. Some appeared to be in a military uniform. No one talked to anyone. First all the seats came flying out and then the bladder was stretched out flat on the cabin floor—all in about thirty seconds. The 55-gallon drums of fuel had already been dollied over. A hand pump was mounted on the drum opening and a long hose was being connected from it to the rubber bladder. Filling the bladder took longer than I expected. I watched mine expand and finally be declared full. The other guys' fuel bladders were full about the same time as mine, and the actual loading began. The marijuana bundles were compressed heavy cubes about 30-inch-square and tightly wrapped in black plastic. I could see why they chose this size. They fit perfectly in the Cherokee cabin—two across and two up; tight against the walls and right up to the ceiling. They were stacked on top of the fuel bladder. I suspected this weight would assist in forcing the bladder fuel through the eight foot rubber line that led up to the engine. Starting against the aft bulkhead in the cabin and then forward right up against the pilot's and copilot's seat, allowed four rows. (In fact the guys loading had moved my seat full forward in order to be able to get in the last row.) This was going to be an uncomfortable trip back. In the cabin were 16 bales; plus two in the copilot's seat, a full load—18 bales total.

The Trip Back

It was at best—twilight, when we positioned for takeoff. I was third. As I anticipated, the acceleration on takeoff roll was frightenly (alarmingly!) slow—*as if I was towing a trailer with flat tires!* Halfway down the dirt strip I considered aborting the takeoff; fearing I was so heavy I might not even attain lift-off airspeed; just plow into the trees at the far end! I kept going (and praying); waited until I had fifteen more knots speed than usual, and eased the yoke back. The nose wheel *did* come up, but the main gear—supporting most the weight, *were still heavy on the ground*. The tree line was rushing up. When I'd gotten as close to it as I dared—I pulled (yanked) the nose up, and *thank God* I broke ground. *I was airborne!* But none too soon. Before I got the wheels up I heard them scraping through the tree tops and snapping limbs. Incidentally, so many guys did crash on these overloaded takeoffs that even tonight, parked alongside the strip was a tractor with a back hoe *to dig a hole and bury the remains of a crashed plane*. (If the pilot lived and was lucky, he could talk one of the other pilots into not taking the two bales in the copilot's seat, and let him ride back in the vacated space.)

Performance of an Over-grossed Aircraft

I was at full power, the engine was screaming for me to give it a break. I was climbing, barely—at maybe 50 feet per minute, as compared to the normal *1,500 feet per minute!* If I would have acquiesced to the engine's plea for a rest and pulled off even the slightest bit of power, I would have stopped climbing and started settling. Rolled into a bank to make my right turn to the north, towards the coast. Maximum lift is produced when the wings are level. Rolling into a bank this lift is markedly reduced. The normal bank angle is 30 degrees. I tried it and immediately noticed my rate of climb go to a *negative* 50 feet per minute down! Quick—lessen the angle of bank! Just hold 15 degrees for longer; a wider turn but I'll eventually get to the departure heading. Once we were "feet wet" northbound, we once again did the verifying all aboard mic clicks. Usually in a Cherokee Six, to get to a cruising altitude of ten thousand feet would take six to eight minutes. It took me fifty minutes—almost an hour, to reach ten thousand feet (and I was never sure the airplane was going to make it). Soon it was pitch black; blacker than you would be familiar with, because on land—always near a town or city, there is a lot of light trapped in the lower atmosphere that reflects back. Out here in the middle of the ocean, you have none of that. We say "it's like being inside a bottle of ink, in a coat pocket, hanging in a closet with the door closed."

Fuel Management - Having Enough to Get Back

Once stabilized, perhaps the most worrisome time occurs: *that time when you to try to switch the engine to the bladder fuel.* This is done by rotating the recently installed "T" handle, which opens the valve to the bladder, *but at the same time cuts off the normal fuel flow from the wings to the engine.* There are a half dozen things that can go wrong when attempting this: *all resulting in the engine quitting!* Starting the process involves first decreasing the power so the engine has less need of fuel, then advancing the mixture control to "Full Rich," activating the auxiliary fuel pump, then and only then do you *muster the nerve to rotate the "T" handle.* Even when it works perfectly, air trapped in the bladder line will usually cause the engine to miss, cough and sputter for fifteen seconds. A big breath and I did it. Two slight coughs and the engine was running smoothly. *Thank you God.*

And, if *beginning* to use the bladder fuel isn't enough of a challenge; since we have no fuel gauge for the bladder tank we don't know when it's going to run dry. The best you can do is divide the gallons in the tank by the gallons per hour you're using, and come up with a rough estimate of the time when you *expect* it to run dry. Unfortunately the way you know exactly when it's running dry is *you hear the engine quitting!* (And to have enough fuel to make it back, you *do* have to let it run dry.) A half hour before the time you estimated it would run dry, you reach down and position your hand on the "T" handle, so it will be there when the engine starts missing and you can immediately rotate it back to normal fuel flow from the wings.

Arriving Back to Florida and Getting Past the Radar

While I didn't know it yet, our takeoff time from Colombia was calculated so as to have us going "Feet-Dry" (crossing over dry land inside Biscayne Bay) *within a tight 20-minute window!* I told you about the "good ole boy" network down here; how one of Daryl's high school buddies worked for the Water Reclamation Bureau, and had given him the key to the gate that kept the public out of the system of drainage canals in the glades. Well Carl's cousin was the senior radar operator at the Air Traffic Control Center in Richmond (just southwest of Miami). Once we were within fifty miles of the coast, even though our small planes only made a tiny 'blip' on a radar scope, there was a chance we could be spotted. Carl's cousin—

based on the time, would know we were approaching and what time we'd cross the coastline. The plan was (and evidently carried out successfully) for him to create some diversion; give his guys some task or a coffee break and volunteer to watch the scopes himself. For us; monitoring the Miami tower frequency we were able to hear them announce the current barometric pressure so that we could adjust our altimeters, and be able to have an accurate reading of our height above the ground. (The dike was only ten feet above sea level.)

Finding the Dike, Landing, and Unloading

I said the landing would be accomplished with no lights. I lied—but not much; we had two guys with flashlights (bright ones)! On the far end of the dike was a guy shining his towards the landing end, and on the landing end—either the bravest or 'stupidist' guy in the world was standing, shining his flashlight straight up the landing path. (On our landing attempt we would pass only five or ten feet over his head!) After about five minutes of searching, twisting and turning around at a thousand feet, scouring the pitch black expanse without being able to make out a single feature on the ground, I heard a long series of clicks. This would be Carl signaling he had found our landing dike. On the trip back and especially now, none of us had our exterior lights on. I therefore had no way to see Carl or Colt's airplanes. Passing east of the strip, and looking back in its direction, I was lucky enough to see a set of landing lights go on, and knew Carl had touched down. A moment or two later, though now west of the dike, I wasn't able to see Colt's landing lights come on, but I did see the dike brighten up again. He'd touched down and was rolling out. *My turn.* I maneuvered the aircraft so as to line up both lights, putting me on a final approach course. Keeping both lights aligned, I put the gear and flaps down and continued my descent. I crossed right over the first guy with the light, chopped the power, and thudded down like a ton of bricks, at the same time flipping on the landing lights to see where I was going and stay centered on the narrow dike. It was bumpy, but thank God the aircraft stayed together. At the end, just to the left, were the other two planes, parked, engines off, doors open.

Off Loading and Escaping

As best I could see in the dark, with a few flashlights bobbing here and there, there were about five guys, shouting at each other and working at a frenzied pace. It didn't look organized but at the rate things were happening, it must have been. After getting bumped into and almost knocked off my feet twice, I backed up to the edge of the activity (where I could more safely survey the frenetic action). Besides Carl's big 550, there was another huge four-wheel-drive pickup. Bales were going into the trucks right and left, sailing through the air and thudding into the truck beds. As soon as the planes were emptied of their cargo, the bladders were coming out. Soon as they were out, from somewhere the original seats were being thrown into the planes. I'll bet we weren't on the ground ten minutes when the job was done. Someone shoved a Dustbuster into my hands, shoved me back into my plane, and told me to get the hell back in the air. Being the last into the widened area and closest to the dike, I was first off—taking back off the opposite way we had landed.

Airborne—of course still with no exterior lights on, I climbed to about a thousand feet, and flew west till I was over the darkest, apparently uninhabited area I could locate. There, and this was something—I set a certain engine power, trimmed the airplane up best I could to "fly itself," *got out of the pilot's seat and went back into the cabin!* (No one is flying the airplane now.) On my hands and knees in the cabin I rolled up the bladder and began using the Dustbuster to vacuum the airplane; suck up every seed, every twig, every piece of a leaf. This took me about fifteen minutes—during which time I had to rush back to the cockpit every three minutes, lean in and activate the controls to right the airplane (which had begun falling off on a wing, or gone so nose up it was losing airspeed and would stall). The plane stabilized, I hurried back to the cabin and continued cleaning. When finally the job was done, the instructions were to "just throw the damn thing out the window!" I did and was glad I never read in the papers *"In the middle of the night, Glades ranger killed by falling Dustbuster."* But that wasn't my only job. Now, while the airplane was doing mostly okay flying itself, I had to install the six seats. I can tell you, by the time I was done with this I was exhausted and drenched with sweat.

The plan was and I carried out my part, for each of us to go to a separate airport; for me it was the same airport I'd taken off from in the morning: the small Fort Lauderdale Executive airport. No airlines flew into this airport, just small private planes, and there should be zero activity at this ungodly hour. Still in all you can imagine, after landing and taxiing to a parking area I was shaking with fearful scenarios that could occur— like the DEA, not aware of Rich's assignment for us, already there waiting to arrest me, or bored personnel from the facility delaying me in a long conversation. I had to sign in and order fuel; didn't use my real name of course. We always bought fuel with cash—though I wouldn't have to stay and pay now. I'd do it when I returned tomorrow afternoon. Right now I just wanted to get miles between me and the airplane. Didn't hail a cab; walked a couple miles to a mom and pop motel, checked in, and tumbled into the hard single bed, wasted and confused, thankful and worried.

Payday and More

I slept past checkout time, left the motel, walked to the airport, and thank God was able to pay for the fuel and leave without any conversations or any contact that would indicate anything was up. I was due to meet Colt at the Homestead airport at five. Got there about 4:30. Colt was in the luncheonette. He had met with Carl, who had already met with his "main guy"—this *Sinclair* fellow: about whom (remembering Rich's request) Colt asked a couple probing questions. Carl wasn't answering, but he was in a good mood. His son Chad—the one with the acute Talipse of the right ankle, in spite of his significant handicap, had just won a jet-ski tournament in Miami. While of no value to Rich, there was some good news for us: Carl had given Colt our compensation for the trip. With a sheepish smile Colt handed me a paper bag. I went straight to the Men's room, looked inside and pulled out about five or six packs of one-hundred dollar bills! When I counted them, it totaled $28,000—*for one night's work!* I was weak, excited, and not at all sure about my activities.

Colt said that he'd been called by Rich and had to meet him this evening, so probably wouldn't be back at the motel till late. I gave Colt a couple questions to ask Rich, and Colt said he damn well had a couple of his own. About ten Colt returned, with only a few sensible answers. Even though he had no more info about this guy called Sinclair, Rich wasn't upset and even seemed satisfied. He asked Colt exactly how many bales we brought back. Colt told him, that he thought we each had 18 bales, so with three aircraft, the total would have been 54. Colt said that for some reason Rich looked askance at the number quoted, but jotted it down and told him that on the next trip to be sure to get the exact number.

The Next Trip and a Heart-Stopper!

It was another week before we attempted it again, another three plane flight; me, Colt, and Carl's brother-in-law—Daryl. Everything went exactly like the first trip: our departure, our flight down, the hectic loading, the white-knuckle takeoff, the laborious climb to altitude, the flight back, *switching tanks*, and even the landing on the dike. Just as we were finishing the unloading; in the midst of bales sailing through the air, lurching black figures and bobbing flashlights, the air was pierced by a shout of alarm, *"Look over there! Look over there! Jesus Christ!"* I saw where the guy was pointing and whipped around to that direction. He was pointing out to SW 217th, where speeding northward on it, soon to be at that dirt turnoff leading to us, were at least *three cars with flashing red and blue lights.* Uh Oh! The cars turned in on the dirt road and were roaring towards us, sirens wailing! In the next three seconds, without having time to throw the seats in, Daryl, Colt and I were in our cockpits and cranking the engines. My heart was in my throat watching the cars' headlights getting brighter. We hurried onto the dirt runway—only ten feet between us. Simultaneously we poured the coal to it thumping down the dike *only a few yards behind each other* (something that's never done—planes taking off in trail, one right behind the other)! Once airborne I rolled into a steep bank and looked down at the headlights and flashing lights. In the few seconds I had to scan the area, it appeared that the cop cars were speeding westward on the dirt road, at the same time our two trucks were speeding easterly *on the same road!* Had to roll back and couldn't see what was going to happen.

I did not feel like I could return to my designated recovery airport—Fort Lauderdale Executive, or any other airport near Miami, or even anyplace here on the east coast. Checked my fuel gauge and had enough to make it over to Naples Municipal Airport on the west coast. On the way, I did the same drill with the Dustbuster, but didn't have the original seats to install. Luck was with me—the airport was deserted and one half-asleep lineman parked me. I signed in (once again with a made-up name and address), left a fuel order and walked out without seeing a single official. *Thank the Lord for small favors.* Tumbled into a single bed in the first motel I came to. When in a few days I met up with Colt and Carl, I found out what happened with the cops. The drivers of both trucks (Carl being the driver of the first truck), played a game of "chicken," acting as if they were going to plow into the incoming cop cars—head on! Their bluff worked and the drivers of the cop cars chose to yank the wheel and go over the side of the road (down into the canal), rather than risk a "head-on." The trucks roared by, turning right and speeding south on SW 217th. They escaped—with the load, without being caught! In spite of this huge scare, Colt and I stayed as Rich's plants, supplying him with names, dates, and particularly, the number of bales we brought in, and what little we could find out about this guy named Sinclair. We both were waiting for Rich to tell us *"Next trip, we're going to bring em down!"* It still hadn't come. Personally I was just as glad. I had become close to Carl, and knowing his story I would not have felt at all honorable being the reason for his imprisonment. The delay continued, either because of the DEA's ultimate objective, that of course I wasn't privy to, or because the DEA is just another example of federal bureaucracy. In any case we just hung in there (accepting paydays like we never imagined existed).

I thought Carl might fire me after one trip to Jamaica. I was on final to one of those short strips carved out of the jungle, and I could see that Daryl who was landing behind me, had not slowed down near enough, and was too damn close behind me. In order to give him space to land, I would have to land much further down the strip than I would have wanted. I wasn't happy with it. Cursing Daryl under my breath, I held off—staying three feet in the air till halfway down the runway. Touched down, and immediately realized I'd held off so long that there may not be enough runway ahead to stop the plane! A few seconds later I realized *I wasn't going to be able to stop before hitting the tree line at the far end!* The only possible solution: ram the throttle forward and take back off. Give up on this attempt and come back around for another landing. When I finally got airborne I wasn't sure the plane would climb steeply enough to clear the tree tops at the far end. *And it didn't!*

My still extended wheels went right into the tree tops. God awful grating and metal bending; limbs and leaves scraping past the windows, while I was being thrown from side to side. Finally: no movement, no sound, and I was (I thought) untouched. The plane was jammed between two trees, still a good fifteen feet above the ground. I forced the door open, climbed out, and made my way down to the ground. It was then I noticed my right ear bleeding. I think the edge of the shoulder harness had sawed into that indent behind my ear, and the ear lobe was now partly detached. By the time I had walked back to Colt and Daryl at the loading spot, the planes were half loaded. I went to Colt and asked him to throw out the two bales on the copilot's seat and let me ride back with him. I could see he wasn't keen on this idea. He told me if I just stayed overnight he'd come down tomorrow and pick me up. I didn't like that idea at all and pleaded with him. He finally agreed and I was just going to be a passenger on the way back. I was responsible for this trip returning with 18 bales less, *and one less airplane!*

A Terrifying Aviation Story

Surprisingly to me, the loss of one airplane didn't bother Rich at all; in a week I had a replacement. It was a two-plane trip to Barranquilla; Colt and I. Everything had gone well on the way down, loading, taking-off, climbing out, and leveling at cruise. What was next: *start using the fuel from the bladder* (which remember, also stops the normal fuel flow from the wings). You can't make it back without using all the fuel in the bladder. If for some reason it didn't transfer, you'd exhaust the fuel in the wing tanks, the engine would quit, and you'd glide down through the unending blackness, into a crushing wall of unending wet blackness, *and a life of unending blackness.* You had to get all the fuel out of the bladder.

I did the "T" handle rotation, the engine sputtered (which I was expecting) and then *quit!* (Which I wasn't expecting!) Of course I immediately turned the "T" handle back to the wing fuel position, double-checked the mixture "Full Rich," the fuel pump on, exercised the throttle, and dropped the nose a few degrees to keep my airspeed. A cough. Another cough. It caught! The engine was running, but that wasn't good enough, I had to get that fuel from the bladder! If I only used the fuel in the wing tanks, it would run dry about 50 miles south of Andros Island. *Gotta get that bladder fuel.* Have to try again. I did—three times! Each time the same result, a cough, a sputter, and silence. Each time when I rotated the "T" handle back, opening the valve from the wing tanks I was able to get the engine running again.

I had one idea: maybe the weight of the stack of bales in the far rear of the cabin (on top of where the rubber hose came out of the bladder), was *pinching the hose closed.* It was the only thing I could think of, but how could I ever get back to it to straighten it out? My right shoulder was against the two bales in the copilot's seat, and the back of my head was hitting the row stacked up tight behind me. Behind it was another three rows of stacked bales. *There was no way I could get back into the cabin even an inch, let alone to the furthest rear stack.* It could be the end of my life; a night ditching at sea had not yet been lived through, and even if I somehow miraculously survived the crash, I'd have drowned by daylight.

My mind was racing—thinking: could I somehow make a tunnel back through the bales and get to the pinched hose? I couldn't just pull one bale forward—out from behind me, because there was nowhere to put it. I eyed the top bale on the copilot's seat. If I could move it down by the rudder pedals. I could the use the vacated space to put the first bale I drug forward. No, there's just not enough space down there. I could end up jamming the pedals in place; making them unusable. But maybe—if I could slice the top bail into two pieces, I might be able to jam one half of it on top of the glare shield, tight against the windscreen in front of the copilot's seat, and the other half, on top of the glare-shield in front of me. Of course after doing so, I wouldn't be able to see out (but that wouldn't matter because there was nothing but pitch black out there; I was flying on instruments). I radioed Colt with my problem; not that there was anything he could do (other than sympathize with me in a heartfelt manner). I told him my tunneling plan—that I would be out of the cockpit (unable to control the plane). I asked him to come around behind me and watch me, and if he saw me peeling off on a wing or going into a dive, to radio me loudly. Hearing that call I would claw my way back up to the cockpit and grab the controls.

I started. After accomplishing the above—with the top bale out of the copilot's seat, I gained one vacant cube of space. I unstrapped, half stood up, and although it wasn't easy I was able to grab hold of the top bale behind the copilot's seat and drag it over the seat, plopping it down where the other bale had been. *Whew,* one hole. Just starting and I'm already sweating. Facing rearward I was able to grab the bottom bundle behind the copilot's seat, lift it, turn, and plop it down into my now-empty pilot's seat. This gave me a chance to scan the flight instruments, and noticed I was in a slow left turn off course. Colt must not have me in sight or he would have alerted me. I returned the plane to on course and rolled in an eighth of a turn of right wing down trim. I was out of breath, but encouraged; *I now had a place to begin my burrowing rearward.* I dropped to my knees, rolled onto my back, and inched my way rearward until the top of my head hit the next stack of bales. I first pulled the top one, then the bottom one, out of the stack, dragged them over my head (face) and chest, and pushed them towards the cockpit.

I was now flat on my back in the cabin, in the dark, with two bales of marijuana on my chest. *Uh Oh!* The sound of the airflow passing the airplane was getting louder. I was gaining airspeed. This meant the nose must have dropped and the plane was in a dive! *Quick—up!* Wrestled my way past the two bales, into the cockpit, grabbed the yoke and pulled the nose back up, arresting the descent. Added a bit of power and a hair of nose up trim, and back to work. Still lying on my back, squirming my way rearward, I was removing and replacing one bale and then another. (Made me think of a giant Rubik's cube.) Finally, *there it was!* With my fingers shoved under the last bale, I could feel the kinked rubber hose—what I was praying had been the problem. *Thank you God!* I smoothed it out and then spent another ten minutes working my way back to the cockpit, restacking the bales behind me as I went. After removing the bale from my pilot's seat I plopped down into it, drenched and exhausted. Now, just one more thing: pull the half bales off the top of the glare shield (so I could see out the windshield), and put the two pieces back on top of the bale in the copilot's seat. For all practical purposes, I was no worse for the wear, ready to resume the flight (although looking at blurred engine instruments I realized somewhere during the process, *I had lost my glasses*). After my calves stopped shaking and my heart rate was down to 120, I rotated the "T" handle to access the bladder fuel; a cough, a sputter, and the engine was purring!

A Month Later and a Different Kind of Flight

Colt was captured in South America! Carl's connections in Barranquilla must have missed a payment to the local police, because they were hiding alongside the runway when Colt landed, rushed the plane and had him. It took two weeks to find out where he was being held, and then a few more weeks to lay the groundwork (get the payments made) to get him freed. (Oh, turns out Colt wasn't completely retired, according to his wife, he was working at home as a manager of the pension plan for the state of Illinois, and three weeks after his mysterious disappearance, the SEC shut down all trading of the parent fund.)

The right people were paid and the day to spring him was set. Since Colt was my friend, Carl assigned me as the pilot on the plane going down there to bring him back. Not only that, but I was bringing down two Cuban guys—each carrying Uzi's (600 round-per-minute submachine guns)! *Made me think Carl wasn't entirely sure things were actually laid on.* I landed at the designated jungle strip just outside Barranquilla (not the one we used on our previous trips). We were met by a military guy driving a jeep. And here's where things took a real twist. My two Cuban guys got in, and waved urgently—*for me to join them!* In the jeep I saw them look at my waistband and pass an approving look when they saw my 9mm.

It was a ten minute drive to a small village. Only a few shutdown businesses and a building with barred windows that I took to be the jail. The two Cubans leaped out of the jeep and ran full speed (with no hesitancy or sign of fear) into the building. I heard three or four shots, and a minute later they came out with an old skinny guy with a white beard, wearing a straw hat. They threw him into the jeep on top of me. *Shit!* I hollered to them that it wasn't Colt! *They had the wrong guy!* In fact I was trying to push the old guy out of the jeep myself when he shouts at me, "Rog! What in the hell's wrong with you"!? Holy Shit, it *was* Colt! He must've lost thirty pounds, and with the beard and the hat he didn't look at all like the Colt I had last seen! It was a high speed, careening trip back to the strip; a quick embarking, engine-start, and takeoff. Safely at altitude Colt began telling his story, and that he only had one friend in jail, who no one else would associate with, a guy named "Mata." I told him that "mata" was short for "matador" which is the Spanish word for "killer." The flight back and landing was uneventful (and it was a comforting feeling to know the cabin contained no contraband).

The Key Largo Debacle

On the trips back we always left the exterior light switch off; safer to fly all "dark." Shortly after takeoff and now well past dusk, I tried to switch the instrument panel lights on. They didn't come on. In another twenty minutes I couldn't read my engine instruments—or worse, my flight instruments (which one needs to fly the airplane)! *Big* problem. While holding the flashlight in my mouth, I tried a variety of things, finally discovering that if I turned the *exterior* light switch on, the *instrument* panel lights came on. Great, I can see the gauges, but with the exterior lights also on, I'd be spotted inbound or crossing Biscayne Bay, or as bad—overhead the dike for landing! Something was wrong with the wiring circuitry, which didn't surprise me. (Carl's maintenance man was always experimenting with it.) The next step—that any pilot would do, was to pull the exterior light circuit breaker out, cutting the electric power to those lights. *It came out, but the lights stayed on!* I had no choice but to reach behind the circuit breaker panel, find the lead wire to the circuit breaker, and try pulling it loose. I did and it worked, the interior lights stayed on but the exterior lights went out.

At the end of the trip back, about fifteen minutes from our landing destination (the same old raised dike), over our discrete radio frequency I heard Daryl's voice: "Divert! Divert! Divert!" This was a briefed call, but in all my trips, it was the first time I'd heard it. And while I knew what it meant (probably law enforcement—not warned off by the DEA, had finally zeroed-in on our dike and were there waiting for us), I didn't know what to do. *I was sitting in an airplane loaded with marijuana*; where in the hell was I going to land? It had to be a decent runway, but also had to be a small airport that would not have any personnel on it or even near it. I had just flown this same aircraft into the Key Largo airport last week and knew it closed down at sunset, and not only that, it was somewhat isolated—being almost a quarter mile in on a dirt road from the Overseas Highway leading to Key West. Only thing was—the runway stuck out in the water, and even in the daytime it was a tricky landing; there were always a couple dozen sailboats moored right on the final approach course. You had to weave your way in between the masts without hitting one. Exterior lights out I flew about forty miles south to Key Largo.

Overhead the airport—as best I could see, it appeared deserted. No activity, not a single solitary glimmer of light! I didn't want to stay airborne, grinding around low enough that I could perhaps be seen, and definitely would be heard by anyone within a mile, so turned onto final, descending and heading for the end of the strip. In the blackness surrounding me, I could just make out the grayish blobs below and in front of me that I knew were the hulls of the sailboats. The masts were too thin to spot visually. No two ways about it, when I get down to about fifty feet of altitude, I would have to use my landing lights to see them and weave my way between them. Going through fifty feet I flicked the switch to turn on my landing lights, *and they didn't come on!* How I made it to the runway without hitting one mast is beyond me, but I did. Hit hard, rolled out to the north end, then taxied at max speed (without landing lights—in pitch blackness) back to the south end parking area. Pulled into the first empty space.

I leaped out of the aircraft and started running back towards the dirt road that would take me out to the Overseas Highway where I could hide in the brush alongside it. *Uh, Oh! Big trouble.* When only halfway to the road and still on the runway, I heard sirens and could see the flashing red and blue hue in the sky; was sure they'd be turning in on the road I was running out on! *They did.* About three hundred feet ahead of me, with the headlights looming larger, I did a sharp right turn into the woods alongside it, which suddenly became a swamp—me finding myself up to my crotch in slime. (Back when I had the respected position at Learjet, my own office and staff, you may remember I remarked, "Boy Mireille would at last be proud of me!" *I wonder what she would think if she could see me right now, hiding; up to my ass in mud?)*

I was only a hundred feet off the road when the cop cars went streaking by. In about ten minutes, based on the shouts and increased commotion, they must have found the airplane. All kinds of activity followed. It was a good two hours before they had all cleared out (minus I think—one cop left to guard the airplane and its cargo). Soon as I could I left my hiding place and started sloshing towards the main highway—or almost to it. I stopped about fifty feet from it, staying hidden in the tall scrub brush. I sat slumped there until dawn, tired, exhausted, and out of ideas. I then (staying sufficiently off the highway) walked about four miles north to John Pennekamp Park. There were lots of people there visiting the Welcome Center and using the restrooms and phones. I had no idea where Colt or Daryl were. I called a South Florida friend (telling him an outlandish story) to drive an hour south and pick me up.

Everything Must Come to an End

Carl had contacted Colt and asked us to meet him at the Stewart Aviation luncheonette. We did, and noticed he was a different person; calm and satisfied. He spoke first: "Guys, this is it. You can retire. I've got the $175,000 and we're already scheduling our trip to Berlin for Chad's first surgery. I had promised Shirley, and I'm doing it. I'm counting my blessings, knowing full well I could be in prison or dead. I'm quitting this whole ugly thing. For good!"

We didn't know exactly how to react. Certainly it was going to affect our lives; and with what we'd saved, and the increasing danger—*surely for the better*. My screwed up life had left me with one interesting thing: sometimes when you just can't seem to make a decision; it gets made for you. We didn't argue with Carl, in fact, I think we were genuinely pleased that he had achieved his goal—he was going to get Chad's ankle fixed, and almost more importantly had enough integrity to keep his word as far as quitting. And that in truth was it. Don't know about Colt, but during the past few months I had been having a more and more skeptical opinion of Rich's government ties, and if what I was doing, might be exactly what it looked like I was doing. Of course the big deal now would be: *what happens when we tell Rich?*

As much of a surprise the end of the operation was, we got a bigger one when we met with Rich. It was true he *was* a DEA agent, but knowing the ropes *he had begun his own smuggling operation:* Carl and Daryl! *And Rich was Sinclair!* Rich had at first gotten us involved to add to his take;

two more planes, twice as much pot, twice the profit! Then he got worried when Colt told him that Carl had mentioned a guy named Sinclair (*who was him*)! That's why he kept asking Colt what if anything Carl had told him about the guy named Sinclair. Later, Rich suspected that Carl was skimming off some of the incoming stuff, and that was why he wanted Colt to keep track of the exact number of bales. Rich thanked us (like we had just babysat his kids for the afternoon), told us we could each fly our planes back to the original airports; just leave the key in them. He'd have one of his guys pick them up. *I would sleep much better in the nights to come, than I had for the past months.*

Chapter Fourteen
A STORY WITH AN ENDING

Chet Falk Again

You may remember Chet Falk, my pilot friend—first from the Marine Corps and then Air America—the guy I was flying with when I got shot down in the Delta. Just about the most dedicated ex-Marine I ever met; only problem: he sure didn't *look* like one. Oh he was tall enough, and he had that military crew cut, but it was on top of a round, chubby, juvenile-looking face. And he was "pear shaped" with narrow shoulders and wide hips (and a flat ass). Perhaps because of this appearance, when he showed up before the board to be accepted as a Regular Officer (a certified "leatherneck"—a "lifer") *they turned him down.* This absolutely crushed him. Took all the wind out of his sales. So he did what almost all passed-over Reserve officers do: when his current temporary commission expired he didn't try to renew it, he left the Corps. Soon thereafter he heard about Air America, applied and was hired. When he walked through my Chief Pilot's door in Saigon in 1967, though I hadn't seen him for five years, I recognized him immediately. Chet was single—in fact never married, which he appeared not to be well-suited for, and everyone assumed he was likely to stay unmarried. He definitely wasn't a womanizer; never was comfortable interacting with the ladies, although he made an exception, conversing with our young Vietnamese secretaries. They felt safe with him, recognizing his intentions were honorable and appreciating his dry sense of humor.

Before too long the other pilots began to call him "Black cloud Falk" because he had so much bad luck. For example: After never availing himself of his scheduled time off, when finally urged to do so, he took a trip to Hong Kong. There—upon arrival, walking out of the airport he was hit by a cab, spending half the week in the hospital and the other half in his hotel room. Unlike the rest of us, he never bought a car and persisted in taking taxis. We finally convinced him to buy his own transportation, and he did—but not a car. He bought one of those Italian Vespa motor scooters. First day out on it, thrilled and speeding to work, he caught the front of his foot on the curb and broke his ankle.

A Serious Health Problem

As you know—in 1975 the war in Vietnam ended and our covert operations in Vietnam, Laos and Cambodia were terminated. The Air America pilots went to the four winds: Malaysia, Indonesia, Alaska, Iran, Africa, and parts unknown. Not sure where Chet went, but about a month ago—ten years after Air America disbanded, I got word that Chet was living in Rialto, California and battling a serious health issue. As the sole offspring, his deceased parents left him the house he had grown up in. Now in seriously deteriorating health—with no living relatives and only in touch with a couple other Air America pilots, he had no one to count on; completely alone. Since he worked for me in Air America, and we were together in the Marine Corps, I decided to give him a call; let him know I hadn't forgotten him (as well I shouldn't have). On the first call I got his answering machine, causing me to listen to the whole "Marine Corps Hymn" before I could leave a message.

When I did get through to him I was able to sense a brave but understandably resigned attitude. He said he'd gone to the emergency room one night with unusual nausea and dizziness. Next thing he knows, it's the following morning and a nurse is at his bedside asking him to sign a permit for them to do a cranial operation—*that he had already undergone!* They had diagnosed an aggressive and usually terminal cancer of the brain stem. They did the best they could. Nothing more surgically could be done. The only question now was, would it be six months or a year? He was now seeing the doctors at the VA hospital in Loma Linda, just fifteen minutes away, and thought they were taking good care of him.

My First Visit to Chet

Feeling as if I might be the only one to do it, and it was necessary, I booked a flight to Los Angeles, which was not too far from Rialto. I arrived in LAX late Friday night, rented a car Saturday morning and made the hour and a half drive to Rialto. It was as warm and rewarding a reunion as could be had under the circumstances. I did my best to cheer him up; straightened up the house, did a load of laundry, cleaned out the refrigerator, and after a consultation, made a grocery run. I could see there was one administrative task he had been putting off. On his open desk was a mound of envelopes; all medical bills and insurance forms to fill out. He told me that a couple times each week, when he first woke up in the morning he would make a pledge to tackle it. But somehow—every time, he'd start, become discouraged and then just give up. He just didn't have the energy to ever complete the job. Before I had to leave on Sunday I at least made a dent in this correspondence, but I'll tell you: not being terminally ill and with all my faculties, even I got frustrated at the unanswerable and redundant questions. Back in Florida I stayed in touch with him. On a call just a month later, he told me that his condition had deteriorated to the point that the doctors told him that *unless he could arrange full time care in his home, they were going to have to hospitalize him!*

Miss Hanh

In the late sixties when Chet was stationed in Saigon, there was one young Vietnamese girl who worked in our Air America Admin Office at the airport. I doubt Chet and Miss Hanh ever went on a date together, and I'm sure they never slept together, but he was sweet on her and she appeared of similar feelings. I guess it could have been called "puppy love." She escaped Vietnam just days before Saigon fell and was flown to Los Angeles—where other Vietnamese had set up a refugee assistance program. They were able to get her an interview with Travelers Insurance. She was hired and rose rapidly through the ranks, ending up eleven years later, still with Travelers, but in Tulsa, Oklahoma as the Vice President of Claims for that state.

At some time after arriving in the states, Miss Hanh and Chet were put in touch, evidently writing and phoning each other from time to time. Miss Hanh (now a still unmarried 50-year-old) learned about Chet's dilemma—*that if he didn't have full time in-home care he was going to be committed.* As hard as it is to believe: she quit her job, put all her things in storage, put her house up for sale, and travelled to California to become Chet's required "24-hour care." Once there she was an angel; she cooked for him, cleaned the house, did all the shopping, took care of all his needs, monitored his medications, and was a constant compassionate companion (and I'm sure—a companion only). Talking to Miss Hanh on the phone I learned that as the weeks went by Chet's condition—especially his hallucinations, worsened; he began to sometimes think there were strangers looking in the windows, and wanted her to pull the blinds. Although she resisted as best she could, the doctors at Loma Linda, instructed her to bring him in; he would have to be hospitalized, and sadly but realistically—assigned to the palliative care ward (the Hospice of a hospital).

Hearing of this latest development I again booked a flight to California to be with Chet, perhaps for his demise. There, daily—with Miss Hanh, I visited him in the hospital. At his bedside I would watch as she mopped his brow, spoon feed him, and when not doing that, would just stroke his forearm, or if he dozed for an hour or two, just sit there silently until he awoke. I was a little hurt because Chet never did seem to take much notice of me, although the doctors later told me (and gave me a pamphlet explaining it) that dying is just about the most personal thing a human can do, and for me not to feel bad, *because it is not unusual for a dying person to completely ignore anyone with whom they are not intimately connected.*

Better Late Than Never

I had been there a little over a week and Chet was undeniably failing. On one of the last visits before he passed, sitting alongside his bed with Miss Hanh I noticed that although it was a struggle, he was making an effort to reach out one thin arm towards her, and form some words. I took this to be something very much on the personal side, so quickly exited the room. After wandering the halls for five or ten minutes I snuck back and peered in the doorway. Miss Hanh was no longer at his bedside, but rather standing at the foot of the bed—trembling. I approached her and saw tears streaming down her cheeks. She looked up at me with an expression of pained rapture and exclaimed, "He said he *loved* me!"

Chapter Fifteen
TAKING ADVANTAGE OF WHATEVER I CAN

My Chances for a Corporate Position Were Nil

The "positions held" on my resumés looked pretty good (factory test pilot and Assistant Chief Pilot for a Fortune 500 company). But in view of that *"Outplaced for Management Convenience"* thing it didn't surprise me the resumés weren't netting a lot of responses. During the last six months I got a few inquiries from halfway respectable aviation organizations, but no corporate flight departments; all charter companies—that weren't carrying lazy executives on boondoggles; they were carrying paying passengers who had paid good money to get to some God-forsaken place regardless of the weather. So these companies weren't so concerned with why you left your last job; rather they just wanted to be sure you didn't mind flying in sleet and blowing snow, making zero-zero approaches, and landing on a frozen runway at 2 in the morning! I think if I would have forced it, I could have been hired each time. But the cities these companies were located in were not choice spots, the aircraft weren't new or well maintained, and the closest one was a thousand miles from Florida. I thusly wasn't all that disappointed when nothing came of them. (Of course at the time I wasn't as motivated to take them either; flying for Rich and making great money doing so.)

Still with no retirement, but being flush with cash, I knew I had to do something with it that would have a good chance of increasing, and be able to take care of me in my old age. (The average cost of a Long Term Care facility being about $4,000 a month!) Of the many recommendations I got, real estate seemed like an investment with as good a return as any, and would be safe. I could have put down more, but it would have looked suspicious, so I put $60,000 down, took a $120,000 loan, *and bought an oceanfront home right there in Hobe Sound!* That transaction, plus regularly making large bank deposits with no ostensible source of income, required a lot of administrative chicanery. (If you make a cash deposit in excess of $10,000 the IRS and the FBI are notified, and you are investigated as a possible "money launderer".) In any case, here I was now with a large mortgage but no job or income. Time to reapply myself to that task; get a job—any job.

Another Voice from the Past

In the spring of 86' an old pilot friend from Air America—who with his Langley connections found out I was unemployed and available, called me from Dallas while on a break from his assignment *in Nicaragua!* You may remember that it was at this time that Nicaragua was in the midst of a civil war. In a not very well-disguised fashion (which resulted in—under Reagan: the Oliver North "*Iran-Contra Scandal*") the US was arming the "Contras" (the guerillas) who were attempting to defeat the "Sandinistas" (the government militia) and overthrow Daniel Ortega, the Communist leader of Nicaragua.

Just like every other one of these so-called civil wars, it had the same makeup: There was a third world regime or dictator somewhere (usually a dirty-rotten communist) that we wanted to "kick out of power" because he was resisting our commercial interests, or conversely: there was a regime somewhere that was amenable to our commercial interests, and (against the will of the citizens) we wanted to "keep it in power." *Every time, no matter where in the world it was, or which side we were aiding, the Soviets were actively supporting the other side!*

In any case my friend was personally involved in this Nicaraguan civil war and was asking me if I would like to join him; do some flying not unlike what I had been doing six months ago, except this time no confusion over who was employing me, so I didn't have to worry about whether or not I was going to prison. Evidently while not yet officially being done under the direct supervision of the CIA it was at least under their auspices. Among other things John hinted the job would pay *really good!* I accepted his invitation and was told I could expect to soon receive an airline ticket from Miami to Comalapa airport in El Salvador.

I GUESS I JUST WASN'T THINKING

Arriving in El Salvador

Soon as I got the ticket, I packed one suitcase of what I thought would be sufficient for my intended activities, and had a friend drive me to the MIA airport. It was only a short flight; a little over two hours. The airport was reasonably modern and I didn't feel apprehensive. Soon as I walked out of Immigration and Customs I saw John waving at me. We joined in as much of an "old friends" reception as we felt comfortable demonstrating in these strange environs. Not long after exiting the airport John pulled up onto a reasonably good highway. After a short time on it he turned off onto a two-lane-wide paved road. Ten minutes later there wasn't a building of any sort no matter where you looked; on either side of the road—just rolling bluffs of bright green foliage and taller palms.

We were definitely in the countryside. He noticed my look of concern and told me that the international airport was about 30 klicks (kilometers) outside of San Salvador, and our safe house was in downtown San Salvador. As we approached it, making our way through an almost middle-class neighborhood, John commented that although nothing looked threatening, people 'in the know' had told them not to wander more than even a few hundred yards from the safe house. Kidnapping Americans for ransom was an ongoing activity here (which was not encouraging). John also told me that our airplanes were based at a much smaller Salvadorian military airport: Ilopango, located just a few miles outside town. That's where we would launch from and recover.

Some Old Friends

Arriving at and entering the safe house (which was in a not-too-bad part of the town) I was pleased to see two other Air America pilots I knew, Bill Copper and Jerry Stemwell, and two "kickers" from Laos: Dan Gamlan and Gene Hasenfeld. Another series of hugs and back-slapping ensued. So far, I had no reason to suspect the danger involved in what I would soon be doing. The mood was light and interspersed with joking and wise-cracking. Although they weren't with us in the safe house—at least now, I learned that two notorious Cubans (who had worked directly for the CIA since the famous but failed "Bay of Pigs" invasion in 1961) were now assigned to this operation. They were actually the intermediaries between the Agency and our manager—Bill Copper. They were the ones telling him where and when we would go, and what we would carry. They were dictating our missions.

How the Operation Was Being Funded
(This will be Important Later)

That night, John gave me a briefing (that you will later see, figures in on a horrendous occurrence). The financial support for the operation came from two different fund-raising groups; each of their remittances went solely to support *their* aircraft and *their* contras.

Funding group "A" provided the money to arm and supply their contras, and to operate a large but old propeller-driven cargo plane—the C-123 "Provider." This one had been upgraded by the addition of two small jet engines to give it better takeoff and climb capabilities. Air America had operated this plane in Laos and John was the senior C-123 pilot there (undoubtedly why he was picked for this project).

Funding group "B" provided the money to arm and supply their contras, and to operate a Vietnam-era, old US Army propeller-driven cargo plane—the DHC-4 "Caribou." In any case, here comes a major glitch: when given my aircraft assignment—the Caribou, I realized that John thought I had flown the Caribou when I was with Air America. I had never even *been* in one, let alone *pilot* one! Holy Shit! That's why I'm down here: they needed another Caribou pilot!

A Real Challenge for me

I was just smart enough to know better than to say "No John, I never flew the Caribou." Too late for that. But what could I do about it? I'll tell you what I did: I got a ride to the nearby military airport where our aircraft were. Upon seeing it I was not impressed. There were dozens of disabled old military airplanes with flat tires, just decaying in the sun. Behind them and alongside them were large piles of junk: broken wooden pallets, rusted hunks of metal and discarded engines, and rows of tarp-covered stacks of who knew what. I located our Caribou, went to it, dug out the Aircraft Flight Manual and brought it back to the safe house. There, I locked myself in my room for the next three days, and memorized that manual— cover to cover; the layout of the cockpit, every operating technique, every flight condition, all the "normal" and "emergency" procedures, and most importantly: the critical airspeeds, such as what speed I needed to attain on takeoff before attempting to raise the nose wheel off the ground, and very important—what was the airspeed to hold on final approach to landing, and a matter of life and death—how slow could you let the airplane get, before it would stall (59 knots). The stall speed is the lowest speed you can allow before the airflow over the wing separates, causing a sudden loss of all lift, and results in the plane "falling out of the sky" Normally these things are learned through a week-long ground school, a week of inflight training, and accompanying a qualified pilot on three or four actual flights. *Not by reading them in a book and trying to memorize them.*

The Two Routes of Flight

Funding group "**A**" that financed the C-123 (with considerably more money) delivered the military supplies for their contras, directly to Ilopango airport. So the C-123—with its long-range capability, could load up here in Ilopango, takeoff, fly south over the Pacific, maintaining a safe margin of at least 25 miles off the western Nicaraguan coast; continue south until they had passed the Nicaraguan southern border and were over Costa Rican waters. Once that far south they'd turn east and fly all the way across U.S.-friendly Costa Rica—about 140 miles, with no fear of being shot at. When they were finally over the Caribbean Sea, they'd turn left and fly far enough north to be abeam their designated drop zone. There, they'd turn west—inland, entering Nicaragua and *for the first time be over hostile territory and likely to draw ground-fire.* So they'd minimize this time; get in quick, drop the load right away, a "U" turn and get back out! Once out, they'd retrace their route south, then turn and fly west back across Costa Rica until "feet wet" over the Pacific. When a safe distance out to sea, they'd turn right and fly north—up the western coast of Nicaragua back to El Salvador.

Funding group "**B**" that financed the DHC-4 Caribou (my plane) also launched out of Ilopango airport, but that was the only similarity to the C-123 routing. We would launch empty. It would only be the first leg of the mission, not for the flight into Nicaragua. This Caribou funding group delivered the military supplies for their contras—for reasons not disclosed to us, to a tiny village named Aguacate ("avocado" in Spanish). It was about a hundred-thirty miles due east of San Salvador, in the neighboring country of Honduras. We would thus always fly our first leg to Aguacate (empty). There we'd load up and launch on our 150-mile incursions into Nicaragua. *Instead of just ten minutes over hostile territory (like the C-123) we'd be over hostile territory for over an hour down, and the same time back!* Sometimes we would have to spend a couple nights in Aguacate waiting for our mission—a flight for which we were given the coordinates of a drop zone deep in Nicaragua, and the exact time to be there—usually about 3:30 a.m., meaning we'd not be taking off until about 1 in the morning. At Aguacate we had a hostel for overnighting; a porous, leaking, dirt-floored shack with one toilet, a homemade shower stall, and four or five canvas cots.

My First Flight to Aguacate

The day of my first flight came soon enough. As the van made its halting way to the Ilopango airport I was a nervous wreck, hoping and praying I'd discover the Caribou cockpit and the panel to be at least reasonably similar to what I had pictured in my mind; that I'd be able to find and locate all the switches and levers, and that I could get through all the checklists and procedures *without my copilot having serious doubts about my qualifications.* My copilot was going to be Jerry Stemwell. While he had been a qualified captain, some pilots just don't like the pressure and responsibilities of being the captain, and chose to demote themselves to copilot, and just assist the captain. That's what Jerry did. My first flight— that everyone thought was my first flight in the aircraft *down there,* was actually my first flight in the aircraft *ever!*

Miraculously (thank the Lord for small favors) purposely acting as if I was not in a hurry (to disguise my lack of familiarity with the procedures) I was able to get through the pre-start, and start. Jerry called for "taxi clearance," I added the power and we were on the way. One big thing different right away: Every plane I had ever flown was steered during taxi by the rudder pedals—using your legs and feet. Not so in the Caribou. It had a wheel-like knob on the left side of the cockpit that the pilot rotated to steer the aircraft. It turned the nose wheel left or right. I had never seen one of these let alone used one. This resulted in a second never-before-encountered procedure. With my left hand on the steering knob and my right hand on the control column, I didn't have a hand remaining to move the power levers (throttles). Every takeoff I'd ever made, my right hand was on the power levers. For the first time, I realized in planes with this steering knob, the *copilot* handles the throttles until lift off. We got to the runway, were cleared for takeoff, and did so, me remembering that speed (66 knots) when I could lift the nose wheel and become airborne. You might imagine the thrill and satisfaction I had seeing the ground fall away beneath me and calling out "Wheels Up"!

About an hour later we spied our destination, the tiny village of Aguacate, which was located in the middle of a several-mile-wide, flat green valley. At the most it contained 50 small one-story dwellings, *but no runway*. Scanning the horizon I noticed the valley proceeded westward (back under me) and continued to narrow the further it stretched behind me. I made a "U" turn, and saw that about five miles east of the village the valley had narrowed to only a couple hundred feet across; and there nestled along the floor of that crease was our runway—a crooked, rutted red dirt path; very much like the strips I flew in and out of in Laos. I couldn't make out any persons on it or near it, just a couple beat-up shacks on the rising ground to the south side of the strip. I entered a downwind leg, got the wheels down and half flaps, and started my 180 degree left circling turn to final approach. Having flown landing approaches in the Learjet at 125 knots, and quickly enough have made the necessary flight position adjustments; now, here in the Caribou at just 70 knots, even though I had never landed it before, I had more than enough time to smoothly make the required adjustments. I'm pleased to say the landing went perfectly (and I don't think Jerry was any the wiser regarding my newness). I *might* be able to pull this thing off!

The Operation at Aguacate

Boy, this "runway" and its surrounding area was remote; only three structures, as I said, all on the rising slope on the south side of the strip. There was one small one-room building that served as our operations headquarters, another, our dilapidated hostel, and a small cottage— manned by two CIA guys. And believe it or not, since Congress was still three months from approving the CIA funding for this operation, the two CIA guys assigned here were not supposed to talk to us, *or even to notice we were here!* However the other pilots told me that every day at noon— when the CIA guys went to lunch, they left their cottage unlocked, and conveyed to us that no one would know it if we snuck in. And we did, since one whole wall inside was a battle map of Nicaragua, showing where the "Sandinistas" (communist government soldiers) were last spotted, and where the anti-aircraft guns were located. That was our "Intelligence Briefing." The first night I was not assigned a mission, but the other Caribou pilot (Buzz Sanders) was. While I had never met Buzz, he had the reputation of being an out and out global mercenary, and had "balls of steel" like no one I ever met (except maybe Colt). Two hours before his flight that first night, he just laid down on one of the cots (wearing a black tee shirt that read *"Kill em all and let God sort it out"*), and slept like a baby. Oh, another thing about Buzz: he had a wife in Miami, a wife in Puerto Rico, and one in Colombia!

Not too far from Aguacate was another and bigger Honduran airport: Tegucigalpa. We were told in no uncertain terms, that under no conditions were we to ever land there! We were told to just crash before landing there. While no one told me why, I later learned that on this airfield was the secret headquarters for the CIA division that ran every operation in Latin America, and even some in South America. For us to even fly *over* it was verboten. There is a story about an incident that occurred there, told to me—in an indisputable manner, by a retired CIA agent who was there and saw it: A Honduran pilot landed his jet at Tegucigalpa, and right there on the ramp, after getting out of his airplane, in front of God and country, a senior CIA officer (whose name was told to me) shot him! Obviously if this story was true, we would choose to crash before going to Tegucigalpa. (This senior CIA official was later promoted to an Under Secretary of State, or maybe Defense. Can't remember which. You'd recognize his name.)

My First Mission

The next day about supper time, or whatever time you decided to eat your "MRE" (which was the latest canned military K-rations), I received my first mission. I was surprised that they would be considering an airdrop because of the weather. Dark storm clouds had begun forming around 1 in the afternoon, and were getting worse. If this same weather were over our drop zone, we would not be able to find it. Once again it would be a 3:30 a.m. drop, which based on the coordinates, indicated the flight time to get there would be an hour forty-five. This meant a 1:45 a.m. takeoff. And let me say, while I had the coordinates, this was decades before GPS and there were no radio navigational aids to use. Finding the drop zone was a major task, and only accurately accomplished by a skilled pilot or copilot, using a years-out-of-date navigation system called LORAN-C. The pilot himself—flying the aircraft, could not keep his head down looking at the LORAN scope (which was alongside his thigh on the center console).

It was primarily the copilot who monitored this ancient navigation device, and some were much better than others in interpreting it. The distorted, unclear screen showed literally hundreds of curved thin red lines, paralleling and crossing each other: half from the upper right corner of the scope and half from the upper left corner of the scope. Those copilots who had demonstrated superior skills in interpreting this maze, were in high demand and often got paid extra by pilots to fly with them. In any case after receiving my flight particulars, I went back up to the hostel to waste the next five hours and take a couple of nervous pees. (I certainly was not of the mettle to take a nap like Buzz.)

I was getting more and more worried. About midnight the thunder started and it was increasingly deafening. An hour later the rain started, and *did it!* A torrential downpour. By the time Jerry and I started our walk down the steep, rutted, rocky path that led to the runway, it was a gushing stream of muddy water about a half foot deep. No sense even thinking about keeping your feet (or your body) dry. Keeping one's self upright and not ending up on your ass in the water was the prime objective. The mechanic for our aircraft (an extremely good-natured Filipino named Alex Custodio) met us at the aircraft, and assured me (but not as enthusiastically as I would have liked) that the plane was "ready to go." It took me four attempts to get the right engine started and running; in fact there were several minutes when I was not sure I could get it started at all. And I must admit, as fearful as I was I relished a few moments of relief when I thought the flight might have to be scrubbed. Taxiing to the far end of the runway in the pitch black was no easy task. It was possible a main wheel would become mired in an unseen hole, and we'd be stuck there (and then the flight *would* be scrubbed).

The Flight Down

It was my third flight in the aircraft; a night takeoff in pouring rain. I did it, taking off to the east, toward the wide low plain the village was located on. It took me the predicated one hour and forty-five minutes to twist and turn my way through towering cumulus ("thunder bumper") clouds to get there. Jerry had his head down the whole way, trying to interpret the LORAN. I was looking outside, but it being pitch black and with a solid cloud coverage, there was no way I could navigate by any terrain features below. Oh, and one more thing: these coordinates I had received—radioed in from the Contras (the guerillas) asking for the drop, were only where they *thought* they were (and after retreating backwards for two hours, in the dark and being shot at, it's real hard to track yourself on a map)! We could forgive them if they weren't where they said they were, which they seldom were. On these trips, back in the cargo bay were two guys: my kicker who would shove the stuff out (Dan Gamlan) and the number two Cuban guy with a hand-held radio. The number one Cuban guy—running the operation, was Felix. He never went on the flights. (In his wallet he carried a photo of him shaking hands with George Bush senior.)

Who Was the Cuban Guy in the Back of the Aircraft?

Raphael! A guy rumored to be a storied "hit-man" for the Agency. And I believed the rumor. Observing him I had come to the conclusion that guys who did what he did, *definitely marched to their own drummer!* No smiles—never; no jokes and certainly no smart-ass "one-'upper'" remarks (like the guys on TV make before they shoot someone). A week ago in the hostel there was a bedroom shakeup and he ended up sleeping in my room. When I went to sleep he was sitting on the edge of his bed, his head in his hands. I don't know if he stayed that way all night, but when I woke up in the morning, *he was still sitting exactly like that.* Tonight it was Raphael who was with us back in the cargo bay, using his radio to try to make contact with his Contras. He did (mercifully) and they directed him to overhead their position. When he gave Dan the sign, the load went out the open rear hatch. As soon as it was clear I turned towards home and poured the coal to it.

The Way Back and Landing

On the way back the weather did not improve; lightning on all sides, thunder cracking our eardrums, and the steady loud drum of rain on the top of the aircraft (and the cockpit leaked). I was (thank you God) successful in finding Aguacate. To make us able to see it and land, the ground crew had put out four or five .45 cal. ammo cans on each side of the runway, stuffed them with rags soaked in gas, and lit them to act as runway lights. Unfortunately the rain had doused the fire in at least half the cans. While circling overhead deciding what kind of pattern I could use to land (without flying into the rising ground on each side of the strip), *my heart almost came out my throat!* The right engine quit! Cold! Not only was it just my third flight in the airplane, it was night and in pouring rain, and now—*single-engine!* Not sure what Jerry was doing, but lots of frantic moves—I'm sure in an attempt to get the engine running; none of which worked.

I feathered the engine—manually pulling the lever that would turn the propeller blade angles so instead of hitting the airflow flat, they would be fared—streamlined. (This greatly reduces the drag, so with just one engine we would be able to keep our airspeed.) Regarding the circling approach to landing, there's an expression that every pilot knows: "when making an engine-out landing, never turn into the dead engine." This can cause a stall and spin fatal crash, so I had to make a tight left turn to the runway (away from the failed engine), almost brushing the trees on the rising terrain to the south. I did, lined up on the few burning cans remaining, and (thanks again God), made it down with a splashing thud. After I parked it was ten minutes before my calves stopped shaking and I could get out. I was drenched, but not from rain. Jerry was slapping me on the back in a most congratulatory and thankful manner.

My Next Mission

While it wasn't a solid overcast with pouring rain (like my previous flight), during the afternoon the sky became crowded with high-reaching, quickly rising, pure white, bubbly, violently turbulent cumulonimbus clouds. Should you try to fly through one of them, you'd get a ride you'd never forget (and which from time to time caused a plane to come apart in flight)! Once again about five p.m. I got my assignment for another 1 a.m. takeoff. *Sure hope those clouds dissipate.* Waiting for our departure time I went through the same drill, nervously wasting the hours in the hostel we shared. And oh, about an hour before we would straggle down to the runway, I walked into the small toilet alcove to take my last nervous pee. While standing there I happened to glance over onto the wood-slatted floorboard in the shower. There—looking up and glaring at me, was the biggest and ugliest giant toad I ever saw! I swear it was as big as a football! I backed out slowly.

The Flight Down

At one-thirty a.m. I was in the cockpit and gratified when I had no trouble starting the engines. And more good news—the taxi-out and takeoff went okay. Airborne, as soon as I had enough altitude to clear the ridge to the south, I turned right and began my route into Nicaragua, turning the aircraft as necessary so as to stay in the clear between the towering "thunder bumpers." Jerry was my copilot again, my kicker was a different guy—Gene Hasenfeld and the Contra liaison guy on board was again—Rafael. About halfway to the drop zone, our LORAN navigation device went out; belly up! Nothing on the screen. If I stayed in the clear, between the cumulus clouds, with good visibility (thanks to a bright full moon), I thought I might be able to identify enough terrain features, to successfully navigate to the Contra position. In particular I was paralleling a wide river presently flowing due south. In about sixty miles I knew it made a ninety degree turn to the west, and if I made that turn and flew another thirty miles down the river, the drop zone should be about a half mile south of the river. I mentioned that plan to Jerry, he checked the map, took a look outside at the terrain illumination, and agreed. I maneuvered the plane over to the left until I was centered over the river, and able to more easily navigate down it by the reflection of moonlight on the slick surface. To avoid being hit by ground fire, there are two theories: first, fly so high that even though they can see you more easily, they don't have the fire power or accuracy to bring you down. The second theory is to fly low and fast. This way you're upon them and past them so quickly, they don't have time to get their guns ready and on you. In order to better stay over the river, I chose the low and fast option.

A Heart-Stopper!

I was still low over the river—almost skimming the surface; pretty much obscured from being sighted from the sides, as I was lower than the tops of the trees on both banks. I was about twenty miles from where it and I would make our right turn westward. The moon was bright and racing on the flat black water in front of me. I had the cockpit window open and the cool air was rushing past my cheek. Things were going pretty good. Well things *were* going pretty good. Everything changed in a flash! Suddenly the cockpit filled with about 10,000 blinding lumens! Jerry and I were struck sightless by the glare. Heart pounding, straining to see through the glare, I spotted the source: a huge spotlight about a hundred yards in front of us on the left bank of the river. It had been flicked on was fixed on the nose of the aircraft—the cockpit! I only had a second to come to that awareness, when the whole sky in front of us turned *fluorescent bright pink! Hundreds if not thousands of tracers going by!* From the left bank, several machine-gun emplacements had opened up on us. Nothing I could do—had to go right through the noisy, hot lead, pink veil, shuddering at the sequence of snapping "pings" as bullets pierced the aircraft, from the nose to the tail. In a matter of seconds we were through it, and departing at an angle the guns could not track. *We'd escaped!* I knew one thing—one *great* thing: I personally hadn't been hit. The expression on Jerry's face definitely indicated he had to be alive, and the engines didn't miss a beat. I grabbed the mic and called Dan in the back; good news: he and Raphael had not been hit either! God knows how many rounds went through the aircraft, and none of us got hit!

I continued down the river till it turned west, and banked to the right to stay centered over it. In 13 minutes I was at the spot where a left turn and about two minutes should put me over the drop zone. I called Dan to tell Raphael that we would be over the drop zone in two minutes. Dan said evidently Raphael already knew that, because for the last couple minutes he had been using his hand-held radio trying to make contact with his Contras. And he did, but was becoming more and more aggravated, because although he was *talking* to them, and they could *hear* the airplane, they were unable to give him clear or accurate left-right directions, or even compass headings to get me over to wherever they were. We pilots knew that we were never to drop the load unless we were sure we were right over the Contras (otherwise not only would we waste an expensive load of equipment, but maybe in doing so, donate it to the enemy)! After a good fifteen minutes of Raphael screaming at his Contra leader, he shoved the radio into his back pocket, grabbed Gene's parachute off the hook it was on, put it on, *and ran out the back of the airplane! In the middle of the night, somewhere in the middle of Nicaragua, maybe right over the enemy!* We had no choice now but to bring the load back, something we did not want to do. The flight back was uneventful, and this time with two engines the landing was also uneventful. I have no idea how he accomplished it, but three weeks later, who comes walking in the safe house door, *carrying Gene's parachute*, but Raphael!

The Most Critical Mission Yet

There was a lull in activity for a couple days and I had returned to San Salvador, just hanging around the safe house; wasting time and waiting. Didn't have to wait too long. About 07:30 in the morning Bill Copper came and got me (in bed) and told me that Jerry and I had to get out to the airport, fire up the Caribou, and get over to Aguacate as fast as we could. A mission had come up; supposedly an urgent "life or death" mission! Funding group B (who financed and directed my Caribou operation) had a couple companies of their most loyal and well-trained Contras, surrounded by the Sandinistas, and likely going to be wiped out to the man, *unless*

I could get them essential supplies right now! These supplies of course, were stock-piled at Aguacate. Jerry and I rushed to the airport and made a quick flight to Aguacate. The head Contra general, General Bruno was already there and was waiting for us, to hold an immediate briefing.

The anticipated serious high level meeting would be held in that third building I previously described as the "Operations" building. It was a small one-story cottage comprised of just one room—about 20 feet square. It had one wall-mounted air conditioner. To keep the cool air in, in the one entrance door there was a hanging drape of thick plastic blinds you had to brush aside to enter. General Bruno was standing on a raised platform at the front of the room, and in command of the meeting—seriously in command. He was using a large wall map to identify the location of his guerillas and the surrounding government troops. As I made a note of the latitude and worked out the distances, there was a big problem—a very big problem: the Contras needing the supplies were much further south in Nicaragua than any of our previous drop zones; in fact so far south, no matter how many ways I planned it, *the Caribou did not have the fuel range to get down there, make the drop, and be able to make it back to Aguacate. No way the Caribou could do it.* With much hesitancy I raised my hand and made that fact known to the General. He was stopped cold, dropping both arms to his side. An expression of pain and disbelief covered his face. *It appeared there was no way to avoid his troops being wiped out.*

About two minutes later a 16-year-old civilian Honduran mechanic standing next to me, knowing I spoke Spanish, whispered an idea to me— his idea, that nobody in the room (including the General or I) had thought of. In Spanish, the kid said "I know the equipment here is for General Bruno's troops, financed by Funding Group "B" and delivered in your Caribou. But you said the Caribou doesn't have the range to do the trip. What if you just load up your plane here, and fly those supplies over to Ilopango, and let the long-range C-123 (financed by Funding Group "A") take them; doing the same route they always do: south off the west coast of Nicaragua like they always do. When they get over Costa Rican waters, turn east like they always do across Costa Rica. Then when they get to the Caribbean Sea, turn left and fly up until they're even with this drop zone, then turn into it. They got the fuel to do it, and will only be over Nicaragua for ten minutes!"

I GUESS I JUST WASN'T THINKING

I was surprised that this young kid knew so much about our operation, and even more taken aback that he was capable of considering all the factors and arriving at this solution. I raised my hand and told General Bruno, that I might have a solution. Understandably he was all ears and gave me the platform. I humbly repeated the kid's plan (not attributing it to him lest it be blown off immediately). It only required that General Bruno get approval from funding group A, *to borrow their C-123 for one flight.* He said enthusiastically and greatly relieved, that would be no problem. Jerry and I loaded all the designated supplies into our plane, and flew them back to Ilopango, and had them unloaded by 10 a.m. If all went well, the C-123 would be airborne by noon, to deliver them to General Bruno's surrounded troops.

The pilots were Bill Copper as captain and Buzz Sanders as copilot. They were airborne shortly before noon—*on the way.* Oh, one thing: while it's true I was a captain in the Caribou, early on Bill Copper said the limited number of personnel would make it necessary to occasionally assign me as a copilot in the 123, which as an old Air America buddy of his, he already had me fly with him on two trips. (Had I not already had two flights in the Caribou this morning, I may well have been his copilot on this trip.) Once his plane was loaded, Bill did the standard C-123 route; first flying south, paralleling the west coast of Nicaragua (a safe distance out to sea). When he was far enough south to be safely over Costa Rican waters, he turned east flying across Costa Rica towards the Caribbean Sea, where, once over the water he'd turn north towards the critical drop zone.

But it was a beautiful day, deep blue skies, friendly puffy white clouds; everything copasetic. As a pilot, flying in hostile conditions (as I did in a handful of third world countries) you've got to be wary of these balmy sunlit conditions. They can give you a false feeling of safety and cause complacency; bringing about a decreasing regard for the ever present danger. This in fact occurred to Bill. Before reaching the designated point to turn north (over the water off the east coast of Costa Rica) Bill opted to turn northeast early; take a diagonal short cut across the southeast corner of Nicaragua. No problem—save ten or fifteen minutes.

This turned out to be a single—just one, but tragic example of a momentary lapse in judgement. Still over Costa Rica and a little south of the Nicaraguan town of El Castillo, Bill turned to a northeast heading, crossing the San Juan river—entering Nicaragua; on what would have been a 50-mile direct leg to the drop zone. Unfortunately there was a Sandinista Special Forces camp on the north bank of the river. They spotted the C-123, and radioed ahead to where it appeared to be going. The anti-aircraft emplacements there were ready, *and blew it out of the sky.* The kicker, Gene Hasenfeld bailed out, but Bill and Buzz were decimated on impact! *I could not help but think, if I hadn't relayed the teenager's idea about this flight, it wouldn't have gone, and Bill and Buzz would be alive.* This event made the headlines and weekly magazine covers, alerting the population to another clandestine government shenanigan. Congress was enraged and voted not to approve CIA funding for this operation; the end of the project and my job.

Chapter Sixteen
A NEW RESPONSIBILITY

Dad

Some years ago Dad was complaining of decreasing vision and pains in his left eye. His doctors concluded it was a detaching retina. Knowing the visual distortions caused by that, I doubted that was his problem. On one of his visits to Hobe Sound I took him to my ophthalmologist (a French-speaking Swiss doctor). After an in-depth examination, he told Dad he should—as soon as possible, make a trip to Miami—to the Bascom Palmer Eye Institute. It was his opinion that Dad may have an even more serious problem. He said he would arrange the appointment. He did, Dad went there, and the verdict was *he had cancer in the back of his left eye!* The eye was removed and Dad got a glass eye (that it took him months to get used to). There were no indications of any cancer remaining, life went on as usual for him, active as ever doing indoor and outdoor projects at the house. We assumed "case closed."

About six months ago, Dad began having pains in his abdomen that were diagnosed as a gall bladder problem. In the process of removing the gall bladder the surgeon discovered that Dad had cancer of the liver. Both my brother Hank and I were with him in the doctor's office when he gave the bad news to Dad. Dad took it like someone talking to him about the weather. Hank and I tried to pry more information from the doctor, such as what could be done; if nothing, would it be terminal? If so—what was his life expectancy? We learned that there was nothing surgically that could be done, and that chemo was not appropriate. As far as life expectancy, the doctor could not or would not hazard a guess. It was hard to believe that noting the stage and extent of the cancerous tumor, he could not come up with even a ball park life expectancy.

There was one part of the doctor's manner that was disturbing to me. When Hank walked Dad down to the car, I went back into the doctor's office and told him I was disappointed that he failed to recognize that half of what he had said, was going right over the top of my dad's head. He should not have used all the anatomical and medical terms he was using, and instead use more common, understandable terms to explain the situation to my dad. We kids took turns making more frequent visits to his home in Ft Myers, being generally pleased with his apparent still-good health. That was up until two weeks ago, when he rapidly began to fail.

Visiting Dad and Listening to Him (for the first time)

It was my turn to be with him and I was over there. I was surprised to see; unlike so many of my older friends in his condition, my dad only had two pill bottles. One was a pain-killer and the other was an anti-nausea medication, in case the first one caused nausea. My dad said he wasn't having that much pain, so didn't take the first medication and thus didn't need the second medication. It was a moving visit. At last—finally, for the first time, my dad shared some of his youth with me; stories of compassion and persistence, that I could hardly believe were ever a part of his life's story. There was so much I didn't know! These tales caused me to have an even increased admiration and respect for this *mashed potatoes and gravy* man. There was one story in particular, perhaps a sign of those times, or the willingness to make sacrifices for a better future. It was 1933, Dad was dating Mom and knew for sure she was the one. He told his "Pop" (my grandfather of course) that he wanted to marry her. His Pop said that was fine and he thought she'd make him a good wife, but he wouldn't give his approval until my father was making $50 a week.

Dad said, "I was floored when I heard that and asked him as a carpenter, how am I ever going to make $50 a week. His advice to me was, if I wanted to make more money, I'd have to learn how to operate machinery. I asked him where in the heck I was going to find a job operating machinery. He said there was a new aircraft plant in Woodridge—Curtiss Wright. They had all kinds of drills and lathes and presses and milling machines, and that was the first place he'd try. So I did, and learned they didn't hire machinists off the street. No way. I'd have to start at the bottom. I got hired as a cleanup guy, spending the whole day scouring the floors, picking up discarded pieces, broken machine parts, and metal fragments. I did that job a few months before I got promoted to a stockman, which was easier. I spent the whole day in a small room behind a screen, handing out parts."

"And how long did you do that?"

"About six months, but it had an advantage. Not far from the stockroom was a large machine shop. So here's what I did: In the morning, in addition to packing my lunch I packed my supper—two brown bags. At five pm when my day was over as a stockman, I'd go down to the machine shop and just stand in the doorway—watching the night shift guys arrive and start their work. After being there every night for a month straight, the workers began giving me a nod or even a little wave when they came in. One night about three or four months later, about midnight, the lathe operate must have wanted to sneak out for a shot or a hot date, because he motioned me to come over to him, and showing me the lathe, said: '*Listen kid, you see these metal pieces coming off here—they're straight. Well if they start curling like this'* he bent down and picked up one to show me. '*As soon as you see that curl, turn this gray knob a half a turn to the right, here to here, that's top to bottom, and make sure the pieces start coming out straight. If something goes wrong, this big red button here stops the machine. Just hit it'*. I nodded that I knew what he meant and he slipped out a side door.

"Well the ice was broken. During the next few months, every time one of the guys wanted to sneak away for fifteen minutes, he'd call me over to his machine and have me run it while he was gone. I ended up knowing how to run every machine in the shop. And like I said Roger, having brought my breakfast and lunch with me, and having stayed all night, I ended up at the plant 21 straight hours. At five each morning I made a quick bus trip home, ate breakfast, made my two meals for the next day, and caught a bus back to the plant. I'd done this for about six months when it happened: someone in the machine shop quit or got fired. *They were one man short*. One of the union stewards brought up a replacement. The shop foreman looked at him, then looked at me in the doorway, pointed at me and said, *I want that kid over there*. I was now a machine operator. Your mom and I got married about three months later!"

I had waited my whole life to have my dad talk to me like that, and it finally happened here in this little kitchen, just before his death. Sadly we had both missed out on something of value.

Dad's Final Days

A week or two later I was back on the other coast—at my oceanfront home in Hobe Sound. It was a Saturday and I was putting down wood flooring on the whole second floor (and it wasn't that pre-formed, self-locking stuff you can get now in Home Depot or Lowes). I was using a yellow pine from Arkansas, *and pegging it!* The raw boards aren't perfectly straight and it takes a couple guys using wedges and 2x4's as levers, to get them straight and tightly enough together. To help me I had hired a crew for the day. It was 10 am and we were just beginning to make good progress when the phone rang. It was Hank.

"Rog, I think you better get over here."

Of course I suspected why and certainly was ready to do so, although it would mean I'd have to let the crew go (and pay them all a full day's wages).

Hank continued: "Laura just finished her week, and I'm over here to relieve her, but she's concerned and doesn't want to leave; so both of us are still over here. Laura told me that Tuesday Dad had been great; had even mowed the lawn. Wednesday he was okay except the whole day he said he felt a little tired. Thursday he napped most the day, and yesterday he slept all day, maybe even sort of in a coma."

"Okay Hank, I'll be over right away." I changed clothes, packed a gym bag with toiletries and underwear, was in the car and on the way (justifiably embarrassed at myself for being upset that I had to let the crew go and couldn't finish the flooring project). Two hours and thirty minutes after leaving Hobe Sound I was stopped in traffic just short of the last draw bridge in Fort Myers. Seemed it was raised half the time, causing large traffic hold ups; the one obstacle each time we drove over to visit Mom and Dad. Once passed it, things went smoothly and in ten minutes I was parked in front of the house. I hurried in, finding Hank and Laura at Dad's bedside.

Hank looked up, saw me, grasped Dad's hand, leaned over him and said, "Dad, Dad, Roger's here!" I saw my father's eyes flicker and his lips move.

He hadn't spoke for a day and a half, and was about to. He said the same thing he did every time any of us arrived, and in this case were the last words he spoke in his life: *"How was the traffic at the bridge?'*

About three in the morning, me trying to sleep on the living room floor, I heard Hank calling. I jumped up and went into the bedroom. It was

117

obvious that some recent sounds or unusual breathing led Hank to think Dad was in his last few minutes. Laura was at the foot of the bed with both her hands over my father's bare insteps. Hank was on the left side of the bed, holding his father's left hand. I kneeled at the right side and grasped his right hand; all three of his children touching him. He took one huge inhalation, blew it all back out, and his head rolled over. It may have just been my imagination, but I swear I heard it: A deep voice from the ceiling saying, *"Roger, for the first time in your life, you're exactly where you should be!"*

After a tiring and not comfortable day; with the coroner, the police, a Department of Health officer, and a mortuary crew, I gave Hank and Laura a big hug and got in my car for the drive back across the state. Not sure I ever had the feeling I was experiencing on the way back. Halfway across the state I came upon a rest stop, pulled in and shut the car off. This was surely the first time I had ever felt these emotions. I thought of all the Yahnkes in the country and Canada—all my cousins. None were older than I was. Of the four sons, my dad was the oldest, and first married, and first to have a child—me. Perhaps that was why I felt as I did. I was now the oldest living Yahnke. *I was the new patriarch; the leader of the clan.*

Chapter Seventeen
A MAN, SHAMEFULLY DISSUADED

Taking Stock of My Own Flawed Life

I will claim the spectrum of expounded-upon activities of the preceding two years would never have evolved were it not for the death blow to a respected career in aviation (that *Outplaced for Management Convenience* thing). But eclipsing the vocational aspect of my life, of more importance was my mounting realization of the inexcusably selfish path my life had and was taking. Unfortunately for as long as I could remember, my actions would be viewed by any third party as unpardonable; with my parents (the infrequency of my adult visits); with my children (my prolonged and flagrant absences); and most especially with my two good wives (my infidelity). To another man my affliction may not have been the enslavement I profess it to be, and if not, I may well be nothing more than a most unworthy male person.

From having read the preceding parts of the Series, you have seen how my life was dominated by that deficiency; each era containing at least one wonderful woman, with whom I little more than experimented, in an attempt to achieve the ultimate intimacy, and if so—a good chance of making it a permanent union. This singular objective resulted in repeated female involvements, and produced the deep and permanent hurt I failed to realize I was causing my fine wives and the hurt I was likely inflicting on other women. Out of a truly, deeply-felt respect for each of them, I'm going to share with you a bit about the foremost of the ill-fated, wonderful women I selfishly chose as candidates to rescue me.

I GUESS I JUST WASN'T THINKING

1959: Sara—Wife Number One

I owe her a debt I can never repay. Marrying Sara was not ordained in any way; in fact it was the result of spectacular short-sightedness on both our parts. Although we shared not a common thought, she was a good woman and well ready to be a devoted wife; full of love for her husband (or as much love as a 19-year-old high school girl can know). Back then if a young lady wasn't married by 20, she was almost a spinster. And the boy—what about him? Once he reached 21 the parents wanted to know all about each new girlfriend, and what were the chances for a daughter-in-law and a grandbaby? Back then it was just the thing that everyone our age was doing: getting married (knowing very little or nothing about your partner, or worse—yourself) and what this act would entail. Hopefully you remember from Part One, the insufficient (maybe a half dozen long-distance calls) and the ensuing chain of incidental events that brought about my marriage to Sara. I knew nothing about her: what she tended to think, or say, or do, and why. She knew nothing about me. And with the mores of the days she did not have the opportunity to experience the absence of my love-making capability (which absence I tragically demonstrated on our wedding night)!

After a single phone call and my poor choice of words, that she interpreted as *an invitation to call ourselves engaged,* I stood by passively, just watching from the sidelines; neither encouraging nor resisting the course of events, while one seemingly insignificant occurrence after another had us moving steadily towards marriage. Even though no one could have asked for a better wife, my evaluation of our marriage was that it would ultimately be doomed by my difficulty in performing (an overwhelming majority of failures in spite of desperate pleas to the Gods of love-making). While I clung to the belief that the one woman who could unlock my manhood existed, *Sara was definitely not that woman.* And almost as bad, besides this wholly disqualifying disability, I had that itching in my bones, that discontent, that restlessness, that damned feeling that my life had become a closed book, and I was missing out—on *something* (though I had no idea what)!

A year after I was married the Marine Corps sent me on an "Unaccompanied" 13-month tour in Japan. ("Unaccompanied" means no family members are allowed.) Not good for any marriage, especially mine. Two years back in the states and the Marine Corps sent me on another unaccompanied tour—a one-year carrier-cruise in the Med. This allowed me to visit the storied European cities as well as the enchanting coastal villages, and what would turn out to be my downfall—sample the Continental culture and meet the exciting persons residing there; particularly the alluring and mysterious femme fatales! This was the beginning of the end, the thing that irreparably changed my life. I was tainted and would never be the same. Tragically upon my return, Sara and the miraculously-conceived kids—in spite of being more than any husband or father could ask for, had no chance. I knew it was dishonorable and I dreaded it, but after multiple determined tries failed, separations ensued, and a divorce finally occurred.

1978: Elsa—Wife Number Two

Returning from France, after my ecstatic, exhilarating, then heart-breaking dismantling of any plans with Mireille, I wasn't ready or motivated to even try to create another relationship. I just had to regard my success with Mireille to be a "one-off"—something that validated my life, but something not likely to occur again. Just resign myself to a life on the sidelines; don't let myself reflect on that one-time event; just try to find other reasons for being. And then, while in the throes of that modus operandi, in a rather unusual manner, I met Elsa, a troubled, struggling single mother of two. I was very much impressed that in spite of battling a significant bipolar condition, and running out of food, money, and ideas on the 30th of each month, she was doing an admirable job of raising and providing for her two girls (each from a different father). And she had a reasonable job and owned her own small home.

One afternoon I observed her making a list of the precise evening meals she would fix for the kids the entire next month, and then make a shopping list for every food item she'd have to buy to accomplish this menu. This plus other brave and disciplined actions on her part convinced me I was in the presence of a valuable person. We did spend the night together, and while it certainly was no Mireille, it was a stateside "first." As soon as I touched her silky, tanned, Scandinavian skin, I was thrilled (and grateful) to feel it begin happening. I was able, and evidently to her it was satisfactory. If not called upon to "do it" too often; I was able to accomplish a passable effort. We soon became a couple, and I developed a caring for her two daughters, especially the oldest, who though she had no reason that warranted it, seemed to have placed me on a pedestal.

We ultimately—in spite of her claims that she considered herself to be "un-marriable" and continued to voice this doubt, I—for some reason, persisted. She acquiesced and we did marry. After about seven years of us making it in a household with five kids from two families, it happened: but not because of some problem with her. No. My own wanderlust again made itself known; that itching in my bones, that discontent, that restlessness, that damned feeling that my life had become a closed book, and I was missing out—on *something* (though once again I had no idea what)! It was this fault, this illusion on my part that caused the divorce. Knowing what I know now; feeling the way I feel now, I would not have divorced her. I would have stayed her partner and taken care of her no matter what. *But I didn't.*

June, the English Dancer

June, wonderful June; remember June—from the cover of Part Two and in Part Three? Of all the women I've had the privilege to know; in fact of all the *people* I've had the privilege to know; June—the always smiling, never down, daughter of a Scottish shoemaker, and invincible captain of the Stafford Ballet, affected and impressed me more than any other woman. She was just 16 when she quit school to learn to dance. The only instruction she could afford was offered by a seventy-year-old Czech woman, in a cold, unheated upper floor of an abandoned train station. Doing her pirouettes while wearing mittens and seeing her breath, paid off. June was now dancing for appreciative crowds all around the world.

It was my good fortune to have met June when the carrier pulled into Valencia, Spain. Inexplicably—since in no way did I bring any special qualities; from "day-one" June knew in her heart, that this American boy was going to be the guy—the one who would change the course of her life. Every expression on her face, every decision she made, every comment she made, every action she took, gave unimpeachable evidence of her love for me. If ever I loved a woman (which I'm not sure I ever did) at least with June I admired and respected her so much, it may well have been love. I at least knew—for the first time, I could have been singularly devoted to this woman—one woman, and have felt the reward of honoring her always and making her life all she dreamed of. Sadly, my impotence was not on vacation when I met her, and as many exceedingly joyful times we otherwise had together, never—*not once was I able to consummate the act with her*; an irony, a tragic overriding obstacle with the one perfect partner. I adjudged my deficiency to disqualify me, and I was unable to consider myself her life's partner. With that most personal, physical, soulful interaction missing, I feared the day would come, when all the good things she felt about me, would not be enough.

However after our work situations caused us to be half a world apart, there was not a day—not a single day that she was not in my thoughts. For twenty years—up until I lost her address, each year I'd send her a birthday card and a Christmas card (each with a $50 bill taped inside) and phoned her when possible. In spite of me letting her down, she was always thrilled when she heard my voice. She never married and honored me by still considered me *her guy*.

June had been a victim of diabetes, and last year her sister Angie located my address in the states and sent me a card, letting me know that after a two-day hospitalization, she had *died!* I would have given anything to have been at her bedside! The card from England had arrived in just four days and I was able to get tickets to England in time to attend her *Celebration of Life*. She had written the whole service. It was comprised of a list of famous hit songs from Broadway musicals, the theme song being "The Show Must Go On." I stood close and watched her coffin being withdrawn and disappear through a parted curtain. I lingered there some time, my eyes well wetted. At the reception I was pleased to meet again, a handful of mature and somewhat rotund women who had been teenagers in her troupe 40 years ago in Spain. They remembered me and were all pleased to see me. I'm glad; perhaps they will find some comfort in now knowing that the guy June picked must have in some way picked her. I am not religious, but I am spiritual, *and hope that June saw me there. I still think of her every day.*

The One—the Only One, Mireille

Undoubtedly you remember her from Part Three and the first two chapters of this part; that tall intimidating French woman who left men strewn in her wake. I had first seen her striding across the lobby in that Dakar oceanfront hotel—in her floor-length fur coat and her 30-inch blonde ponytail bobbing with each strong step. The men she passed looked down to avoid being caught in her razor gaze. *Mireille validated my existence!* She was the woman—who for reasons still unknown, may have found in me something she had not yet found. She was the one (the *only* one in my whole life) whose tears, trembling and declarations of undying love, let me feel the pride and power of consummating the act. She was and still is, the only woman who awoke my manhood; aroused within me a force that allowed me to at last consider myself a male! She blessed me with a glorious hope; gave me a reason to live!

But... as I told you earlier, it was a way too-short life of elation. Back in France, after a week of uninterrupted, unabated glorious physical unions, she confessed to me that *she was afraid she could not live with just one man!* No need to tell you what a crushing blow this was! I was truly awestruck. It fell on my ears with a stunning resonance. Both dumb and numb, I was forced to realize that her wildly demonstrative pleasure was not me, it was her. She was evidently vexed with an usual sensitivity that demanded the reactions I had reveled in, thinking of course I had inspired them. Seconds after she said those words, I was only a shadow of my former self. Hearing that proclamation I knew that I had to give up on this dream. I had to forget any thoughts of marrying Mireille. If I did, there would surely come a day when she would break my heart. Anticipating the sorrow and humility that would bring was sufficient to eclipse even the most pleasurable recollections. I had to leave her; not contact her again; blanch her from my mind; erase everything and go on (if at all possible) like it had never happened.

Chapter Eighteen
1984

My Undeserved Good Fortune: Wife #3

Now—after twenty discouraging years of humiliating failures to please a woman (except the "one-off" with Mireille), I had no other choice but to conclude *I was not going to have the resources or time (or luck) to bring it about again.* I was therefore able to emerge from the depths of despair, not by succeeding, but rather by resigning myself to the fact I would *not* succeed, and hopefully be able to discount the impact of this deficiency with any possible future partner; strive to minimize its importance in my life from here on out. Just forget the fulfillment, pride and power it had showered me with for one week, long ago and far away. (Or, although it would not be likely—find a woman to whom the act was not a "be all end all.")

I Now Believe in Miracles

Buying the oceanfront home in Hobe Sound entailed a lot of visits to the bank, finalizing the mortgage loan particulars and finally the "closing." The agent—Kathy, who began helping me and stuck with me through the whole process, was a cheerful, always smiling single mother, just a few years younger than me, with a high school age son. I found—perhaps for the first time, and who knows why: a totally non-stressful, complementing "other." It was an easy and fun relationship, and mercifully to me—without her giving any indication of being the least desirous of future intimate acts! We began dating and it went well. The revelation—the clincher, was after she felt comfortable enough with me she had a confession; *a confession that made her the perfect partner for me!* Several years ago she had uterine prolapse surgery, requiring a mesh implant. It slipped, penetrating the forward wall of her vagina. This condition was irreparable, and forever more: *intercourse—if even possible, would be more painful than pleasurable!* (For which she and about a hundred other women received a significant financial settlement.) I was rescued! *An answer to the unanswerable!* Finally, a union was possible. I had just found a woman, whose enjoyment, whose daily pleasures, I would be able to provide! One who didn't need that *other* satisfaction. No longer would it be necessary to pray for a manly raucous bedroom encounter! All this being true, it was not a long courtship. Three months later I bought a ring and proposed.

I know—even understanding the difference, and a *huge* difference this time, I can't blame you if you're saying "Not again!" But Kathy's wonderful gift (although unknown as such by her) made this a "first." And this time I knew it would last; or—that I would. In fact, I was so convinced of its permanency that shortly after making it official, I had the deed for my oceanfront home changed to show Kathy as the co-owner. Although I must admit: unfortunately, like the reason for both of my previous marriages, there was a bit of the same motivation: *do something to save another woman; rescue her, make Kathy's dreams come true.* In the previous two unions I failed to realize this personal reward would be short-lived and certainly nothing to make a marriage decision on. Of course Kathy and her son were excited (thrilled) to be able to move out of their rented one-story, two-bedroom 1960's concrete-block home, and move into my three-story custom-built oceanfront home.

Most people would not be impressed with my furniture (half of them bought at Pier One), but Kathy was a doll—showing no disapproval of my décor of questionable furniture and wall coverings; in fact praising me for this and that. It wasn't until a month after my encouraging her to do so, that she made some recommendations and we bought a few new items— all of which I agree were an improvement. We furnished the downstairs bedroom for her son Neil with the kinds of furniture and wall decorations a kid his age would like (including a bunch of Pittsburgh Steeler posters and memorabilia). Things went well, especially aided by the fact that—except on rare occasions, I did not have to sweat out the hours before bedtime, wondering if I'd make it or not. What a relief! No pressure. I was able to reflect less often on the fulfillment and euphoria I had experienced with Mireille.

In Spite of and After All the Above

The major project now was, find a better job. The one I had was barely tolerable. I had been able to get a job in Fort Lauderdale (an hour's drive south) with one of those "shoe-string" "mom-and-pop" charter companies: "AAA Aviation." They owned and operated one old and poorly-maintained jet (one of the first Lear jets ever manufactured). Don't think I ever did a pre-flight inspection on the aircraft that I didn't find corroded hinges, a half dozen seals leaking oil, or tires that should have been changed twenty landings ago. The company was a "last resort" choice when someone couldn't get airline reservations, and couldn't afford a more highly regarded charter company.

Here's an example of a too-typical flight: One evening I was called at about 10 pm, to fly down to Cozumel, Mexico, to pick up a woman tourist and her daughter who had been injured in a traffic accident. Not at all what I felt like doing this night and at this late hour, but I dressed and jumped in the car. Arriving at the airport, I discovered they had not yet found a copilot. I had to wait over an hour while they scrounged up one; a woman who owned a *Sea-Doo* dealership in the area, and had just recently gotten a Learjet rating. This made her qualified to fly one, and in spite of having practically no time in the Learjet, once or twice a month they were short one copilot. Not the best crew complement for an international, over water, night flight.

About 45 minutes after takeoff, halfway to the west end of Cuba, AAA Aviation contacts me on the radio and tells me I have to turn around and come back, but not to Ft Lauderdale, rather I should land at Miami Opalocka airport and park at Lejeune Aviation, and phone them when I got there. *Geez!* I had Sue call Miami Center and tell them what we needed to do. They gave us an okay and I reversed my course back to south Florida; landed at Opalocka and taxied to the ramp in front of Lejeune Aviation. I didn't have to walk into the office, since the manager met me at the plane. "Here's the deal captain, triple A hasn't paid their Mexico Overflight Permits for the last six months, and your aircraft would be impounded if you landed down there. George and I worked out a deal. You can just leave your plane here, and take 25 XL over there. We've kept our "Overflight and Landing" account paid up with the Directorate de Aeronautics."

I did a pre-flight inspection of their airplane (which was no more impressive than the on one I had done on ours). We departed and flew to Cozumel, arriving about 2 am. Two problems: The first, our passengers weren't going to be at the airport until 8 o'clock the next morning! And second—while we were waiting (and I now had a bone to pick with the guy who met me at Lejeune Aviation): Mexican officials here, informed me that the Lejeune account with the Directorate of Aeronautics (for their aircraft to fly over and land in Mexico) *was also delinquent!* I had enough experience to know these kinds of "SNAFU's" occurred frequently, and that Third World officials often would not take a credit card, demanding cash (to allow for all the skimming that would take place on the way up). I therefore never left on one of these international trips without a hidden wad of cash. This time I had just enough to pay the fine, and fill out forms to renew Lejeune's account. The passengers arrived; we took off and flew back to Opalocka. Landed a little after ten a.m., unloaded the passengers and escorted them to my original aircraft, *which had a flat tire!* (I suppose I should have been relieved; if I had taken our aircraft to Cozumel, it would have gone flat there.) It took another two hours to get a new tire and get it mounted. Took off and arrived back at my home base of Fort Lauderdale about two in the afternoon. *On duty all night and half the day—16 hours straight!* This was only one of many similar flights with AAA Aviation. Still, with no other positions available, I remained with them—one of George's "go to" guys.

Something I Had Actually Considered On My Own

Exhausted from the contorted and prolonged disorder of my Mexico flight, I slept-in the next morning. At a late and leisurely extended breakfast, Kathy and I conversed about a string of topics—all light and pleasant. (Just one of the pastimes that made our marriage peaceful and rewarding.) Nearing the end of our chit-chat she became quiet. By her facial expression I correctly guessed she was mulling over something to say. I didn't wait and asked her what it might be. Hesitantly—she was reluctant to speak at first, she started. For once (embarrassingly—maybe for the first time) I realized I was going to be deservedly on the listening end.

She began. "Roger, I've never mentioned this to you before, but it has crossed my mind a couple times, and it could be a good thing."

"And what's that?" I asked.

"God knows you've been—and still are, the most loving and involved father of any divorced father I've ever seen; always at your kids' beck and call, such as quitting that good job in Wichita to move to Hobe Sound and provide them a domicile to continue at St. Michaels, and so many other things, but..."

"But what?"

"Have you ever thought of apologizing to them for how you must have hurt their mother? It may be a good idea. I've noticed they worship her. Maybe when the time presents itself, you could pay a visit to each one of the kids—alone; one at a time and make a formal apology."

Although I was not accustomed to being on the receiving end of instructions, I knew this was something that had also crossed my mind more than once, and probably due. I started to offer my side of the story: "Yeah but..." But that's all I got out.

She had more to offer: "No, I don't mean you should try to explain why. No excuses, no matter how valid you think they are. Just an apology; how sorry you are about that period in your life, and how your actions hurt their mom. Be humble. You don't have to ask for their forgiveness, but recognize what you did to their mom was more than just a little wrong."

I was a bit taken aback by this proclamation—for two reasons: First, because with my overly self-assured perspective and frequent position as 'the guy in charge' I don't think I had enough experience with people telling me what I should do, and especially someone so close—like Kathy. I knew she was right and should have thanked her. It would be an appropriate action on my part, and I finally vowed to bring it to pass.

Chapter Nineteen
AN ALMOST FINAL EVENT

July 4th, 1988

In addition to being a nationally celebrated holiday, July 4th was Kevin's birthday and Donna's wedding anniversary. Having these two family milestones occurring on that day we chose the three-day-long holiday weekend as the perfect opportunity for a family reunion (giving an extra day for travel time). In years past, my first wife, myself, and each of the four kids travelled from wherever to take advantage of this annual event. The last few years it was held at Sara's new house in the upscale town of Windermere, just 20 minutes from Orlando. (She had long since returned from Okinawa with her USAF—now colonel, husband.) If it wasn't held there, it was held at Donna's house. She had her Ph.D. and was happily married with two children. Being a professional with her own business she could live anywhere she wanted, and as a still-avid surfer, had chosen to live on the beach, back in Hobe Sound where the kids had grown up and her father lived.

In spite of the above, for some reason—this year it was being held at my oceanfront house. Weather-wise, the morning of July 4th did not dawn as a sunny and warm Chamber-of-Commerce-type Florida day; in fact it was an uncomfortable, low pressure, gray-skied, "bad vibes" day. I felt antsy. Sitting out on my balcony (if you can believe—with both Sara *and* Kathy), Donna's son Ike asks me if I want to go out surfing with him. I didn't. Like I said before, it was not a "user-friendly" day. Also, instead of having my "baggies" on (the standard knee-length surfing shorts) I had just finished my jog and was still wearing a pair of skimpy nylon running shorts. (Going surfing in these would be sacrilegious, but I would.)

A Shortened Surfing Session

He kept hounding me until I gave in. Walking into the surf, too easily scaling my board ahead of me, confirmed that the surf was definitely not "up." The waves were low and slow-moving. We paddled out (me not at all enthusiastic and hoping this would be a short-lived activity). While waiting for a good set of waves (which didn't come) Ike spied a half dozen kids on boards, a couple hundred yards south of us, *and starts paddling down to them*, leaving his old grandpa alone. *Not* a courteous or even safe thing to do. I was pissed and anxious to reprimand him for leaving me. Rather than take the time to paddle down there, I decided just to catch a wave, ride it to the beach, drop my board and walk down there. Once again there were no good waves and I had to satisfy myself with the best facsimile available. I caught one and was quickly leaving the deep water and would soon be in shallow enough water to "skag" a tail fin (have it dig into the sand). So, and this was my mistake: still moving at about 20 mph, instead of just jumping off feet-first and catching my balance, I decided (God knows why) to do some crazy jack-knifing dive off the board. Evidently the water was more shallow than I thought. My forehead rammed full force into an under-the-surface, raised ridge in the sand. I heard the snap in my neck!

Instantly I was completely paralyzed! *It was the most terrifying sensation I had ever experienced! No body parts! No neck, no chest, no hips, no arms or legs.* And I don't mean I couldn't move them, or that I couldn't feel them; *they weren't there!* My entire being was no more than a set of eyeballs. The shocked awareness of my situation was too much to accept. It was so bad I had the fleeting desperate thought that it was a nightmare, and if I could just shake myself awake, it would be over and I would find myself raising up in bed. I mentally labored at that effort for no more than a few seconds before disastrously concluding, that no—this was no nightmare. *It had happened. I was a quadriplegic!* I thought of the kids who dove into the shallow end of the pool and ended up like this. I thought of the Hollywood Superman Christopher Reeve, who as a result of an equestrian accident became a quadriplegic. And although my mind was churning furiously I was not in possession of any idea that could salvage me, and now recognized and accepted that I too was going to be a quadriplegic. I'm ashamed to admit that I considered all those lifestyle concerns about becoming a quadriplegic, before realizing I was going to be a *dead* quadriplegic. I was not going to live a long and handicapped life. *I was going to drown. I was going to die!* Believe it or not, while my whole life didn't flash in front of my face, while I was too frantic to devote sufficient time to doing so, I could visualize Kathy's face (and importantly, reflect on the advice she had given me about apologizing to my kids, *which I had not yet put into action*).

My eyes were open, and when I rolled face down I could see nothing but the sand bottom two inches in front of my face, then as I continued the roll and was looking upward through six feet of water, I could see the clouds drifting by, and then continuing the roll, my nose again in the sand. I didn't recall taking a breath before I went into the water, but in any case, I did know I was going to be running out of breath—and soon! By now I knew there was no hope and I was going to die. This thought surprisingly did not scare me, although I can still remember the terribly imposing melancholy that swept over me. Amazingly, it came to mind that just last week—for $9 a month, I bought a policy from the lender stipulating: *in the event of an accidental death my mortgage would be paid off!*

The oxygen situation was getting worse by the second. My lungs were on fire. I actually had time to consider whether: (1) I would just hold my breath until I passed out, or (2) if I would—even knowing it would be the end, be unable to resist the urge to inhale—take the fatal gasp which would fill my lungs with water. I am here to tell you—first-person, that you cannot resist taking that desperate inhalation. Even knowing the certain consequences, I did! And shockingly to me—and I remember this vividly, I did not gag or choke or cough, but rather felt a sudden sensation of complete relief and comfort; *no longer was I out of breath! My lungs immediately felt full and satisfied; no longer any discomfort!* I probably had this thought for four or five seconds before I lost consciousness.

Mercifully Spied!

What follows here was relayed to me by Kevin and other members of the family: He was inside the house, standing by the bay window, burping his one-year old son and perusing the other family members down on the beach. Miraculously—through the bows of the pine trees; through a small space between two limbs, I happened to appear in his gaze. Evidently the surfboard leash was still connected to my ankle, and as the board was making its way out to sea, it was pulling me with it. In so doing, parts of my body would momentarily bob above the surface. Ken shouted to Kathy, "Dad's screwing around again!" Fortunately for me, it wasn't a half minute before he reevaluated his previous impression that I was screwing around. He dropped the baby, hollered to Kathy to call 911, burst out through the sliding glass door onto the balcony, down the steps to the beach, and into the ocean at a full run. Kevin is just about 6' and 180 pounds, and a natural athlete; having been a high jumper, point guard, and 800 meter track star; a real gazelle! (Thankfully for me.) I was a good 50 yards from shore and Ken, also a surfer and strong swimmer—made short work of the distance. I say "short work" but doubt it could have taken less that two or three minutes for him to get to me. I was not an appealing sight—forehead split open, a bloodied face, and skin blue! Kevin at first tried to drape me over my surfboard, intending to push it to shore. Shoved up onto it from the left; I slipped off it into the water on the right. Shoved up onto it from the right; I slipped off it into the water on the left. With no way to keep my wet dead weight on the board, Kenny got behind me, reached up through my armpits, clasped his hands, rolled over on his back and started a strong, quick frog kick towards shore.

Once up on the beach—much of the family now crowded around, they started CPR. Most fortunately at this time an off-duty EMT (Emergency Medical Technician) happened to be walking by, saw what was going on and jumped in: "No. no. That won't work yet, his lungs are probably full of water. No air can get in. Roll him over on his stomach! Yeah, now put your hands down here like this, grab him under the pelvis and lift it up—way up, high. High as you can! Yeah, just let his torso hang, you can let his head touch the ground, that's okay. Great, that's it. That's it." Evidently, a second after they had me draped in half—head hanging low, my full lungs just let the water pour out; what looked like gallons of it. So much was coming out that when my eyes flicked open, Donna was kneeling in front of me, her hands digging in the sand by my mouth, fashioning a drainage ditch for the water to run away from my nostrils.

The ambulance arrived and I was in it and on my way to the hospital. In the ambulance I was fully conscious and able to evaluate the ride. It was horrible! They had a fold down cot from one wall of the ambulance; snapped the legs in place under it, and then using wide leather straps, lashed my chest and lower legs to the cot. Halfway to the hospital, the cot legs collapsed and the cot went down, swinging back flat against the ambulance wall. My feet were secured high at the lower end of the cot, and my chest was secured high on the upper end of the cot, and my body was a sideways hanging contorted boomerang! My hip was against the floor, where it was being jarred black and blue with every bump they went over. In having fallen to this new position, the oxygen mask was pulled askew on my face, with the bottom seal now covering my nostrils and the top seal on my forehead! After this ride, what I now say, is: If you ever do have an occasion like this; yes, call 911! *Then have your neighbor drive you to the hospital in his Lexus.* You can meet the ambulance at the Emergency Room entrance.

My arrival and first few hours are not real clear. As I came in and out of consciousness, I heard Kevin speaking forcefully to the Emergency Room personnel. "You have to give him that injection for swelling! You have to avoid the swelling!" When Kevin was playing basketball at St. Michael's, Dudley—the Center on his team had gone up for a rebound and came down on his head, violently twisting his neck. After ten minutes he claimed he was okay, sat out the rest of the game but joined the team at a McDonald's after the game. The next day he was a paraplegic, and would remain so the rest of his life. This tragic condition was attributed to the swelling that increased and lasted all night, causing a pinching of the spinal cord. Kevin never forgot it, and was going to make sure it didn't happen to me!

A Shaky Recovery

Miraculously—after a day and a half, the feeling and ability to move my limbs came back and I was released from the hospital. For the first several days, all I could do was sit in one chair, my head lain back against the seat. I was still flying for AAA Aviation, and fortunately—knowing this family reunion was coming, I had asked George to be left off the schedule during the holiday weekend and the next two days (never thinking I'd be using the extra days to learn how to stand again). I still had two more days before I would be susceptible to be called for a flight. And a good thing too! One of the reasons I spent so much time seated, is when I stood up and tried to walk, it was all I could do to keep my balance; wobbling and tending to veer from side to side; seemingly to have little control over a left or right lean. After three days I was better; but not much better, and the bad news is, I did get a call for a flight that would launch early the next day. *Foolishly I said I could do it.* At 05:30 the next morning I got up, pulled on my dark blue trousers, my light blue shirt with the captain's epaulettes, and black flying jodhpurs, had a small breakfast, and I must admit—somewhat unsteadily made my way down the steps to the garage. Sitting in the car in the dark, I realized I was fading in and out and felt like I might have a fever. Kathy was in the stairwell doorway monitoring my progress, with obvious concern. I didn't feel well enough to even get out of the car. Slumped in the driver's seat I hollered to her (as best I could) "Phone George tell him anything. Tell him I've got the 'runs' and can't make it. I know Jerry is standing by and only lives ten minutes from the airport."

I was measurably better a couple weeks later and could maintain a straight line while walking, however if someone passing me would have just put their hand on my shoulder, and lightly pushed, I would have gone tumbling off to that side. And one other strange lingering thing: it took a month—a full month for the color to come back to my face. I truly remained "white as a sheet" for that long. In fact, two weeks later I did get called for a flight to take a gambler to the "Redneck Riviera" (Biloxi, Mississippi). I knew the guy from having flown him there before. As evidence of how I wore the effects of the brain stem shock and drowning, when the guy was handing me his suitcase he looked at me with visible concern and said, *"What in the hell happened to you!?"* I never told anyone about this drowning incident, because if a licensed Airline Transport Pilot (me) ever lost consciousness, it was the end of his piloting career! His medical certificate would be withdrawn. (Funny this applies to a pilot, but not a neurosurgeon). It was six months before I could stand on one leg, consider venturing down stairs without reaching for the handrail, or turn around quickly. I kept on flying for George at AAA Aviation, but there wasn't a day that I didn't check out another flying job.

Chapter Twenty
A RESPECTABLE JOB, THE AGENCY, AND THE MIDDLE EAST

Having Been a Factory Pilot and Speaking Spanish

October 1988: I was still living in the oceanfront home in Hobe Sound, and not knowing how long I could put up with AAA Aviation (driving an hour to the Fort Lauderdale airport, the 3 a.m. flights, the poorly maintained aircraft, and not well qualified copilots). *But a break!* Not once but now twice. Having a Lear rating and speaking Spanish had first netted me that job at the Learjet factory, and now I'm lucking out again. Right here on the West Palm Beach airport (where I flew out of for SSL Systems, and only 20 minutes from home) there was another aviation employer. It wasn't a corporate flight department or a charter company, but the most respected and advanced aviation training company in United States: FlightSafety International. Their specialty was giving FAA annually-required recurrent training to *already certified* jet captains; and in particular: *Lear Jet Captains!* They were being overloaded with Mexican and South American Learjet captains and needed a Spanish-speaking experienced Learjet pilot. They scheduled me for an interview that included me giving a classroom presentation to all the other instructors—one sentence in Spanish, the next sentence in English. (With my lack of fluency, the only way I was able to do this was to practice it a hundred times the night before.) I was hired!

Working at FSI and a Surprise Offer

I can't really complain about the job. I very much enjoyed instructing and I could possibly end up with that long-sought-after retirement! I had nice co-workers, good visual aids equipment, and the satisfaction of administering realistic simulator sessions. Although everything else was just fine the pay was not great, and that was enough of a downside for me to at least keep my eye open. Not long after I was released as a "Platform Instructor" and a "Simulator Instructor," one of my Learjet students was a Chief Pilot for McDonnell Douglas, flying for some kind of operation in the Middle East. While other students always related anecdotal stories about their flight department activities, Bob was mum on whatever they were doing in Saudi Arabia.

One day—out of the blue he asks me, *is that right—you were the chief pilot for Air America?* I had no idea how he found that out, but I said, "Yeah, Bob, that's right. I was." He confidentially informed me that his company was flying in support of the Saudi Air Force, and would I be interested? He implied I would be *real* pleased with the pay. I said sure, and not a week later I received tickets to the McDonnell Douglas headquarters in St. Louis. There I had two interviews, the second one being from a government guy who said he was from Langley (which I knew was the CIA headquarters). I passed the interviews and was offered a job with Middle East Logistics Support, in Riyadh, Saudi Arabia. They told me they understood it was a big decision, *and to just go home and think about it, but give them an answer in one week.*

An Old Friend and a Big Surprise

Just down the street from FSI was a Hilton hotel, whose parking lot I used for my evening jogs. A day or two after returning from St. Louis, while running clockwise around the lot, a guy running counter-clockwise approaches, waves as he passes and continues behind me. He somehow looked familiar. I stopped and turned around, to see him stopped and turned around looking at me. He hollered at me, "Roger, is that you?"

"Holy Shit—John, what are you doing here?" It was John Kundell, a young pilot I flew with when I was at Learjet; one of the first Navy Seals (in every way). He wasn't big but my kids still joked about shaking hands with Mr. Kundell and then having broken knuckles. I had been in Wichita for about a year when he and his beautiful, freckle-faced athletic wife and two high-energy boys arrived—all stuffed in a bright red sport model Jeep Wrangler. It was an All-American family if ever there was one. They went skiing together in Aspen, scuba diving in the Bahamas, and every one of the family participated in a half dozen competitive sports. (Everyone was jealous of the Kundell family.) I asked what he was doing now and he said he was the Chief Pilot for US Airways and living in Charlotte, North Carolina. I asked him what he was flying and he said he was qualified in the Boeing 737, 757, and 767 models (the current mainstays of the airline industry). I asked him about his wife.

"We're getting divorced!"

You could have knocked me over with a feather! The famous Kundell family broken up?!

"And there's more. You may be able to help me. I've got to get me and my money out of the country—quick! In court, I got pissed and told the judge to get fucked. In three weeks he's going to take me to the cleaners."

"Well how in the hell can I help?"

"The Sultan of Brunei just bought a Boeing 737, and I'm one of the most qualified 737 pilots in the world. Please, can you call Boeing for me—they're the ones who gave me my type rating in it over five years ago. See if there's any way I can get the job of flying that 737 for the sultan. And soon!"

An Unexpected Outcome

To help John, the next day I called Boeing, trying to get some info. I got the Boeing chief pilot on the phone and began feeling him out about the possibilities of him being able to give John some contact information for the sultan (or maybe even recommend John for the job of flying his new 737). Halfway through the chief pilot says, "And who are you again?" I explained who I was, and what I was doing with FlightSafety International. He asks, "Did you say you are a qualified instructor in a six-axis, motion, full-visual simulator?" I told him that yes, I was. He then commenced to tell me that Boeing was in desperate need of simulator instructors for the new 737, and would I like to come out for an interview." *Shit. I was calling for John and I end up with a possible job offer myself!* He goes on to sweeten the pot by saying "At Boeing, after three months as a simulator instructor, you are promoted to an actual inflight instructor!" Wow—*me*, a "little-plane" pilot (first, that Swiss Porter, then those "puddle jumpers" across the ocean, and finally the Lear Jet), now with a chance to fly the big stuff, the *"heavy iron;"* what every pilot wants to do!

I accepted the offer and received the tickets to Seattle two days later. I told John I'd failed in his mission (without mentioning anything about how the call turned out.). At Boeing I was interviewed by several of their pilots, given a short session in the simulator checking my reaction to engine and systems malfunctions, and then a flight check in an actual 737 (which I had never even been inside)! This was my first flight ever in a big jet, and I was more lucky than I deserved: everything went much better than I could have hoped for. When it was all finished the chief pilot shook my hand and told me *I could consider myself hired!* But then added, "Of course to be officially hired you have to be approved by the board, and they meet the end of the month; I think the 25th. I'll be calling you then. And don't worry, they have never opposed even one of my recommendations.

A Welcomed but Unusual Conundrum

After years and years of trying to find a good flying position, I now find myself with not one, but *two* job offers, and two *good* ones! The one from McDonnell Douglas was a "done deal" while the one with Boeing (that I was *assured* of by the chief pilot) wouldn't be confirmed till later this month (after the board met). And here's the problem: Boeing wasn't going to be calling for two weeks, and I only had two more days before my time was up to give McDonnell Douglas a yes or no. In line with "a bird in the hand is worth two in the bush," with a lot of "what ifs" and hand wringing, I came to a decision (maybe a cowardly one). I called McDonnel and gave them an affirmative answer. *I'd be going to Saudi Arabia.* Only not as soon as I thought.

A Couple Setbacks before Joining McDonnell Douglas

Before officially being hired I had to take a "new hire" drug test. I did, *and it came back "positive." I'd failed it.* I found out why: In addition to working at FSI, I was in the process of getting my Flight Instructor's Instrument Rating during my off-duty days. This had entailed an unbelievably long and complicated day, the day before my scheduled drug test. I knew I had an FSI class early the next morning and needed a good night's sleep. As "wound up" as I was—to be sure I slept, *I had taken a valium*, and that was what caused a "positive" on my drug test. I had a second test, and guess what: when McDonnell called for the results, the clerk misunderstood the first letter of my last name, and told them they did not have a "negative" test result for that name. It *appeared* I failed again! (At this point I was surprised they were still considering me.) Fortunately it only took a couple days (me becoming involved) to clear up the "name" thing.

I was told each employee had a probation period before his wife or family could come over, so Kathy wouldn't be able to join me for ninety days. She was able to coordinate renting our house—with all our furniture in it, to her brother Ted and his family. They agreed to moving in the day after she left to join me. I packed two suitcases of clothes and special personal things, *and was on my way to the Middle East!*

Oh, In Case You Were Wondering, I Did it

I had this three-week delay thrust upon me, and though the thought of doing it weakened my knees, I knew Kathy was right. I had thought about it many times since she brought it up. No matter how I dreaded it, I had to apologize to the kids, specifically for how I had treated their mother. After the drowning incident (which almost excluded this apology forever) and now with my coming tour in the Middle East (which could delay it many years); no two ways about it, I had to do it now. And doing it was not an easy job. Two of the kids were out of driving range; had to take the airlines. Not surprisingly, the nature of each apology went the same: I was successful in getting them alone (like Kathy said, no sibling present) and just came out with it—as hard as it was to voice the words (even though in preparation, I had mouthed them to myself a hundred times). I didn't know what reaction I was expecting; certainly I knew they wouldn't thank me (and they didn't). Each one just took it in silence—an extended silence (while they appeared to be weighing its merit), and then accepted my hug. Donna was matter of fact. Mark was the only one to offer his perspective on it (and it wasn't easy to hear). Stacy was the best, apparently never for a moment having doubted her wonderful father. Kevin seemed to be the most hurt. I now recognize him as the one most sensitive and affected by my waywardness. But it was done. I did it. And though they gave little or no indication of it, I hoped it meant something to them. I know I didn't deserve that it should have produced some, or any forgiveness.

Chapter Twenty-One
EAST IS EAST AND WEST IS WEST

Arriving In a New and Strange (Very Strange) Country

My flight touched down at the Riyadh, Saudi Arabia airport a little after two in the morning. I was a little worse for the wear (three flights and 20 hours). The terminal was a spectacular architecturally enlightening experience. I entered a huge, glistening, cavernous, stadium-sized interior space. All the walls and the ceiling were made of polished cream and taupe marble, with lots of apparently real gold trim! It was the most ostentatious, garish display of opulence that I had ever laid my eyes on. Five times the size that would be required (now or ever), and displaying way too many statues and forms carved from probably prohibitively expensive materials; a décor that in majesty eclipsed the foyer of any palace. I had arrived with two other McDonnell Douglas guys who were—like me, stumbling along, their heads turning left and right, eyes upward, sweeping the interior with disbelief.

Coming out of Customs and Immigration, I spied Bob (the chief pilot I trained in Palm Beach, who got me the job). He was there to meet me; gave me an enthusiastic greeting, hustled me to the car, and we were on our way. It was about ten miles to town; ten miles of five-lane wide highways, bathed in the amber light of sodium lamps atop towering 100-ft tall stanchions. (Highways which by the way were completely deserted.) We arrived at the compound in which I would live; located well outside the city limits and isolated by miles of flat sand in every direction. It was a half-mile square block, completely enclosed by a ten-foot high concrete wall, the top of which was embedded with shards of glass. The guard at the gate waved Bob through and he took me to my new Saudi domicile. I was amazed; it was a much larger and grandiose home than I would have anticipated, or that was necessary. (A smaller facsimile of the airport.) He gave me the key and told me he'd pick me up at seven. *Seven? Geez.* Checking my watch it was already past three!

A Trip to Town and My New Employee Briefing

And he was there at seven sharp. I was ready, although only a yawning replica of a half-awake, barely ambulatory human. As we left the compound (now in daylight) he showed me the pool, the gym, the tennis courts, the bowling alley, the movie theater, and the dining hall. *Holy Shit! This place was nothing short of a resort!* I was of course excited, and anxious to share this news with Kathy a soon as I could. Bob told me he'd get me a line to the states that night. It was a twenty minute drive to the McDonnell Douglas Admin Offices in downtown Riyadh, where I was to get the standard "new employee" briefing. Most of this was given by Louis Martin—the head of Human Resources. He covered all the "dos" and "don'ts" of being a McDonnell Douglas employee in Saudi Arabia.

Throughout the briefing he threw in supposedly humorous asides about the Saudis; one I remember being: did I know what the shortest unit of time was. I responded, no what is it? He said *the time between the light turning green and the Saudi behind you beeping the horn.* This and other surprising admissions led me to believe that there was no love lost between Louis and the Saudi's. At the end of the briefing he took me to the Disbursing Office (pay window) to change my US dollars into Saudi Riyals. As I was arranging the money to put it into my pocket, Louis said, "No, no, don't do that." He was referring to my habit of turning all the bills so the sides showing the face were up, and then organizing them in ascending order so the larger bills were on the inside of the fold. "We're in a Muslim country, and that's how Jewish people arrange their money. *You don't want the Saudi's to think you're Jewish!"*

A Hint of What We Had to Deal With

Louis told me that to appease the Saudi government (a clause underlined in the contract) McDonnell Douglas had to employ one Saudi national for every American employee in-country. And furthermore, employ them as managers or senior office workers—*each and every one with their own desk and an elevated title.* He said in his office he had 19 Saudi office workers, 16 of whom were related and claimed to have royal blood. They never came in before ten, read the paper till eleven, had tea till twelve, took a two hour lunch, came back at two, and left at about 3 (knowing that no performance issue would ever result in their being fired). The company understood that they absolutely could not hire Saudis as errand-runners, or cooks, or janitors, or to do handy-man jobs around the buildings. And that's because it was beneath a Saudi man to be asked to carry something heavy, or do any manual labor.

A Briefing on Our Flying Routine

After my session at headquarters Bob was anxious to show me our flight department, which I found was not located at the International Airport. We operated out of a smaller airport run by the Saudi Military. Once there Bob gave me a walk-through of the hangar and offices, introduced me to our maintenance staff, Rick, Tom, and Ken. I didn't get to meet any pilots. The only two out here were gone with the Lear. During the time there he gave me the rudiments of our operation: our two Lears were owned and scheduled by the Saudi Air Force, and I would be a Saudi Air Force pilot, *reacting obediently and without question to the whims of any Saudi Air Force officer.*

Our primary (published) mission would be flying a daily, canned (not challenging) fixed route that spanned the Kingdom—landing at five military airports. Each of these airports was operating the F-15 Eagle; a state-of-the-art fighter/bomber manufactured by McDonnell Douglas. (Unknown to me at the time of my hiring was that having been in the military and flown jet fighter/bombers was a boon to my being hired.) At these airports, most frequently we'd drop off the parts needed to get one of the aircraft back in a flying status (there was always at least one not in an airworthy state). We'd also drop off the Saudi pilot who hopefully (if he got around to it) would fly it back to Riyadh. Many times we'd drop off a cadre of senior Saudi Air Force pilots to attend a supposedly urgent "Aviation War Plan" strategy meeting at one of the bases. Meetings which Bob had been invited to attend and discovered in every case were no more than a chance for a half dozen old friends to have a private social gab session, conducted during an all-afternoon lunch (while seated cross-legged on the floor, greasy handedly, tearing out choice morsels from the prone roasted goat).

I GUESS I JUST WASN'T THINKING

A Surprising, Awkward Invitation

About 3 pm Bob left me off at the compound. I paused a moment outside my home to wonder at it as my abode; and inside was again impressed by the extravagant furnishings. I knew Kathy would be very pleased and surprised. Tired as I was, I decided not to give in to taking a nap (in my four-posted "king-sized" bed). Instead—being the Florida "sun-freak" I was, decided to go to the pool; a beautiful Olympic-sized pool only about 50 yards from my house. I put on my bathing suit grabbed a towel and was out the door. The fellow—Louis Martin, who I had met for the first time this morning when he gave me the new-employee briefing, was just being dropped off at his house, which was next door to mine. We met on the sidewalk and seeing I was bound for the pool, had a few words of caution for me: "Roger, you must be careful over here, even at this late hour of the day one can get burned real easy. After supper if you'd like, come on over *and I'll give you a nice back rub with aloe lotion.*"

Which Brings up A Unique Appeal of this Country

The above incident I was to find out, was my first indicator that there was a pervasive and understandable prevalence of homosexual Americans working here in Saudi Arabia. And why? Just like many homosexual men seek out the priesthood, because it is a celibate lifestyle that disallows intimate association with the feminine gender, *it is their perfect "cover."* Here in Saudi Arabia—Kingdom-wide, it was absolutely prohibited—against Sharia law, for a man to ever be seen—anywhere, with a woman who was not his wife, mother, or sister. If he was, strict punishment evolved, including prison sentences for both! So here, since men were rarely seen with a woman, it was commonly accepted behavior for two men to be seen walking together (even holding hands), eating together—even in candle-lit darkened corners. This was not only not uncommon it was considered quite normal behavior. And listen to this: while I could not check into a downtown Riyadh hotel with my wife without showing the same surname on both of our passports, and the notarized copy of our marriage certificate (that I was required to get before leaving the states), *two Saudi men could walk in (holding hands) and check in to a single room!* Saudi law and its strict application, prohibiting men from associating with women, like the priesthood, was the perfect cover for a gay gentleman.

In our flight department there were two pilots that everyone knew were gay. In the five years I would spend here, not once—on no occasion did I ever see them with a woman, or did they ever mention one with any indication of attraction (or even mention one—period). It was as if both these gentlemen were aware of their sexual orientation, but through upbringing or other influences, they themselves somehow considered it possibly inappropriate behavior. Without a single lapse, they refrained from ever openly displaying their inclinations. Among the McDonnell administrative personnel, there were another two so-inclined male employees. Once again they were highly respected individuals, and never acted in a way that would have indicated their preferences. That one incident with Louis and the back rub, was the only indicative advance I had, or heard of. (I did notice that when vacations were taken, the two above individuals often chose the same destinations.)

Flying the Line

It did not take long for me to complete my "training and in-country familiarization," and find myself flying the daily schedule to those five military bases. One thing: the weather was always clear, no thunder bumpers, snow, sleet, rain, or fog. Easy flying. No real challenges; in fact it was a boring routine, but the pay was good. Almost an 8 to 5 office job. Transporting the same few Saudi Air Force pilots to and from these outlying bases, I learned that these pilots had undergone training in the F-15 at Eglin AFB in Florida, and were supposedly qualified and proud to say they were a "Jet Captain." *In fact it may have been the most prestigious position a young Saudi could hold.* However, even trained stateside, and assumed to be thrilled and anxious to "slip the surly bonds," Bob told me they were just smart enough to recognize their lack of aptitude and the inflight danger involved, so it took considerable urging to get them in the air.

One of our pilots remarked they were like chickens; *you had to throw a rock at them to get them off the ground!* A year ago a rumor emerged that the Yemeni Air Force was going to launch an attack on Saudi Arabia on such-and-such a day; and on that day 70% of the Saudi Air Force called in sick! There was no attack. I later heard a popular joke that panned their questionable fighting spirit: *the Saudi government said they would spare no cost in defending their country! And so they were going to hire the North Korean Army.* During my first three months I learned a lot about the Kingdom.

The Respect due All Saudi Men

No Saudi man would engage in any activity that required the slightest bit of manual labor or subservience. No Saudi man would ever let himself be seen holding a broom or a paint brush, or carrying anything heavy. If they had a flat tire in their Mercedes they would step out grab their cell phone and call a friend to pick them up. All—every conceivable bit of manual labor, and especially driving those smoke-belching, mud-caked trucks, was done by "third-country nationals:" mostly Filipinos, Koreans, Bangladeshis, Indians, and Sri Lankans. In fact the 1985 census of Saudi Arabia showed that one out of five persons living in the country was a third-country national—not a Saudi-born individual. In fact recently Saudi Arabia had won the MEEA (Middle East, Europe and Asia) Little League Baseball Championship, *without a single Saudi kid on the whole team*; every last one was the son of a Filipino worker. Of course while the imported third-country men occupied every last one of the undesirable manual labor jobs, the third-country women and young girls were not that lucky. They ended up as poorly treated servants, maids, cooks, or nannies (and were forced to provide other services you might imagine). Upon arriving every one of these third-country nationals had to hand over their passports to their employers. No matter what abuse they suffered, they could not leave the country on their own; only when released by their employer (who holding their passport could destroy it at will).

But Not Much due Any Woman

The status and treatment of women of course, is what Saudi Arabia is known for, and deservedly so. Even now in 1989, not only were women forbidden to drive a car, to even be seen in public they must wear the face veil (niqab) and the completely-covering, floor-length, black gown (the abaya). The good news was that while American women also had to wear a head scarf and long black dress in town, they didn't need to wear a veil; and they were seldom bothered by the "Religious Police." (An official vice-squad called the Muhtawah.) They patrolled the streets in Riyadh carrying switches, while searching for some female not properly covered. And once again, under no circumstances could a Saudi woman ever be seen at a table, in a car, walking on the street, with a man who was not her husband, father or brother. No exceptions. Strict punishments including extended jail times could result! I could count on the fingers of one hand, how many times I saw a Saudi man walking with a Saudi woman. As best

I could tell, the largest segment of Saudi women, not being able to work, just stayed in school—most going on to college and earning Masters or PhD's, and then after becoming highly educated and capable, *they were still not allowed to work!* The main reason so many Saudi women tried to move to Lebanon or Syria or Jordan—was to work! (In the Saudi women's colleges, if a course was taught by a male professor, he could not be in the same classroom, he had to teach it via closed circuit TV.)

Receiving Mail

Bob told me there would be no trouble getting mail, since rather than using the international post we used the US Military mail service to foreign bases, called the "APO." (Army Post Office.) And that was good, because here in Saudi Arabia there was no postal delivery. No mailmen. Everyone had to go to the main Post Office to claim their mail. And why was there no home postal delivery? Because even in the big cities the streets did not have names, nor did the houses have numbers. The streets here in Riyadh (the capital) were referred to by the activity or large business known to be located on that street: The street holding the Coca Cola bottling plant was called "Coca Cola" street. The street on which every night the roast chicken vendors set up their stalls, was called "Chicken Street. The street leading up to the town-square in which was located the high platform and guillotine—where each Friday the criminals were beheaded, was called "Chop Chop Street."

The Things Necessary to be a Good Muslim

One thing I noticed when out driving, was that most of the Saudi men passing me in their modern Mercedes or BMW's were not wearing their seat belts or shoulder harnesses. Seeing this often enough (almost without exception) caused me to question one of the old hands who had been in the country over twenty years. He explained to me the reason for this unsafe behavior: if a Saudi driver were to wear his shoulder harness, it would be viewed as him taking personal measures to assure his livelihood, *demonstrating that he did not have confidence in Allah to protect him!* And no Muslim wants that on his record.

Also, many westernizers have seen supposedly devoted Muslims (drinking alcohol or womanizing) in the open society of foreign cities (Dubai, Hong Kong, Las Vegas, etc.) and thus concluded they are all hypocrites. To some extent that may be true, but here's an example of how serious they can be: One day passing overhead the city of Khamis, on the way to Jeddah, I gave the standard—universally approved inflight "Aircraft Position Report." It's a radio transmission that lists: (1) your aircraft call sign, (2) the name of the city you are over, (3) the altitude you are flying, and (4) the time you will be over the next point on your flight plan. I did just that. "Saudi air traffic control, this is Hotel Zulu Golf, over Khamis at 45 minutes after the hour, 41,000 feet, will be over Jeddah on the hour." One of my passengers—a full colonel, sitting on the rear divan must have heard me. He undid his seatbelt and came up to the cockpit. There, in a firm and very business-like manner, instructed me to make that call again, only this time, instead of just saying *"Jeddah on the hour,"* say *"Inshallah, Jeddah on the hour."* Inshallah means "God willing." It supersedes any human intentions or efforts, and I would not be arriving over Jeddah on the hour unless Allah willed it. I would go on to hear Inshallah a hundred times a day as long as I was there. I'm here to tell you that many Muslims are *not* hypocrites, they are true believers!

The End of the Canned Routine and a New Assignment

I had been flying three or four days a week, doing that fixed 5-base Kingdom-wide run for about three months when word came down that I had been selected by a board of senior Saudi Air Force officers, to head up a new and high-profile program. (Perhaps because I had two Flight Instructor ratings and had been a jet flight instructor at both Learjet and FlightSafety Int'l.) But for whatever reasons I was selected to (single-handedly) administer initial jet training to young, newly licensed civilian Saudi pilots, *who in spite of minimum (no) experience, were (for some reason) being given the opportunity to start their career as respected Saudi Air Force pilots!*

And there was another reason I was excited, not just being off the boring daily milk run, or because of this new challenging assignment, but rather that 90th day had arrived. I had successfully completed my probation! *Kathy would be cleared to join me!* I was sure she was going to be excited at being able to sample such a different culture and enjoy her leisure.

Chapter Twenty-Two
KATHY'S ARRIVAL AND THE
IRAQI INVASION OF KUWAIT

Right on Time

The company was good to their word. Two weeks after my 90-day probation was over, Kathy had her tickets. I was really nervous and anxious on the day of her arrival, and was an hour early at that magnificent King Khalid International Airport. She was scheduled to arrive at the same time as I did: 2 am. From a high balcony I spied her coming into the terminal—just like I did, head spinning and eyes scanning the treasure of marble and gold encasing the arrival foyer. I was proud of her, a woman who had never been out of the States, now walking bravely across the huge marble expanse of a Middle East public shrine. She dutifully joined the end of the immigration line. While making her way forward she glanced up and saw me, and waved enthusiastically—raising up on her tip toes, obviously glad to see me there and waiting.

When her place in the queue made its way under the edge of the balcony and out of my line of sight, I hurried downstairs to meet her coming out of Customs and Immigrations. We had a joyous hug before gathering her luggage and walking to the car. She was at first quiet and then began with an enthusiastic narration of the details of the flight, none of which (I was happy to hear) were uncomfortable for her. Starting the drive to the compound, she was—like I had been, impressed (or dismayed) at the modern, wide, well-lit, *completely deserted highway*. At the compound I thought it best to skip a tour and drove straight to our carport. Out of the car she asked where this was that we would be staying the night. I told her it was our house and she was motionless in disbelief; a wonderment only surpassed by the one displayed when she entered the home and observed its space, design, and furnishings.

Bob had assured me the next day off, so in the morning—we walked to the dining hall, (just getting in five minutes before they went to the lunch menu), and availed ourselves of a great breakfast of a bacon and onion omelet and hash browns. (We could've been in Denny's.) During the meal several of my friends came over to give her a hearty "welcome on board." I was grateful to them for their efforts. So far in the compound, there were no indication we weren't in some upscale residential development in Florida. In the afternoon we drove into downtown Riyadh to buy a week's worth of food stuffs and household items, and marvel at the many towering and ultra-modern buildings under construction. They were being helped skyward by dozens of tall cranes (jokingly referred to as the Saudi national bird). She of course spied the women on the street (completely covered in black and not a single one with a male escort). Before leaving, the company had thoroughly briefed her on the Saudi culture and this kind of dress, so she wasn't shocked. I also gave her my take on all the "ins and outs" of how she would have to carry herself. She was not disappointed and in fact demonstrated some excitement about the challenges. Back at the compound I gave her the famous "Cook's" tour of all the great diversions included within the compound, and that she could use any one of them at any time, for no charge! Her arrival had been a success.

Meanwhile, My New Assignment and a Stark Realization

My first student was a young—well not so young, aspiring Saudi pilot (Mohammed, as you might guess). The first thing I did was administer a week of in-classroom ground school—with slides, videos, and numerous training aids. Only after this ground school was completed, and he had finally passed (barely) a written test on the subjects covered, did I schedule him for his first training flight. On it, I put myself in the left seat to handle the controls, so he would not be under any pressure to manipulate the aircraft. He could just observe how I managed the five basic phases of any flight (take-off, climb, cruise, descent, and landing). I did these in as uncomplicated a fashion as possible, so it would not seem overwhelming to him. He just rode in the right seat as copilot, watching me and holding the operating checklists. I'd ask for the checklist and he would call off the items. However, on our second flight—I put him in the left seat, where he would begin handling the controls, and start the perhaps lengthy process of gaining the confidence that would be necessary to someday be qualified to fly the famous F-15 Eagle. (Which was the final objective of this Lear training program.) This move (putting him in the left seat) provided me with a shocking awareness and premonition that was *not* encouraging!

Forget about the import of the syllabus—what the higher-ups thought should be taught; *forget* about teaching the high-bank, unusual aircraft attitudes, and stick-yanking dogfight maneuvers. Although the powers to be envisioned the program to be imparting these skills to their young pilots, I found that I would be starting way back—*way way* back. One "way" back would mean having to first teach them how to perfect their takeoff and landing techniques. For Mohammed that would have been *Advanced* Training. He was having real, persistent (and hardly believable to me) major difficulties before we even moved! Still parked, just doing the checklists, he worked at understanding the nomenclature of the systems and their associated switches. And this difficulty was in spite of me—just before the flight, having given him a thorough, sequential and detailed, hour and a half briefing on each thing we would do on the flight. Just doing the simple start procedure was a time-consuming drill of hesitancy and reluctance. By the time we got the engine started (half the total flight period had already expired). He was completely baffled attempting to understand and do the "after-start" checklists. (Two thirds of the allotted time was spent when we finally moved out of the chocks.)

Ah Ha, an Explanation!

Big trouble! I soon discovered that *aviation aptitude played no part* in a young Saudi gaining access to this program. Every new pilot I got was either a prince, related to a prince, or a dear friend of a prince. In addition to that first indispensable connection, there was a second requisite: having adequate funds to buy their way into this prestigious program. Large sums of money had to come into the hands of certain senior air force officers before the applicant was approved. The third requisite was that the concerned pilot had to be in possession of a *USA Commercial Pilot's license.* This should mean he had already made a trip to the States, taken the required flight training courses and been awarded a *USA Commercial Pilot's license.* It wasn't long before I became aware of something that could not exist in the States, but was a common practice here among the concerned applicants: The aspiring applicant gave his passport and $10,000 to an older and experienced *Saudia Airlines* captain, who then—carrying the aspiring pilot's passport, traveled to the United States, underwent the training and received the necessary US Commercial Pilot's license, *but in the name of the guy who had given him his passport.* And so frequently when I got supposedly properly-licensed young pilots, while many of them did have a US *Private* Pilot's license (requiring only 40 hours of propeller aircraft flight time!) many of them knew better than to try to qualify for the more demanding *Commercial* Pilot's License, and resorted to the above shenanigans.

And What if I Couldn't Produce a Single Captain?

It was obvious to me that if ever, it would be years before these guys could operate jet aircraft in an even reasonably safe manner; and in no way would they ever be F-15 fighter pilots! No potential "top guns" in this group I can tell you. I wasn't sure how I (or anyone) could achieve any laudable results in this program, and *the Saudis historically dealt harshly and quickly with any American mentor who failed to bring his Saudi charges up to speed.* To get rid of the American, usually the Saudis claimed to have found something disqualifying in his application and deported him. I knew no one could salvage the guys I was getting—in any amount of time. I couldn't imagine being able to ever show the big wigs even one young man, and say, "Here he is—a red hot, qualified captain, a future "top gun"! *Consequently I was real concerned about whether or not I'd be able to finish my first year.* Although one thing existed that I think saved me: the "bragging rights" of these students! They could rightfully claim they were jet pilots (even though they weren't a captain, and probably never would be). Evidently just being able to flaunt their "flyboy" status was more than enough for these individuals *to be perfectly content making no progress whatsoever, and with the full knowledge they would be students for the indefinite future!* If they had to be in training the rest of their lives, that was perfectly okay. It was a prestigious and highly paid pastime.

Wow, Talk about a New Wrinkle

There were State Department rumors about the intentions of the neighbor state to the northeast (Iraq). These concerns included the possibility of a military encroachment into Kuwait, *and perhaps even into Saudi Arabia.* In July US troops and Air Force squadrons began pouring into Saudi, and McDonnell— in fear of the worst, ordered that all dependents (wives and kids) immediately leave the country! Kathy was back in the states by mid-July.

On August 2nd Iraq invaded Kuwait (which area they claimed was Iraq a century ago), and they wanted it back. There was an unpublished, pivotal event that influenced Iraq to invade Kuwait. A week earlier the Iraqi Minister of Defense spoke personally to the US Ambassador to Iraq (April Glaspie) and point-blank asked her, *What would the United States think, and what action, if any, would they take if Iraq attempted to take back their land in Kuwait?* Obviously somewhat on her heels at this question, she responded she would contact Washington and give him an answer the following day. And here is why Iraq *did* invade Kuwait: Washington told April to tell him that the US would consider it a matter solely between two sovereign states *and not become involved!* Had Washington responded, *"Don't even think about it!"* the invasion would not have occurred! There would have been no need for our "Desert Storm" offensive. Keep in mind both Reagan and Bush had maintained close (even friendly) ties with Iraq and Saddam himself, especially in Iraq's long war against Iran, when we gave huge support to Iraq (including *chemical weapons*), hoping they would defeat our arch enemy Iran. And here's the ironic part: when after three months it looked like Iraq would make no attempt to invade Saudi Arabia, in the first week in January (1990 now) to the pleasure of all the married employees, McDonnell Douglas authorized the dependents to return to Saudi. *Kathy was back in the house on January 12th.*

Day One!

On the evening of January 17th I was sent to a small, hard-packed dirt strip in the An Najaf province *of Iraq*. My mission was to pick up some personnel and equipment. On the strip (living in tents) was a small contingent of —I think, US Air Force personnel doing I don't know what, but I'm sure whatever it was, it was for the Agency—in advance and support of some clandestine coming activity. Shortly after dark three or four individuals (I think everyone that was there) carrying aluminum cases scrambled and banged their way on board the aircraft. To say they were in a highly excited state would be an understatement. One of the individuals—who appeared to be no more than 20-years-old, couldn't contain himself and blurted out, "We can't tell you why, but you gotta get outa here quick! Something's gonna happen!" Without needing that vague but ominous warning, I fired up the engines and promptly took off.

Not sure what time I got back to Riyadh, but it was late and pitch black, no moon—barely could make out the lights of Riyadh some miles ahead.

Whooaa! The aircraft rocked violently right wing up, and I heard and felt the "whop" of diverted air hitting under that wing! I had almost hit something! Or something had almost hit me! *Shit!* It happened again, only this time on my left side. Unknown to me, two squadrons of US Air Force fighter/bombers had launched from Riyadh, "silent"—without radio transmissions, and "dark"—no exterior lights on. I was arriving and they were departing—in the same airspace! I had just missed being rammed by two of these departing unlit bombers! *Tonight—right now! The US had initiated our aviation reply to Saddam's attack on Kuwait!* These planes would take part in a late night brutal, city-rubbling, neighborhood-leveling, body-dismembering, aerial and naval bombardment of downtown Bagdad and other Iraqi cities! *Kathy had gotten back just in time to see the war start.*

Saddam's Scud Missile versus our Patriot Missile

Shortly after the US attacked Bagdad, Saddam began flinging his Scud missiles into Saudi Arabia, which he boasted would destroy their major cities as well as all the US installations in the country. In response, one of our defense contractors—Raytheon, came out with the much-hyped anti-scud missile called the "Patriot." Its success in defending against the Scud brought fame and fortune for the manufacturer; *albeit truth be known, the missile was a failure.* True it did hit the incoming Scud (maybe half the time). But, it zeroed-in on the heat of the tail-end-located rocket *motor*—hitting it, but leaving the forward-located *warhead* to continue its ballistic trajectory, to wherever. And I say "wherever" because there was no guidance to Saddam's Scud. It was a primitive device that when launched went like a thrown stone; its point of impact dependent on the luck of the thrower. Several—by sheer accident did hit random buildings in Riyadh, but most landed harmlessly in the desert outside the city limits. A safe time after each attack we'd drive into the desert searching for a crashed missile. In finding them we were amazed at their lack of sophistication. It looked like they were built in a 9th grade metal shop, with wooden 1x2 stringers and chicken wire! The rivet lines were crooked, not evenly spaced, and about two out of ten rivets had not been installed.

Living in the compound, the most frightening thing for Kathy and I was when an incoming Scud rocket was detected, and the battery of Patriot missiles launched a salvo of rockets. The battery was a half-mile from the compound, and every missile goes supersonic within one second of being fired, which meant that while Kathy and I were crouched in our bedroom hallway, every few seconds for five minutes, *we were deafened by a sonic boom and the house was shaken to its foundation!* (At first we frightfully thought these were the retorts of incoming Scud rockets hitting nearby.) Regarding the Patriot missile, I was assigned a flight to bring the commander of these Patriot missile batteries (a full colonel named Jay Garner) to a strategic high level US Defense Department meeting in Jeddah. I had occasion to speak to him for some time, and was very impressed by his circumspect view that putting US troops on the ground in Iraq would have long-term negative and costly consequences. (Remember his name; a most interesting anecdote involving us later.)

A Testimony to Inhumanity

In February, Desert Storm—the ground assault of US troops into Kuwait and eastern Iraq began. As anyone could have predicted, it was an immediate and decisive victory. The Iraqi troops in Kuwait—poorly trained and not well-equipped, fled in terror towards their homeland in stolen Kuwaiti SUVs, on the only paved road leading northward. They had loaded the vehicles with Kuwaiti women and children, to serve as hostages and hopefully discourage air strikes. With our satellite imagery we were able to see this several-mile-long caravan of crowded SUVs, and chose to launch airstrikes. (I'm hoping without knowing half of every vehicle contained Kuwaiti women and children.) Since the terrain on each side of the paved road was soft sand, no car could leave the pavement. Our F-15 Eagles (flown by Americans, not Saudi pilots) rocketed the first (lead) vehicles in the caravan, leaving them a twisted impassable obstacle, *thus bringing the caravan to a stand-still and unable to move off the road!* Hard to believe (with a clear conscience), but what then ensued was an hour of our aircraft either doing it or anxiously awaiting their turn to empty their complement of rockets into the line of vehicles (as the old saying goes, "Like shooting fish in a barrel"). An hour later what remained was a three-mile long blazing queue of furiously flaming, twisted black metal. And horribly, in many of the vehicles, the distorted charred bodies of those that had burned to death while clawing their way out the windows and doors. Local GI's who were able to travel there the following day, took photos of the remnants of a thousand trapped cremations (which they then reproduced by the hundreds and had the gall to sell to anyone willing to pay five bucks apiece for them)!

I GUESS I JUST WASN'T THINKING

Post War

The war was—thankfully, short-lived with only a few residual effects. Weeks after it was over—when I flew into Kuwait, the fires Saddam's troops had started a the oil pumping stations were still burning. Billowing black smoke stretched from horizon to horizon *and even at high noon it was as dark as midnight!* After refueling the Lear I could not read the quantity or cost on the invoice without holding a flashlight within six inches of the clipboard. In addition to my pre-war mission of trying to make jet fighter pilots out of individuals that had no aptitude whatsoever for handling an aircraft, I received another more exciting and much easier post-war assignment, and did it for the next four years. The USA had—almost alone, arbitrarily declared a "No Fly Zone" over all of Iraq. Any and all Iraqi airborne activity was "off limits." No plane of theirs—any type, could leave the ground (although a couple times an old Mig-25 did—for five minutes). But guess what our Air Force did? They used me and our Lear as bait, to fly back and forth across the country, just to antagonize some controller at an Iraqi ground radar station. Remember that "Oh Shit" gauge I used with Air America when flying those low level flights into N. Vietnam? Well the Lear had been fitted with one of them. It would let me know by both a visual and audio tone, when I had been "locked onto" by ground acquisition radar. (Perhaps I had gotten this assignment because of me previously using this equipment was somewhere in my records.)

As soon as one locked on me—the operator merely carrying out his normal duties (not remotely considering pulling the trigger) I had to make a transmission to an airborne US Air Force C-130 orbiting over southern Iraq. As soon as he got the word that I had been locked-on, he contacted a waiting F-15 Eagle or F-16 Falcon to fly to my position; which they did—arriving in no more than five or ten minutes. They would ask me if I still was locked on. If I replied *Yes I was*, they called some command post for a "clearance to fire"—which they were given just about every time. They then rolled in and made as many runs as necessary to blow the radar installation off the face of the earth! And we did this if not daily, at least weekly, throughout the 90's! *For the ten years preceding 9/11.* (Now, credible historians—knowing this decade of US presence in Iraq and Afghanistan caused the deaths of over 100,000 "liberated" Muslims and the homelessness of five times that many, understand it created a feverish level of Middle Eastern Islamic resentment—resulting in what they viewed as a justifiable "retaliatory" attack on the USA.)

An Incredulous Face to Face Experience

I continued my high-profile (but impossible) assignment to transition the most inexperienced (and unmotivated) pilots I had ever seen, into *jet fighter pilots*. I was truly surprised that I had not been relieved of duties. In the first two years, I still—in all good faith, had not been able to instill in even one applicant, the determination and level of skill needed to be promoted to captain. Don't know why I hadn't been canned. Alas, in my third year I finally got a very westernized Saudi pilot (who had often traveled to the States and other European countries) and who I felt would be the first one to have a chance. I worked hard with Amir and he recognized and appreciated it. I began to feel like—for the *first* time, I had met a Saudi I could consider a friend. In fact we met for dinner several times, to which he invited his friends, and enthusiastically introduced me with both respect and affection; a real first! However something happened between Amir and I that vividly demonstrates one of the tenets of the Islamic faith, and confirms Rudyard Kipling's famous line.

You and I will admit that from time to time in our lives we told a "white lie," or maybe even a real lie. But in each case we knew *the listener did not know it was a lie*. If they already knew it was untrue, we would not have been able to speak it, knowing he or she would know while we were mouthing the words, it was entirely untrue. You've heard that in the Muslim religion a lie is not a lie if you tell it to an infidel. Well, you can believe that! One day when I asked Amir a question, about whether or not he had done a certain thing—to which I absolutely knew the answer was "Yes," and—a question that *he* knew that *I* knew the answer was "Yes," *he looked me straight in the eye, never wavering, and calmly said "No."* And was able to do so, fully aware that I knew this was a bald-faced outright lie. This Muslim capability left a lasting impression on me with regard to all future conversations with Saudis.

One Last Revelation on the Saudi's View of their Destiny

Every international business headquartered in Saudi Arabia was necessarily owned by one or more princes. However the Saudis themselves—recognizing none of them were capable of directing an enterprise of this scope, consistently hired experienced American, British, or German executives to be the CEO and run these companies. Finally—this year, the Saudis had an epiphany: it was now time to incept a large international, commercial, for-profit venture *with a Saudi-born national as the CEO!* Of course they were smart enough to know they would need a "shadow" CEO behind the assigned Saudi CEO to keep him out of trouble. The man they chose was my old friend Earl Richman (from that Banner Flight project in upstate NY in 1974).

Al Salam—this new and large Saudi-only, for-profit venture had been hyped to the Saudis by Boeing. Every six years 747 airliners must undergo a lengthy and very expensive heavy maintenance "D level" check. It is the most comprehensive check for the airplane—requiring taking the entire airplane apart, removing every piece of the interior, even removing the paint to inspect every rivet! It can take up to 50,000 man-hours and 2 months to complete, and costs 1.5 million dollars! Obviously—being this intensive, it was presently being accomplished by only a handful of well-established installations. Once Saudi agreed with the project, Boeing presented them the building plans for an ultra-modern, huge, circular building that would have easily held the Dallas Cowboy's NFL stadium inside, in which these inspections would be accomplished.

Boeing then presented the business plan (which in exasperation, shaking his head, Earl gave me to look at). It claimed that since this giant building could hold nine 747s at the same time, and since they could do six inspections a year; nine times six times equal (54) "D" inspections a year. (54) times 1.5 million dollars each, equals an annual revenue of over $81,000,000! Earl said this revenue forecast was outrageous; foolishly assuming that *the day they opened, they would receive a 747 from nine different airlines, and two months later, they would be able to again fill up all the spaces with 747s from another nine airlines,* and so on every two months throughout the year! Any aviation businessman would have realized it could be a year—or more (if ever), before Air France or Lufthansa or *any* airline, would consider risking their aircraft being sent to a brand new facility in the Arabian desert and manned by Filipino, Korean, and Bangladeshi aviation technicians!

A few months after construction began—the building was still a shell and a year from the grand opening, Earl was alarmed; there were twenty-some manager's offices on the upper balcony beginning to have furniture installed, *and Saudi nationals appearing behind the desks* (with their newspaper and cup of tea). Of course at this time there was absolutely no work for them to do. After a couple more weeks, all the offices were full. There must have been a hundred Saudis already hired and at work—*a year before there would be anything for them to do!* He went to the Saudi

CEO and explained that the salaries for these unneeded managers would drain their financial resources, and by the time they did open, *they would have no money left for operations!* A week passed and the Saudis were still at their desks. Earl went to Khalid again and told him that letting these employees go was an absolute must! Mercifully, during the next week he saw less and less of them there; until finally, none were left. He went to the Saudi CEO and complimented him on having done what was necessary. A couple weeks later, when checking the financial records Earl noticed that while none of these employees were showing up, they still were getting paid! *The CEO had only told them not to bother coming to work!*

Discovering this he again briefed the CEO on the financial conundrum coming. He was told, "Mr. Richman, there is something you don't understand about Saudi Arabia: We are not going to be in trouble. *Allah put oil under our land, and if we run out of that, He will put gold there.*"

Chapter Twenty-Three
OUR LIFE IN SAUDI ARABIA, AND ELSEWHERE

Living the Good Life

I couldn't complain: Kathy and I were having a great life, the both of us spending a lot of time lounging around the pool and engaging in our new sport: tennis. Most of the McDonnell personnel—husbands and wives played tennis, so it was a physical and social plus for compound life. As the months came and went, I have to admit life on the compound went just fine. The US military had even installed satellite TV dishes, and we could watch our favorite programs. (For me the NFL.) Kathy was a great sport. Even when some inconveniences did come along, she never complained.

Something New for Kathy

At the end of the second year; not that we needed the money, but for an interesting change (after having had all the sun-bathing and shopping trips she could handle) Kathy got job! Some embassy friends got her a secretarial position with the US Treasury in downtown Riyadh. The Treasury had a large staff here to advise the Saudi government on financial matters. Of course in Saudi Arabia, while no Saudi woman is permitted to work, women from other countries with certain specialties could hold jobs with foreign entities located within the Kingdom. Kathy was assigned her own driver, was picked up at 8 sharp and driven to her place of work. There, she was snuck in a back door before any Saudis had arrived, and then quickly hurried to her office (hidden in the basement). Well, she couldn't avoid being seen once in a while, but the Saudis who did see her were so excited to catch a glance of a blonde woman, they weren't going to say anything that would bring an end to these sightings.

The Brits! Gotta Love Em

The CIA used established international corporations such as McDonnell Douglas as a cover—hiring persons (such as myself) to accomplish certain tasks or acquire sensitive information. Likewise, Her Majesty's Foreign Intelligence Service—MI6 also used established corporations from the UK—such British Airways, to position their agents worldwide, and now—here in Saudi Arabia. I never really had any English friends in the states, or in any of my world travels, until now. But let me tell you: they know how to 'make the best of it', in fact create rousing good times no matter where they are! I now have a high regard for all of them—by any measure. Kathy and I had the good fortune to meet and become friends with several of the BA guys (and their wives), not only playing tennis with them, but being invited to parties honoring any number of English or Scottish or Welsh historic personalities. And it seemed every month one of them had a birthday. The most memorable is the one occurring each January, when they celebrated Robert Burns' birthday with a spectacularly prepared and presented Haggis dinner (including the bagpipes)! And, don't know how they did it here in this alcohol-free country, but they seemed to have no problem smuggling in as much wine as they wanted.

A Real Perk

When Kathy first arrived I shared with her something that caused a lot of excitement: Each year, each employee (even "contract" employees like me) got a 30-day vacation. It was called "Home Leave," although almost no one actually went home. More likely, the McDonnell Douglas employees I knew used the time (and our generous travel benefits) to visit some exotic or remote world destination; anxious to try their hand at the Monte Carlo casino or stand in wonder viewing the famous Machu Picchu Inca ruins in Peru. As a pilot, I actually only had three of these weeks free, since I had to use one of them to undergo my annual recurrent Learjet training (coincidentally administered by FSI in West Palm Beach, where I used to be an instructor and met Bob who hired me for this job).

Our Annual Vacations and One in Particular

Like most employees, Kathy and I also chose to use those three weeks to "see the world." The first year I took her to my favorite part of the world— the Mediterranean coast: visiting Cannes, France, Porto Fino, Italy, Barcelona, Spain, and a couple days up in Switzerland. The second year we toured the Scandinavian countries, especially enjoying Stockholm and seeing the "Vasa" (that gigantic, specially preserved sailing vessel built in the 1600's, and sank to the bottom just a few hundred meters after leaving the dock on its maiden voyage). Both trips went great and she had the time of her life. A year later, on our third vacation we toured several Far East countries, which provided a variety of "firsts" for us; one country— the "Land of the Rising Sun" delivering one we would not be anxious to repeat (embarrassedly explained next).

A Special Kind of Japanese Would-be Hotel

While visiting Japan we took a train from Tokyo to Kyoto, to visit its revered temples and Zen gardens. After a so-so stay in Kyoto we boarded the train back to Tokyo. On the way back it stopped at the Shin-Fuji station—the jumping off spot for anyone planning on climbing Mt. Fuji. On the spur of the moment we decided to do just that—well maybe not climb it, but get as close as we could and take some photos. We disembarked and boarded the next bus to the small village of Fujinomiya, located in the Mt. Fuji foothills. Off the bus there, I decided to first off find us a place for the night; and I definitely—very definitely, had one in mind: an authentic Japanese ryokan! That's one of those stilted but single-storied, bamboo structures with tatami-matted rooms, sliding paper-paneled doors, communal baths, and geishas hand-delivering each of the day's meals to your room. (And then—while you ate, sitting in a far corner playing a three-stringed samisen.) Ryokans are usually located within a high-walled, large Zen garden of raked white sand, carefully placed polished rocks, precisely clipped shrubs, soft-textured plants, and small ponds of colorfully patterned fish. Able to observe this woodland setting can do little other than create a mood of great serenity. For centuries Ryokans served as calming respites for tired Japanese businessmen (but nowadays would also take a fatigued foreign traveler). My noble goal was to give Kathy a real first. She would have never sampled, or even imagined, anything like a ryokan. I was committed to this objective!

Finding One

After spending half the morning walking the length and breadth of the village (lugging our bags and wearing our knapsacks) I finally found one. I checked it out but was disappointed; it was not at all what I was envisioning. I knew there had to be another more traditional and appealing one nearby. Only a few hundred yards from this ryokan, was the south end of a five-mile long lake. Alongside its west shore was a narrow road that I thought would be bound to have a couple ryokans somewhere along it. With high hopes we started up it. There—on the south end of the lake I saw a commercial-appearing entranceway to a dock where tourists could take a lake cruise on a faux 16th century sailing ship. Walking over closer to get a better look, at the water's edge I spied an old galleon, crewed by individuals dressed as mean-looking pirates. I made a note for us to take that cruise later in the day or tomorrow.

Unfortunately, after trudging northward about five miles and well over an hour (with Kathy lugging her stuff and doing her best to keep up behind me), I still hadn't spied a likely candidate. At about four in the afternoon, arriving at the end of the road—adjacent to the north end of the lake, I spied one that might fill the bill. *Shoot!* As much as I was hoping, it just didn't measure up to what I was envisioning. But the owner said he was sure he knew what I wanted. He owned another one; that would be just perfect. He said it was just a short drive south, at the other end of the lake (where we started this trek about ten in the morning)! After a forty-five minute wait he drove us back down that same road alongside the lake, to the south end of the lake, and to the same ryokan I had turned down at 9:30 this morning! I gave up and just checked in (and a good thing too. I don't think Kathy could have taken another step). Needless to say we were both asleep by nine.

A Promise Not Kept and an Unwise Journey

The next morning I did want to see—at least the foothills of Mt Fuji (only a few miles away), but promised Kathy that today (unlike yesterday) I'd make sure it would be an easy day: no more ten mile walks wearing rucksacks! Being the great sport she was, she agreed to be part of whatever plan I had in mind. In keeping with my promise, instead of walking I hailed us a cab to take us to the base of the mountain. There, beyond a somewhat official-looking entrance arch, we saw a not too-bad looking path starting up the side of the mountain. I certainly wanted to give it a go; at least some distance up, and see what kind of view we would get. After some mild encouraging, Kathy gave me a "thumbs up." While the upward trek started out at an acceptable grade, it was not long before it steepened, and we were bracing one hand on a rock and hoisting ourselves up by grabbing a hanging branch with the other. And to make things worse, the path was full of loose rocks and acting like a stream, carrying muddy water down the side of the mountain. We both slipped more than once, and I realized the "easy" day I had promised, was not panning out. (Not by a long-shot!)

We saw signs indicating there was a rest spot with an advantageous view not too far ahead and above, and struggled on up to it. Arriving there, getting our breath and aware of our legs, we agreed we didn't need to climb any higher. However with the loose rocks and water rushing down the path we had just come up, we realized we could not take it back without risking a serious fall. At the rest stop, off to one side I spied what could have been, and hoped would be—an alternate downhill path. We decided to take it and started down. Unfortunately, after about a half mile and descending to a level maybe five hundred feet lower, the path just petered out! We found ourselves in a spacious, not too-bad grove of scattered trees. Now we had to just pick our way downward through them—to who knows where we would break out (other than it would be an unknown area).

A Long Walk to Our Ryokan

An hour later, Hallelujah! We did break out, on a strange paved road, but who knew which road and where? I had no idea where we were. After rambling a few hundred yards to the left it began to look strangely familiar. *Oh no!* Guess where we were? Halfway up that north-south road along the west side of the lake! Limping, almost staggering, Kathy bravely joined me as I reversed our direction for the three or four mile walk back down the road toward our ryokan. Finally—almost there, passing the south end of the lake I saw again that shoreline office where tourists were buying tickets for that pirate ship cruise. It just so happened that while we were standing there, an announcement was being made over a PA system, that this would be the last voyage of the day. Don't know where I got the nerve, but if you can believe it, I asked Kathy if (instead of continuing the last 500 yards to our ryokan) we could avail ourselves us of this unique cruise. Not that she needs any more credit or recognition, but she was able to muster the energy to nod a "Yes" (although not real enthusiastically). After receiving her approval, I purchased two tickets, we boarded the galleon, and it shuddered away from the dock.

The cruise hugged the right side of the lake as we made the first half of the trip north. There were lots of interesting sites on the shore (and the crew dressed as pirates acted out various shenanigans). About 45 minutes later we reached the north end of the lake, where I was anticipating the vessel would make its sweeping turn to return to its mooring at the south end, where we had boarded. But instead it made its way into a berth at a large wharf, perhaps to pick up tourists from the north end. *Wrong!* My heart sank as I felt the vibrations in the soles of my feet lessen and stop completely. They had shut down the engines! We were not on a tourist attraction! We were on a ferry that brought people from the south end of the lake to the north end of the lake, and this had been the final trip of the day! We were now marooned, ten miles from our Ryokan, for the third time in two days! This may have been the closest we ever came to a divorce.

Chapter Twenty-Four
MY ANCESTORS AND A STUNNING REVELATION

Periodic Maintenance on Our Learjet

In a previous chapter I wrote about the periodic inspections done on 747's. Well every twelve months a Learjet requires a yearly comprehensive (somewhat preventative) inspection, understandably—called an "annual." It requires the use of equipment rarely in possession of the flight department operating the Lear. We were in that category—not having the capability; so each year we flew our Lear to "Jet Aviation," a well-respected facility in Basel, Switzerland. They were the closest (and perhaps best) approved maintenance facility to accomplish this inspection. The flight up had the standard two pilots, plus on this trip: two of our aircraft mechanics as passengers. They would oversee the inspection and perhaps even learn some things new about the aircraft. The time required for this inspection was about ten days. It was 1994 and for the first time, I assigned myself to the trip. Ever since the carrier cruise had exposed me to the Continental culture, for many reasons Switzerland was a country that I held in high esteem. (We've all seen that photo of the steep, craggy-peaked, north face of the Matterhorn.)

Switzerland shares its northern border with France and Germany; so while there is a Swiss national language, in the west (in Geneva) it is half French. In the east (in Zurich) it is half German. The Basel airport was right on the French border; in fact one runway stuck a mile into France. *Hmmm, France—an idea*: What little I knew about my father's ancestry, was told to me by my mother. (I don't think Dad much cared about this type of thing.) She said the Yahnke family—originally from Eastern Europe, had migrated to France as mercenaries during the first Franco-Prussian war. They lived in France for several generations before Grandpa (at 16 and alone) emigrated to the States. Not only that, the Yahnkes lived in the Alsace Valley *which started just 25 miles north of where I would be*—in Basel, and stretched 60 miles north along the west bank of the Rhine, to the historic French town of Strasbourg. On the first day in Basel (having no duties, just hanging around until the inspection was done) I got the whim to try to locate a distant relative.

Searching for a Yahnke

I started by examining a surprisingly thorough copy of the French phone book for the area called the *"Grand Est"* (the Alsace valley). I found several Yahnkes—the closest being in the town of Mulhouse—only 20 miles into France from where I was in Basel. I drove there, found the address (an apartment), climbed the stairs and knocked on the door. It was swung open by a kindly looking, matronly woman about sixty or so years of age. She spoke no English. I started in my best French to explain the reason for my appearance. Not making a lot of progress, I pulled out my driver's license with the letters Y-A-H-N-K-E. That did it. Without a moment's hesitation she took me in her arms and gave me a giant hug. Unfortunately—after a pause, she sadly explained I was several weeks late; her husband had just passed away. She led me across the room to a wall upon which was a framed, under-glass, newspaper clipping with a photo of her husband—receiving the most prestigious medal for heroism: the "Croix de Guerre." *And it was being pinned on him by Charles de Gaulle himself!* I'm embarrassed to admit it, but when we finally parted company, she insisted I take the framed photo. Besides this moving gift, she gave me a lead: another Yahnke who was a history professor at the University of Strasbourg, and lived in Selestat, a small town just another 20 miles further north.

Found Another One!

I felt a strange sanctifying mood as I viewed my name on the engraved brass plaque, and pressed the doorbell just beneath it. Once I identified myself and my quest, I was welcomed in with an enthusiasm and warmth that even exceeded that of the lady in Mulhouse. I was eagerly introduced to the head of the household—Jean (John in English), his wife Marguerite, and their two children. Jean insisted I stay for supper and overnight, and he would show me the local sites and a couple other Yahnkes tomorrow. Marguerite prepared a delicious roast so loaded with wine and fat-soaked sweet gravies, that halfway through the meal I felt my stomach and colon begin to rumble, and had to excuse myself for a bathroom run that was not a short or minor event. Jean said in the family tree he was not the closest relative; the next morning he would introduce me to another Yahnke, who lived in neighboring Achenheim, and may well have been a cousin of my grandfather.

When we visited this old but sturdy man, he *was* the spitting image of my grandfather; bald and with a large bulbous nose. Next Jean took me to a Catholic church that for the past couple hundred years had maintained ledgers of all the births, deaths and marriages in the diocese. In a small building across from the church, in a decaying 4-inch thick loose-leaf binder, we *did* find a pen and ink, hand-written record of my grandfather's birth! (First spelled Yahnkel and then the "l" crossed out.) After staring at that entry for some almost-sacred time, Jean walked me to the cemetery behind the church where my knees were weakened. *I was able to stand in front of the tall headstone of Alphonse Yahnke—my grandfather's father!*

No future visit could top that of course, but he next took me to another church—the St. Georges church; a real tourist attraction, supposedly built under Charlemagne in the 16th century, and a place that had been the site of a fierce WWII battle; still showing hundreds if not thousands of deep pockmarks from artillery and small arms fire. We took the midday meal in an old wooden-benched restaurant in Strasbourg that *had been in the same building, run by the same family, for seven generations.* (Confirming this was a framed document on the wall, which held the signatures of seven generations of owners!) Leaving the Maison Kammerzell Jean said the day would not be complete without a visit to one of the cabbage farms. When I arrived, I saw why: the average cabbage head was bigger than a basketball!

I left for Basel the next morning, but when doing so, I was surprised and moved to see not a face without tears. We would remain in contact from then on. In fact, Jean made up an *"arbre généalogique"* ("family tree") of my French ancestry. However in it, scanning all the lines and names for my Grandpa, while we easily located his two brothers and his sister Camille, neither Jean nor I could find Grandpa. After further investigation Jean pointed out that the feminine-sounding name of Camille—in France, *used to be a boy's name as well!* And *she* was Grandpa! When Grandpa arrived in the states bearing a girl's name, it was so embarrassing he changed his first name to the name I was familiar with. *Mystery solved.*

When not taking my once-a-day walk to the Restaurant Aeschenplatz for some delicious bratwurst, rosti and kraut, I was just sitting in my hotel room. While wasting away the next day I read that a big tennis tournament was being held in Lyon, with the then famous Pete Sampras being one of the competitors. As the fanatic tennis fan I was, I checked the map and found that Lyon was about a three hour drive from Basel; far, but then again all I had was time. I asked my copilot and the maintenance guys if I could hog the car again for a day or two. They said no sweat. The maintenance guys couldn't go anywhere anyway—being required to monitor the inspection, and my copilot had his own reasons to prefer exploring the city unaccompanied.

A Tennis Tournament and a Questionable Idea

I arrived at the stadium fifteen minutes before play commenced, and was pleased to not only see the famous American player Pete Sampras, but Andre Agassi as well (and the number one and number two French players: Henri LeCount and Guy Forget). I was able to work my way down to an almost front row seat and it was a great night of tennis. It was midnight when the last match ended. Too late to make the drive back to Basel, so got a motel on the edge of town.

Perhaps you were awaiting this: sitting on the edge of the bed I reflected on the last time I had been in Lyon—*with Mireille!* By now you're well aware: the first (and to this day—*only*) woman who magically, immediately and intensely aroused me with everything and more than I would need. But that was twenty years ago; by now she would certainly be remarried, probably with teenage kids. Could I? *Should I*—just give her a call to say hello? *Probably not.* It was such a long time ago. She may have forgotten me, and is probably happily married now (and I know I am).

A Revolutionary Twist to the Most Painful Words I Ever Heard

You may remember the unqualified but instinctive caring I felt for her, and of course the lifetime breakthrough, when she allowed me to know— for the first time, the feeling of unremitting joy, pride and power that all other men knew regularly. Of course I had dreams of a blissful future with her; dreams which were dashed when in the airport, just before I boarded my flight back to the States, in her native language, she made a shocking confession to me—which I translated to mean: *she did not think she could live again with just one man!* When I had digested these words and was able to regain my sensibilities, I realized her pleasure was not because of me, it was the pleasure of having a man inside her, likely—*any* man. If this was so, right then I knew *there would come a day when she would surely break my heart.* As you may remember, crushed, I boarded my flight back to the States. Many times in the following years—to avoid a great hurt, I resisted frequent longings to contact her. She could never have contacted me, because back then when I first met her—in 1974, while I was ferrying airplanes worldwide, I had no address or phone number to give her. When I was in the States between flights I would just bunk with my parents. Early on I had assured her I would send her an address as soon as I had one. But now, *should I try to visit her now,* irrespective of her shocking admission to me, and my then (because of it) never contacting her again. And now, *with me being married I probably shouldn't even be considering it.* But if we only touch base, say "Hi" and reminisce for an afternoon; that could be okay. *I decided to do it!* (And maybe any thoughts of not doing so, had received only token consideration.)

I had long since lost her phone number so had to first inquire with the French telephone information service. I was given the phone number of a person with Mireille's last name, and a first initial of "M," living in her area. *Perhaps, just perhaps.* I called it and unfortunately an elderly woman answered. I was just about to hang up when she told me that while she wasn't Mireille *she knew who she was*—she had received calls for her before, *and here was her number!* I couldn't believe it. She was giving Mireille's number to a complete stranger; what a trusting soul. I called the number and *good news*—a woman answered. I apologized for the call and asked if I had reached Mireille Piccio. Before responding that I had, she blurted out "Roger c'est vous? C'est vous Roger?" *She had recognized my voice in just a dozen words, and after twenty years!* Through a stumbling conversation—half French, half English, I was able to get her approval to stop by and visit her the next day! She said I'd know where, that she was still in the same faux 17th century cottage atop the same high meadow.

Arriving at Mireille's

In spite of an acute case of nerves, the drive north out of Lyon was surprisingly familiar; especially when I went through the center of one small village where the road narrowed to a barely two-car width. Fortunately I didn't meet any oncoming traffic, because I wasn't sure I would have been able to pass without scraping a building to my right or the passing car on my left. It was another twenty or so miles before I entered the outskirts of her town—St-Martin-du-lac. I barely recognized it; twenty years had made a big difference: many new structures and a confusing change of appearance in the roadside foliage. (Crowded tall trees where there had only been scrub brush, and cleared land where there had been wooded areas.) I was hoping that even with the changes, I would be able to spot the partially hidden, right-side turnoff to the private drive; the one that led up the long hill to her house. Oops, arriving in town I realized I had to have passed it. A "U" turn and back-tracking with eyes peeled to the left. Son of a gun—*that could be it*. I came upon what—although it did not convincingly fit my mental picture of how it should look, was what must be her private entrance.

After turning into it and making my way uphill through a wooded area, I wasn't so sure. Then the grassy meadow appeared on the left. *I was there!* Another hundred yards and there ahead were the two stone pillars with the wrought iron gate. *I'd made it.* Within a minute of turning off the engine I spied Mireille, out of the cottage and walking towards the gate. As she got closer I was taken aback noticing her stern expression, with no smile or indication that she was glad to see me. And then I thought back, about me leaving and never contacting her again; why *would* she be glad to see me? We had what would be called a civil greeting, with no embrace (although we did have the cursory peck on each cheek). The first surprise was: there *was* no husband or children! She had not remarried (making my visit even less fitting than I had rationalized).

Twenty Lost Years! A Numbing Explanation

During the next couple hours Mireille slowly warmed to my presence, and every once in a while, I may have seen the barest hint of that warm smile. We sat in two chairs facing each other, speaking mostly French (although her English had improved). It was not long before Mireille brought up the subject of my long ago, unexplained, sudden and permanent disappearance. Her questions were in earnest and with gestures and expressions of dismay and concern. "*Pour quoi, pour quelle raison?*" (Why, for what reason) she asked. Certainly I *knew* the reason—that damned thing about *not being able to live with just one man!* But how was I going to accuse her of being a woman who needed more than one man; a woman who had that sexual need? I had no choice but to do so. It took a couple minutes to get it out, and was hesitantly voiced, but I refreshed her memory of the statement she had made. As I was finishing, she appeared stunned—bodily wounded, raised both hands to her face and stood up abruptly, not speaking, just twisting and turning, in fact—moaning aloud! When she calmed herself, she dropped to her knees on the floor in front of me, put her palms on my legs and looking into my eyes, exclaimed that *"living with just one man"* in French, is an idiom meaning *"being married!"* And the reason she said she didn't think she could re-marry, was *because she still loved her first husband so much!*

Oh my God! Here was a woman who was the epitome of loyalty and devotion, that because of my lack of familiarity with French idioms, *I thought she meant to admit something entirely opposite!* My critically flawed translation caused me to throw away my dreams, never contact her again, resign myself to a life without ever knowing again what I had known with her.

That Night

Shortly after I arrived I had told Mireille I was married, and happily married; something she may well have guessed after all these years. I suspected at this late date, neither she nor I harbored any thoughts of attempting to recreate a life together and the bliss we had known twenty years ago. Late in the afternoon, after agreeing to stay the night, I had thrown my overnight bag on the bed in the guest room and hung my jacket over a chair at the foot of that bed; making it apparent I was not anticipating us sleeping together. And now, after her revelation—her explanation, and the tragic irony of the translation error, I realized what I had thrown away, and was plagued with a hundred considerations. Mireille prepared the evening meal—and a good one, but it was a rather quiet dinner; both of us preoccupied with "what-ifs." After dinner she offered me a Sandeman Porto *digestif* and we ruminated about that which might have been. When it was time to retire, I gave her what was intended to be a polite kiss on each cheek and walked straight to the guest room. Sometime later—on a trip to the bathroom I noticed she had left her door open and I saw the flickering light of a candle. I returned straight to the guest room without entering her room. I was proud of myself for ignoring the wonderment that was in my mind. As you might imagine I did not soon fall asleep, only managing to begin slipping away about one a.m. This respite was interrupted *when Mireille slipped under the sheet next to me.* Of course I knew what she or anyone would have expected, and in spite of everything, *especially my thoughts of Kathy*, I felt the same strong and capable arousal, but resisted—as best I was capable of. With her head on my chest, I found myself stroking her hair; certainly a mistake. That was all it took for her to begin kissing me, and draping and contorting her thin body over me.

It transpired (in spite of my guilt) and was just like Dakar. After lying there the time I knew I must, I went to the bathroom. There alone with my culpability I took a shower, almost scrubbing the skin off my bones; racked with guilt—severe and deserved guilt! I could not believe I let it occur, with a loving wife back in Riyadh, likely incapable of imagining this behavior on the part of her husband. I was sick—physically sick. The next morning I left early, but not before she said in French *that she had lost me once and didn't want to lose me again.* The drive back to Basel was uneventful though mournful—me only a shadow of the man who had left Basel two days ago. The inspection was completed in another three days. Throughout the flight back I was haunted by my transgression, which I vowed would never happen again. And it would not! I made a personal pledge to spend every day the rest of my life making Kathy happy and proud. Though I knew, nothing now or ever could erase my wrongdoing. It was like a huge rock I would drag around behind me the rest of my life.

Back in Riyadh

Even just five minutes from the compound no matter how hard I tried, and how improper, even perverse it was, I could not erase the image of Mireille's face, or cease hearing her saying *I lost you once and I don't want to lose you again.* Even if she didn't, I knew it was over; never to be. If you suspected my guilt and deserved discomfort would be difficult to hide, you would be right. I felt like I'd been shot at and hit, and couldn't believe my overwhelming sadness wasn't apparent on my expressionless face. Kathy's joy at seeing me was perhaps the thing that helped me respond in an apparently normal manner. And as you might imagine, that first day back I dreaded when the hour would come that we would retreat to the bedroom; just hoping this would be one of the usual "holding hands" nights. It wasn't. As much trouble as I had on the rare occasions that Kathy felt up to it, tonight would surely be worsened by my guilt. Mercifully I was able to at least enter her. Undeserved as I was, I thanked the god's of love-making. I was able to get through the first couple days, and then a week, and in the weeks to come, was gratefully able to think of Mireille less and less (sort of).

Time to Leave, and Our Plan for a New Home

About three months later we came to a decision: as much fun and diversion as our Middle East sojourn had provided, including the more than comfortable compound life, the good pay, and the annual exotic vacations, we decided it was time to return to the States. We might even have enough savings to compensate for me having no retirement. One thing I failed to mention: during our years in Saudi Kathy and I had spent many nights designing a small Spanish-style home with terra cotta patios, archways and shaded walks. Our dream house if you will. One of our neighbors had been an architect, and had taken our drawings and made a set of building plans—for free. We knew that at some time after arriving in the States, we would use our Saudi savings to build our new home, and then after selling the oceanfront home, hopefully have enough funds to live out the rest of our lives. In any case that was our plan. We gave Kathy's brother (renting our oceanfront home) a month's warning so they could find another home, held a garage sale for much of the Middle East memorabilia we had bought, and began making preparation for our Saudi exit and return to Hobe Sound.

Chapter Twenty-Five
"BORN IN THE USA"

And Back Again!

The 1995 move back into our oceanfront home in Hobe Sound went smoothly. Having rented it fully furnished, all our stuff was there and in place. It was just like it was when we left. Kathy's brother and his family had taken wonderful care of the house. There wasn't a mark on a single wall or any digs in my pegged-wood floor. The only downside; Ted—who in lieu of rent, dropped off the small mortgage payment at the local bank on the first of the month, had missed one month (which surprisingly knocked 20 points off my credit score). In spite of this I was grateful to him and Ashley for having taken such good care of my house. Still being worried about my old-age retirement (even with a much better savings than before the Saudi tour) I felt I still needed to work for a few more years. This being the case I continued to investigate any flying job within an hour's driving time. I succeeded finding another "mom and pop," "shoe-string" charter company in Ft. Lauderdale. I got in at least a couple flights a week and was still able to enjoy the rest of the week relaxing in or working on the house. It was several months before I realized how much our house on the ocean was worth. I was pleasantly surprised and even considered giving up my flying job; perhaps in selling the house I would have enough money for our old age. At last we could begin thinking seriously about building the home we had designed while in Saudi.

My Kids

A lot happened in the few years before and while I was in Saudi—now affecting my chances to visit the kids. Donna with her science Ph.D. was fortunate enough to have been picked by a government-sponsored agency supporting STEM (Science, Technology, Engineering, and Math) training. Instead of having to market her own consultant services she now had this organization contacting her and sending her tickets to both national and international destinations to give lectures or be the keynote speaker at seminars for teachers. Mark with a Masters in both Electrical Engineering and Business Administration was working for a large IT corporation in southern California (and at 5'8" trying to play competitive Beach Volleyball with the likes of Karch Kiraly). Stacy—the only one that knew what she wanted to do since she was twelve, was the Chief Flight Attendant for Continental at their Houston base. Kevin was a successful architect living and working in Atlanta.

My Beautiful Adopted daughter

The only grown child still living in Florida was Iris. She was living in Orlando and working for a large IT firm there. (Her sister Marisa was the manager of a GAP store in Daytona Beach). Iris was still unmarried. Having been born with the inability to bear children was perhaps the reason one or two earlier possibilities did not materialize. I was thrilled—when in the midst of considering a two-hour drive to visit her, she phoned me saying she was coming down the following weekend, since it would be Father's Day. (Something that I had completely forgotten about.) And the good news, she would be bringing her fiancé—Nick.

She and my kids (her step-brothers and sisters) had remained very close—on the phone with each other at least once a week; something that made me happy. I was especially proud of her when I learned she had been more successful in the IT business world than I thought, now the Vice president of US Operations for a German "voice activation" company (and making frequent trips to Berlin). Through the years and even from the very beginning, Iris and I had grown exceedingly close. She loved me more than I deserved, and was not bashful about telling me that me coming into her life when I did, *saved her life*. (Never sure what she meant there, as outwardly everything in her life was going perfectly.)

During her high school years, even though she and my son Mark were the same age and in the same grade, it appeared that neither the student body nor faculty ever paused to think that *one of them had to be adopted*. Maybe because they looked and acted like brother and sister; both were outstanding athletes, had blonde hair and blue eyes, and similarly thin and attractive facial features. In fact when they graduated from St. Michaels in Hobe Sound, they were voted king and queen of the Prom and were driven to it on the back of a red Corvette. We had a wonderful visit including a great seafood dinner on Father's Day. And it was a very special Father's Day, as Iris presented me with a framed poem she had written (that I have on my bedroom wall today).

Who Am I?
They say I have my mother's legs and my father's eyes of gray
My thirst for life? My quest for peace?
I have looked into the corners of my heart, my soul, my brain,
Tried to figure out the pieces of me....precisely who's to blame
For my love of life, of people, of kids, for stuff that makes me laugh.
Who put this here, this spark of mine. Who led me down this path
Who put this here? My search for answers...this quest I cannot dodge
There is no one other than my father, my friend, my dad, my Rog!
All My Love, Your Iris

Mrs. Diakos

A month later I was invited to Orlando for the wedding, and listen to this: not only did I walk Iris up the aisle, I was also Nick's "Best Man," carrying the ring. I don't know if I've ever seen two people more happy. Iris's mom (my second wife Elsa) was there, and surprisingly, though I didn't deserve it, she was kind and sweet to me, and Iris was happy to see us side by side in the church and together at the small

reception. Iris's half-sister Marissa had moved to Illinois and working two jobs, so couldn't make the trip. I left with a certainty that this was a marriage that was going to lovingly last and be envied by many! He adored her.

In Lieu of Flying Charter

During this first year back we mostly lived off my charter-flying pay checks, and were able to avoid going too much into our Saudi savings. This was good since the plan was to use those savings to build that house we designed, and then hope there would be enough money from the sale of our present home to keep us solvent in our old age. Moreover to possibly make things even better I was contacted by Rich. (Remember? the DEA guy with his own business on the side, and the flights to Colombia.) He had another deal for me; one that was only a little bit illegal, not near as dangerous, and would pay real good.

Everyone remembers back in 1980—the controversial Mariel Boat Lifts, bringing asylum seekers from Cuba to Miami. Well it was a rough trip—often tragically ending up marooned at sea, and the boats were only carrying certain types of individuals: felons and the poorest most illiterate peasants. But there was another type of Cuban wanting to get to the States: rich Cubans, most of whom had lost much of their wealth under Castro. However they had been able to sneak a healthy portion of it into Florida, and now wanted to get there and use it! Rich was somehow in contact with an intermediary representing many of these individuals. Believe it or not he mentioned the name Felix several times, and I suspected it was the Felix I flew for in Nicaragua. (How in the hell they got together now is beyond me.)

For several months—a couple times a week, I made clandestine night trips to Cuba and back. I'd takeoff about midnight and wrap up about five am. I would vary my takeoff locations among several south Florida airports and landed (about an hour and forty-five minutes later) on a small dirt strip outside Cienfuegos. Cienfuegos was on the south coast of Cuba, about an hour's drive east of the famous Bay of Pigs (where the CIA made their invasion of Cuba in April of 1961). I'm sure the guys working the Cuban Air Traffic control were part of the operation, because for sure they were tracking me. Since this immigration was illegal by both Cuban and American law, yup, you guessed it: Rich had me returning to land on that same dike in the glades! Not only did Rich pay me a thousand dollars a trip, almost every trip the passengers tipped me!

Chapter Twenty-Six
LIFE IS WHAT HAPPENS

A Controversial Airline Crash

July 17th, 1996. The nation was shocked by a fatal crash. *TWA 800 went down just a few minutes after taking off from JFK*, a ball of fire, shredding parts—into the Atlantic Ocean, just a couple miles off the southern shore of Long Island. During the next 48 hours numerous eye-witnesses volunteered their observations to inquiring news outlets, including four Long Island high school teachers who were playing cards on their porch. They as well as all the others stated they had—without any doubt, seen a "flare" streaking upward towards the airliner, just before the fire ball. Not only that, contributing to the "it was shot down" theory, a marina manager on the south side of Long Island, relayed an interesting story: The day before the flight two Arabic guys had paid cash to rent an 18 ft. boat for the next day. When this manager returned to the marina the day after the TWA plane went down, the rented boat was there, returned—without the two guys having bothered to pick up their $500 deposit! *A theory was that it was from this boat that a shoulder-held SAM missile was fired.*

Further corroborating this "shot-down" theory is that just moments before the incident an El Al (Israeli) airliner was number one for takeoff, but at the last minute asked the TWA plane behind them *to take their place*. The theory holds that the observer at the airport had radioed the guys in the boat, telling them that the next plane to takeoff was going to be the Israeli airliner, not being aware of the last minute switch. *The guys in the boat thought the American plane was the Israeli plane.*

The National Transportation Safety Board's public statement was that a faulty relay in a half-empty center fuel tank had sparked, causing an aircraft-destroying inflight explosion. Not a single pilot group and especially Boeing 747 captains accepted this as the actual cause! If it was, they said that TWA would have either grounded all the planes to replace the faulty relay, or since it's easier and cheaper—published a change to the flight manual instructing pilots to deactivate this circuit during and after takeoff. Neither action occurred!

More about the Crash — Bob and Don

Hopefully you remember the Part Two stories about Marine squadron 331 on the Forrestal, and from Chapter 6 of this part, those two young lieutenants—Bob Harmon and Don Goft. (In the photo, Bob is sitting and Don is standing.) I may have never known two young men of such fairness, honesty and integrity, and they were about the sharpest looking pair of bachelors you could picture. Not only that, their flight skills belied their ages; they truly worshipped the art, apparently born to fly.

They'd been together since junior high school in South Hampton; now—one almost never being seen without the other. As I mentioned earlier, after the carrier cruise both these guys received orders to non-flying positions (which is not uncommon) and sadly for the Marine Corps, decided to leave the military and join the airlines. They both went to TWA (the then third-largest airline in the world). They were based in San Francisco, Bob flying the Lockheed 1011 Tri-Star, and Don flying the Boeing 747. Initially (1967) while in San Francisco, they bought condemned homes in the "Hippy"-invaded Haight-Ashbury district,

renovated them, and flipped them for good profits. No grass grew under their feet. And their flying activities were not limited to carrying two hundred passengers at 41,000 feet from coast to coast; together they bought an aerobatic, staggered wing, bi-plane (the Christian Eagle), which because of their love of flying and skill level, they took turns flying at various air shows.

Don Goft

Don's nickname was "The Genie," because while he sometimes appeared to be a stumbling, accident-prone individual on terra firma—knocking over coffee cups or stepping back into chairs, when he got into the cockpit his plane appeared to be "painted in the sky." During our Mediterranean cruise the US Navy was assigned to show our war capabilities to the head of NATO and scheduled him a visit aboard the USS Forrestal. We were going to impress him by demonstrating the precision of our aircraft's air-to-ground weaponry. The ship would tow a target (a 30 ft. by 30 ft. sled) a quarter mile behind itself, and then have the best pilot we had roll in on it and fire the new Zuni rockets at it. Most of us were not too confident

about this demonstration, *since no pilot had yet hit the sled!* After two days of competition, among the two Navy squadrons and our squadron, Don Goft emerged as the one most likely to come the closest. On the day of the exhibition, the head of NATO saw "Oh, just one of our pilots" completely demolish the sled by *scoring a direct hit on each of his four runs!*

Minus One

Don was happily married to a Finnish lady, and they had reservations to Helsinki on FinnAir the day of the controversial TWA accident. 30 minutes before takeoff the FinnAir plane sprung a left wing fuel leak, and *the passengers were bumped to TWA 800.* Bob gave a moving, heartfelt eulogy at Don's funeral, saying, "He wasn't the cream in my coffee, he was the rum in my coke." Don's son Eric *gave Don's Marine Corps Cadet brass belt buckle to his dad's best and life-long friend—Bob.*

Bob Harmon

In Part Two I wrote how when I stumbled on board the carrier (a day late) after a questionable Roman adventure, Bob met me at the top of the boarding ladder with a sign that read, *Benvenuto a bordo Signore Fortunato.* (A reference in Italian to the then-popular TV series, *Mr. Lucky.*) In Chapter Six of this part I wrote how while with Learjet in Wichita, I had occasion to fly to San Francisco and visit with Bob and his wife. During that visit I asked him how he and Giorgi met. It is a tale I've never forgotten, and worth another short recount:

After piloting a flight to New York City and having a late night snack at a small bistro, *he concluded his "bachelor days" were over.* He was smitten—sure he had met "the one"! But in the two minutes they spoke he didn't get her phone number; only remembering she lived in White Plains and her last name started with a "B." He finagled every flight he could back to JFK, but after many visits to the same bistro, never saw her again. *But something!* Not able to recollect how it came up, he remembered she had said the people across the street from her were named O'Reilly and had seven kids. With a page ripped from the Westchester County phone book, he was able to—on his fifth call, find the right O'Reillys—*the ones with seven kids.* Surprisingly they gave him the name and number of the prominent Italian family across the street—the Biancinis. He called it and got the baby-sitter. She told Bob that Giorgi and her parents were out for the evening—*attending Giorgi's engagement celebration* at the country club; an event her parents had organized for Giorgi and the man they had chosen as her husband.

After a harrowing drive and a little after 11 pm Bob arrived. In desperation he hurried inside towards the sound of dance music. Arriving on a slightly raised terrace, he found himself looking at the engagement celebration. The darkened dance floor was empty minus one couple centered under the mirrored globe and swaying to a romantic ballad. His heart sank—*it was Giorgi and her fiancé!* The broadly smiling crowd encircling them must have been the approving friends and family members. *She spied him!* And no way she could miss the look in his eyes. She stopped dancing, stepped back, caught her breath, faltered and stood frozen for a half minute. She looked at her fiancé, looked to the crowd—to her undoubtedly startled mother and father, back at Bob, *then lifted the hem of her gown and ran to Bob, who grasped her, spun around and hurried out to the car.*

When Bob turned sixty—the age when airline pilots were no longer allowed to fly (the age recently being raised to 65 after an elderly Captain Sully made the successful water landing in the Hudson River). Bob—still feeling full of energy and able to make a contribution, was contemplating not retiring; just transferring to a non-flying administrative position with TWA—maybe as an operations manager or crew scheduler. That was until another recently retired pilot said to him: "*Yeah Bob, I'm sure you could stay on, but how many summers do you have left?*' Pondering this thought, he retired. And in celebration of this event; knowing he was an avid collector of old locomotive memorabilia, and a lover of trains in general, his wife Giorgi secretly got them reservations on that popular train trip along the Canadian border, from Chicago to Vancouver. And not only that, but also secretly scheduled about twenty of his best friends (me included of course) to meet them at selected overnights along the route! I did so on one stop—wearing a rubber Bill Clinton mask that I didn't pull off until (uninvited and surely to their wonderment) I had approached their table and sat down. You should have seen the expression on Bob's face!

Six months after he gave the eulogy for Don, Bob was scheduled to perform in a local airshow in his now solely-owned Christian Eagle; doing those loops and other acrobatic maneuvers. Coincidentally on that weekend another Forrestal squadron-mate of Bob and I—Mike Barrow, was visiting Bob. Mike was now a captain for the Taiwan national carrier EVA. He had a two-day stop in San Fran and decided to visit Bob, and Bob convinced him to ride with him in the Eagle for the airshow. Mike now being a 747 captain had long ago decided "little" planes were not safe, so it took a lot of convincing before he agreed. The show was going to be held at a nearby state park, over the central attraction which was a large lake. Of course Bob's wife Giorgi attended, and for the best "seats" to view the show, spread her blanket on one grassy bank of the lake. After a few other aircraft demonstrations Bob's Eagle came into sight; the first maneuver was the loop, where the pilot pulls the nose up until it is pointed full skyward, and then continues pulling until the nose passes through the rear horizon, the nose continuing in its downward arc until it is pointed straight down, and then at the last moment the pilot pulls the nose up, leveling the plane and avoiding impacting the ground (or water). The first part of the maneuver went perfect, and almost all of the second half, *but Bob did not level at the bottom.* The plane continued straight downward, impacting the water at over a hundred miles an hour! *There was no doubt both occupants were killed.*

When Bob's wife called to give me the tragic news, she also mentioned something that may well have contributed to her husband's accident: she said that the morning of the airshow Bob complained of being light-headed when he stood up, declined breakfast and said he may be coming down with a head cold. The guy who shared a hangar with Bob said that before the airshow Bob had asked him to help him pull out his Eagle (a job eas-

ily and always done by one man). Stan told her that after being asked to help, he kidded Bob, "Hey Robert, didn't you have your Wheaties this morning?" Bob had responded that he thought he might just be coming down with a head cold. Stan said, "That's bad vibes dude, maybe you should skip it today." (Doing a loop involves a "G" load that can cause the oxygenated blood to be pulled from the brain—often causing even a fit pilot to black out for just a second or two.) *Giorgi later mailed me the belt buckle that Don's son had given to Bob.* Although Kathy never met either Don or Bob, she expressed heartfelt concern as she saw me numbed by the impact of losing not just two good friends, but such extraordinary individuals. A month later when it came due to replace my license plates, I chose letters dedicated to these two guys.

Chapter Twenty-Seven
BAD NEWS

The First of Many Trips to Orlando

Not a month after Iris's wedding I got a call from her husband. He said that just two weeks after they were married *Iris felt the lump*. (And only three months after an "Okay" mammary exam.) It was increasing in size by the week, if not the day. She made an appointment with a breast cancer specialist and a few days later got the bad news: "stage IV, metaplastic, triple negative;" just about the worst—most aggressive type of breast cancer a woman can have; and at just 41! Nick said she underwent a battery of tests in the hospital last week, spending three days as an in-patient; with no good news.

Living only a couple hours away, as soon as I could get some things

Iris and Nick

together, I left for Orlando, hoping to comfort her and give whatever support I could. I stayed all the following week, accompanying them to the hospital on each visit. These visits determined only one good thing: it had not yet metastasized (spread to other tissue or bone). Nick was wonderful. He began as best he could to run his business from home (importing those huge inflatable setups you see in the front yard of a kid having a birthday party). He rarely left the house; and when there—every thirty minutes

185

he walked to her room and sat down, soothing her for a goodly time. While he was bringing in some income, his attention to the business was cut in half as he was spending most of each day taking care of my daughter. So money being somewhat a problem I volunteered to take care of the costs of her health insurance.

The Schemes of Health Insurers

The monthly premium was (at least to me) much more than I would have imagined. And I'm pleased to tell you my loving wife Kathy not only didn't object to this expenditure, but insisted I do it. I soon came to a low opinion of the insurance industry. While they can't legally "drop you" as a matter of course, *they present you with every administrative and bureaucratic obstacle to increase the likelihood of you causing a similar event to occur.* Her original health insurance company wrote and claimed to be transferring her to one of their subsidiary companies, and she'd be hearing from them. She did, and it was a reef of detailed questionnaires to fill out (basically the same ones she had originally submitted), including a request to send the new company just about every doctor's report she had ever received, and do all this within fifteen days, *or not be enrolled.* Believe it or not, two months later this second company transferred her to a third company, which sent her the same batch of questionnaires to fill out, a request for all her past doctor's visits, and once again, return everything within 15 days, *or she would not be accepted for enrollment!*

Chapter Twenty-Eight
THREE SURPRISES

Remember Colonel Jay Garner, the Patriot Missile Commander?

One day strolling across the living room I happened to see now-*General* Jay Garner being interviewed. Having been so impressed with him in Saudi some years ago, I paused to watch and listen. Once again I heard the wise words of a rational, forward-thinking individual. It would turn out his insights were so highly regarded that in 2003—at the conclusion of the "Iraqi Freedom" War, President George Bush would install General Garner in Bagdad as the head of the Office for Reconstruction and Humanitarian Assistance, saddled with the daunting task of supervising the reconstruction and stabilization of Iraq. (Similar

General Jay Garner

to how the US installed General McArthur in Japan to supervise the reorganization of that country after they were defeated in WWII.) General Garner, in his position, argued with the Administration that their dictum that no member of the "Bathist" party (Saddam's party) was to be assigned to any position of authority. The general informed Washington that it was only members of the Bathist party that had held responsible positions in the past, and thus they were the only ones with experience and qualified to oversee the new Iraq. The answer was still "No." His other objection was our Administration's order that the Iraqi army be disbanded. General Garner said it would definitely not be a good idea to stop paying 100,000 men with guns. He was again overridden, but as time would tell, he was 100% correct on both counts.

I was so impressed with his current comments that I decided to check him out on Google. I did and found out he was living in Windermere, Florida—about 60 miles away. On a whim to maybe give him a call I went to "White Pages" and surprisingly, found his phone number. I called to tell him how much I respected what he had said, but only got his recorded greeting. I left a message that I had seen him on TV, expressed how impressed I was by his ideas, and gave my name and number. I was not surprised when I did not receive a call back. However, three weeks later I did get a call from him, in which he apologized for not having done so sooner; having been on a vacation with his wife. We spoke for several minutes and then he said, "What's your last name again." I told him and then spelled it out. After a several second pause, he said, "Did you ever do a tour at the Marine Corps Recruit Depot at Parris Island"? I told him that yes I had. He then said "As a teenager, way before I went to West Point and graduated as a commissioned officer in the Army and ultimately became a general, I was an enlisted man in the Marine Corps and I still have my first ID card that I got when I was a Private at Parris Island, and it's signed by you—*Capt R Yahnke.*

An Alarming, In Fact—Shocking Event

We'd been home almost a year when Kathy and I took a drive up to Charleston, South Carolina, to visit perhaps my oldest and dearest friend, Stu Carlton. You may remember him from Part Three, when in 1974 I was hired as the Director of Operations for Banner Flight in upstate New York. That's where for the first two months, no matter who explained it to me or what records I checked, I just could never figure out where the company was making a profit. In contrast to my ignorance the other managers (particularly the marketing department) were celebrating and high-fiving the coming lucrative contracts. This made me even more convinced I just had no business acumen. One month later the owner announced we were declaring bankruptcy and shutting down. My chief pilot there was Stu. He was the guy who one day I told him: "Stu, as good of friends as we are, I have to point out one habit you have: when asked a question you raise your fist to your mouth and give a couple of *Harumphs*. Anyone can see you're just stalling while trying to think of an answer."

Stu then responded to me, "Roger, as long as we're such good friends, I wonder if you're aware that frequently after you've approached someone—even our secretary, before you speak you put your left hand in your trouser pocket, pinch the elastic in your jockey shorts, pull it away from your legs, and wiggle your hips to shake your balls free."

Stu would not work for a manager he didn't respect and voted with his feet, quitting job after job, but being an extremely qualified captain was immediately hired by another Fortune 500 corporation. In so doing, in the intervening twenty years he had many residences, and I had visited him at several of them. He was finally retired. Today at his house, while out in the sun room snacking on a great plate of cold cuts, cheese, veggies and fruit, he and his wonderful wife Sally had occasion to remark about the time when I had visited them in Charlotte in the late 80's (just before I married Kathy). I told him that although I had visited him in Fredericksburg, Columbus, Richmond, and New Orleans, I hadn't visited him when he was flying for that bank in Charlotte. Upon saying this Sally and Stu exchanged glances of concern, and began filling me in on the details of their previous home there. Nothing they said brought the slightest recollection to mind and I again said "No" I had never been there. This second refusal caused them to look at each other in barely disguised disbelief. For the next few minutes they continued to brief me on the visit, and I continued to deny any recollection of it whatsoever. It was more than a bit discomforting that each of us were sure of contrary remembrances.

The Bourne Identity, or Me

I'm sure you're familiar with those Matt Damon thrillers where an unspecified agency (perhaps our CIA) had sent Jason Bourne on certain clandestine missions. And then (with pre-administered drugs or some type of hypnosis) denied him the ability to have any memory of the assignment—a sort of 'selected period' amnesia. Until this particular day I had scoffed at those plots as entirely fictional if not preposterous. *In the next hour all this would change.* We had a lovely dinner (which Sally was famous for) and after dinner, their perplexity caused them to bring up again, my visit to their home in Charlotte. It was beyond a doubt that both these people—the most honest and upstanding couple you could ever meet, and longtime dear friends of mine, would ever lie to me, or anyone, and of course had no reason to do so. Stu went on to add one shocking detail: "And Roger, you had that neat aluminum briefcase." While I certainly knew about those aluminum briefcases and always wanted one, I instead saved money by buying those cheaper naugahyde-covered types.

I GUESS I JUST WASN'T THINKING

"And I remember yours well, because it wasn't the normal silver color, it had been lacquered to a bronze-like color. Oh, and one more thing. The handle was really cool, it was braided leather." All the while Sally was shaking her head in confirmation of each new thing Stu added. I had no logical alternative but in wonderment—in fact dazed, to believe their account was true, although I had absolutely, positively, no recollection of it whatsoever.

"But Stu did I tell you what was in the briefcase?"

"Well we knew it had to be important, because you didn't leave it in the guest room, and even brought it to the table when we ate supper. After supper—and the two bottles of Bordeaux may have helped, you let us take a peek inside and it contained $150,000 cash?"

"What! $150,000? Did I say what I was going to do with it?"

"No, but I think—and Sally correct me if I'm wrong, I think it was either in December 1986 or January 1987—which was about six months after you were flying for Oliver North in Nicaragua, and I got the idea it had something to do with that."

When Kathy glanced my way I would have to describe her expression as bewildered. She didn't question it later, holding my hand in bed as we went to sleep. Me, while I always thought that conspiracy stuff about the CIA and mind-altering drugs, and the Jason Bourne stories—were purely fictitious, I was now not so sure; shaken to my roots—questioning many of my previous activities, including the lack of clarity about my not infrequent trips to DC. For the next many weeks I was doomed to spend nights awake—striving to remember, without ever succeeding.

And while I didn't think it could get worse, some months later in the Miami airport, a man ran up to me, as if I was a long lost friend, extending his hand. "Roger! Never forgot you, you conniving son of a gun!" While we were shaking hands he continued. "The Brussels airport—remember?" Maybe ten years ago, when we were picking up those two CASA 212 Aviocars for you know where." I responded as if he was familiar and in as friendly a manner as I could (but having no idea who or what his name was). Fortunately he was in a hurry to make his flight and had to run. I stood there stunned. My passport holds no entry stamp for Belgium and I remember absolutely nothing of this event. *Hopefully I won't meet another new stranger.*

On a Lighter Note

It was St. Patrick's Day—Kathy's birthday! I wanted to do something nice for her and so took her to a distinguished (and appropriately priced) restaurant in downtown Palm Beach. Entering the lounge I was amazed; it was packed! I spied a corner table with two empty chairs. It was occupied by a well-dressed, in fact elegant-appearing woman and her husband. I directed Kathy in that direction, to occupy one of the two empty chairs. I would order our drinks at the bar and join her in a couple minutes. Soon as I had the two drinks I went to the table, smiling nicely at the lady already there, acknowledging her kindness in letting us join her. She was well made-up, with chandelier earrings, and dressed very smartly in a long sleeved white silk blouse and a black sequined vest. I spoke first: "Really crowded in here isn't it."

She answered, "Fucking A!"

Chapter Twenty-Nine
A MAN TO BE REMEMBERED

Alex Weber (There's a Reason I'm Talking about Him Now)

Back in 1967 when I was with Air America, the Defense Department agreed to an arrangement with an aircraft engine manufacturer—Garrett AirResearch. The government would do the initial "test-bedding" of their newly-released TPE-331turbo-prop engine. And it would be done by Air America in Saigon *while mounted in my Pilatus Porters!* To supervise the maintenance of these new engines, the manufacturer always sends a factory "tech-rep" with the new engines. The guy they sent to us in Saigon was Alex Weber; not only an experienced engine mechanic, but probably the most agreeable and smartest man I ever met, and not just in engineering and physics (at which he excelled) but also in world affairs, economics, history and science (reading every issue of the Atlantic, the Economist, Barron's, and Scientific America). Being what most of us would describe as a nerd, he was prone to an assortment of mathematical and to most of us—*boring* dissertations. Of course few women were drawn to this conversation, so he was a yet-unmarried 50-year-old bachelor.

I Will Always be Indebted to Him

Most unusual for a tech rep, Alex asked if he could attend my monthly pilots' meetings. I said sure and he began a series of interesting and educational classes about operating his new engine (and engines in general). Using the physics law named *"the conservation of energy"* he showed us how—by continuing to compare the precise readings of certain power instruments on the instrument panel *a pilot could recognize the indications of an impending engine failure long before the event.* I'd venture to say the guidance he provided to my pilots saved his company a half dozen inflight engine failures. Not to mention what I picked up! In the years to come I would owe my enhanced reputation for implementing sound and appreciated aviation procedures, not to myself or my aviation experience, *but solely relaying what I learned from Alex!*

A Rank Injustice

I wrote in Part Three about my efforts to save his job. Bart—our Chief of Maintenance was jealous that Alex was spending most of his time—*not* in the maintenance hangar with Bart's mechanics, but instead—with my pilots. Alex's goal was to instill among the pilots the best operating techniques for the engine, which would result in fewer problems for Bart's mechanics. However, Alex's enthusiastic and vital instruction just seemed to inflame Bart all the more. Bart as a long-time Air America employee—by sheer seniority had gained a respect he may not have merited. He made a request to our head offices *that they contact Garrett AirResearch and have them recall Alex as unsatisfactory.* I was shocked that the company had forwarded Bart's complaint to Garrett. It contained gross inaccuracies; a flagrantly negative piece of correspondence meant to discredit Alex.

I told the company that if they didn't immediately make clear to Garrett that Bart's accusations were entirely false, and point out Alex's marked contribution to our efficient operation of their engine, I (without thinking too far ahead) said *I was going to quit!* Several days later I heard that at least three of my pilots told management that *if Roger quit, they were quitting.* Moreover I wrote a letter to Garrett, pointing out all Alex had done, what an honorable and dedicated man he was, and what an asset he was to their company. Alex had a sort of girlfriend, or maybe just a longtime dear lady friend—Pat. Years later she had occasion to contact me and said that Alex (being so damned smart) didn't have many friends, but no matter where he went, *he carried a copy of my letter in his wallet.* After being shot down in January of 1969, when I returned in December of that year, they assigned me to Vientiane, Laos, and I never had a chance to interface with Alex again.

Alex and My Son the Entrepreneur

In 1995 my son Mark, while working for TRW Electronics in Los Angeles, invented a vertical jump trainer for highly competitive athletes. It enhanced a muscular capability called "Maximal Rate of Force Development" (the neuro-muscular response essential for a high jump, quick start, or numerous other required athletic moves). Mark rented a room over a gas station and began building them, and was able to sell three or four a month. However, shortly after this he came up with an avant guarde system to train thoroughbred race horses. Through wireless telemetry it applied resistance to the horses. This much grander and much larger revenue-producing potential caused him to concentrate on it and show less enthusiasm for the jump trainer production and sales. Somehow— me, semi-retired, just flying a couple times a week or visiting Iris, agreed to do what I could to keep it as a viable, current product. This entailed ordering all the raw materials and parts, doing all the assembly work, and then marketing them. Many of the arriving cast parts still needed finishing work: mostly filing, sanding, etc., so I was gainfully occupied every night while watching TV. During the day, and while building them, I was on the phone with athletic trainers, strength coaches and football coaches trying to sell them.

For the first six months I did this in my garage (having bought a drill press, a band saw, a lathe, and a couple other required tools). Later I rented a small one-room building to do the assembly work. Sales improved and to do the required marketing I was having less and less time to assemble the units. I hired Danny (the most conscientious kid I ever met) to do the assembly work. Ultimately Mark realized we could have a much better profit margin if instead of having our parts manufactured in the states, we took advantage of the "maquiladora," where just across the Mexican border into Texas, factories were allowed to hire Mexican laborers (at much lower wages). We also investigated having the product built in China, but found out that quality control in China was at the bottom of the list. (Although if you wanted pay $2,500 a week you could hire a Chinese-speaking American to supervise the production on-site.) Of course that was out.

Old Friends Make Contact Again

While contemplating these production changes I received a voice mail message from a lady who had been a secretary in Air America. The message said an old friend was trying to locate me, and left a phone number with a foreign country code (Taiwan). I called, and *it was Alex!* What a joyous reunion. We had both been trying to contact each other for twenty years, and Alex succeeded. He was married to a Chinese woman and was an engineering consultant for several manufacturers there in Taiwan. The conversation made its way around to Mark's jump trainer. I told Alex that to save production costs we were thinking of trying to do it in China. He quickly confirmed that for the most part—in China the work was done by military units in out of the field, and the following month it would be another military unit. So as we had heard: quality control was almost impossible to assure.

He said that there in Taipei, he was friends with a Chinese gentleman named Walter, who was the owner of a large Taiwanese manufacturing company—Concordia Products. Alex asked me about the parts—steel, composite, and fabric. I described the parts in detail and he gave me the approximate costs if they were made in Taiwan; *less than half the price we were presently paying!* Alex set up a time for Mark to give Walter a call. Mark did and it went pretty good. Only problem; well two problems: in comparison with Walter's other customers, our monthly order would be so small it was almost not worth the setup costs. And second, Walter was (justifiably) concerned about the financial position of Mark's company— not being in Dunn and Bradstreet and no way to check, and no certainty that he would be paid. I found out later and was honored. Alex told Walter: "I know the boy's father Walter, and you don't have to worry." We commenced all our production in Taipei, using Alex as our production supervisor—at $500 a week, for the next three years; *during which time Alex tore up every check Mark sent him!*

Chapter Thirty
WITH US ALWAYS

Good News

Iris had been battling it for almost two years—bout after bout of chemotherapy and radiation, when Nick called and said he had a nice surprise for me. Could I drive up to Orlando that Saturday afternoon? Of course I said I would; especially for some good news. The two of them plus Iris's mom were going to go out to dinner and they'd spring it on me then. (I didn't bring Kathy inasmuch as Elsa would be there, and we would of course act like the supportive parents we were, and Kathy would feel like the proverbial "fifth wheel.") After the oysters and while waiting for the grouper, they told me the good news: Yesterday Iris had been declared "NED," which stands for "no evidence of disease!" (Supposedly you're cured!) The way the medical experts conclude "no evidence of disease" is you submit to a nuclear scan, during which any cancer cells left in the body "light up." If the picture shows none of these illuminations, you're declared cancer-free. To me while this was ostensibly good news, Iris had been declared "NED" a year ago, before it reappeared with a vengeance. Of course I didn't let my doubt show and celebrated with them the best I could.

Good News Day

After her last "no evidence of disease" declaration, Iris herself told me that she didn't believe in them. She'd done a bunch of research on those nuclear response scans and told me she had discovered that in order for the cancer cells to light up, there must be a cluster of no less than 100,000 of them! *If you only have five-hundred they don't light up, so the scan shows you're free of malignant cells, which you aren't!* In spite of this we tried to exhibit unrestrained joy.

Two months later we got more news, and not good news. Another scan showed illuminations in her pelvis, her thighs, and her back. More chemo. If that wasn't bad enough, a month later a second scan—of her head, showed it in her brain. Cranial radiation.

Prescribed Medications for Terminal Conditions

She was still ambulatory but with measurable discomfort, and now an in-patient at the renowned MD Anderson Clinic, and a prized one at that. Because of her good looks they used her for TV advertisements. In return for these appearances (and I think the affection she had garnered from the entire staff) they offered us a reduction in costs. Her doctor recommended a final stage medication called Herceptin, which had been proven to extend the lives of women with metastatic (terminal) breast cancer. Even with the discount the cost was about $2,400 a month! One day visiting her she said to me. "Rog (I guess, being adopted, she called me by my first name more than "dad) I've been researching some advanced studies on Herceptin from Germany. And while it *is* true that it extends the life of a terminal patient, *the actual extension is between 5 and 6 weeks!* I don't want you to keep buying it. Please." Of course I argued. She was realistic and convinced.

Something (Very Controversial) I Just Have to Say

The last year and a half—month after month, Iris's life was non-stop, devastatingly invasive and dignity destroying procedures. Not just

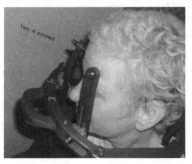

repeated bouts of chemo and radiation, but having holes drilled in her head, and composite head masks molded of her face, so as to be able to bolt her head down. I find it hard to believe that a team of experienced oncologists, having seen hundreds if not thousands of cases similar or even identical to Iris's would not have known for this whole last year, that her condition was emphatically, definitely terminal. There was no way she could be saved. Why? Why didn't they just sit down with her; state the known, certain outcome, just suggest a peaceful palliative care regime for her at home and do away with this year of fruitless torture? Could it be, that if they did, it would mean no more revenue.

Hospice

It wasn't long before the situation had deteriorated to where Iris reluctantly agreed to return to her home and consider availing herself of in-home Hospice service. During the next week, I watched her battle with that decision—to opt for hospice, and believe that decision may be the most difficult decision to make. It is the same as saying, *"There's no hope. I give up. I'm ready to go."* I don't think she would have done it were it not for the fact the Hospice nurse assured her that if any new medications came up, or even if she just changed her mind, she could dis-enroll. One thing I told her, sitting at her bedside and holding both her hands, "Sweetheart, when it comes to the big "C" you got screwed, but let me tell you, when it comes to husbands, you're in the top one tenth of one percent of married women, because you have a husband who to this day, worships the ground you walk on."

Iris with Stacy and Donna

As the outlook dimmed and she was ostensibly failing, her two step sisters, Donna and Stacy took leaves of absence from their work to be there during Iris's final days. Iris said something to Stacy that she quotes to this day: "Stacy I'm not afraid to die. I'm just not ready. So please, since I can't, the rest of your life, appreciate each day a little bit—for me."

A day or two before her passing, both of us fully aware of this fact, once again sitting at her bedside and holding her hands, I said, "No matter what sweetheart, I will never be further from you than I am now." It was about a week later at 3 in the morning when she took her last breath. In the hours after Iris had passed, Donna bathed her, did her nails, and dressed her in her favorite blue dress. I was very proud of my oldest daughter that morning, and will never forget her lovingness.

The Celebration of Her Life

Iris wanted one third of her ashes scattered in the ocean—outside the breakers at Hobe Sound; another third—as an avid Florida Gator fan, she wanted scattered on their football field; the last third was to be split among me, Elsa, and her sister Marissa; For the first third, her brothers—Mark and Kevin, and her sisters—Donna and Stacy, all four paddled out on their surfboards, with the ashes and roses. Kevin had just finished building his own kit airplane, so dropped one third of the ashes from 1,500 feet overhead the Gator gridiron. Me, Elsa, and her sister got the last third. (My share, in a cutely decorated jar is on the bookshelf behind me as I type.)

Chapter Thirty-One
BUILDING YOUR OWN HOME
(AT SIXTY-ONE YEARS OF AGE)

The New Home

Let me tell you about the neat home Kathy and I designed during our time in Riyadh. The front of the house was a garage. The back door of the garage led to the house by walking across a walled-in but unroofed, terra-cotta-paved 20 ft. by 20 ft. patio, with a fountain in the middle and benches around it. The left and right side (exterior) walls had two arched openings in them, from which we would hang a couple appropriate flowering plants. It would be our private and protected (hopefully sun-drenched) Mediterranean getaway. Just before entering the house; stretching completely across the far end of this patio were three (20-foot-wide) steps that led up onto a spacious terrace (both also terra-cotta-paved). From it one entered the house through a pair of multi-paned, glass double doors. Once inside you were in the far right side of a Great Room (the right side being the living room, the middle a dining area, and the far left side containing the kitchen, a bath, utility room, and stairwell. Above this living area was a second floor with two bedrooms, two baths, and a third "office" room. A door from the master bedroom led out onto a sun-bathing balcony. After our work designing it and imagining its ambiance, we were excited at the prospect of now seeing it come together.

The Property

Together we agreed on a new setting for our "Golden Years;" a peaceful one; an isolated one; confident we'd be content with little more than each other's loving company. To achieve this (and having had our fill of an ocean view) we were going to build our small home in an inland area;

and not in a manicured development, but preferably alone, in a wooded area with no close neighbors. Any day I wasn't flying Kathy and I would hop in the car and drive out west of I-95, where there were miles of yet unbuilt-upon wooded areas. The most promising locale was out towards Indiantown; about 30 miles west of Hobe Sound. It had lots of tall pines and wasn't swampy. In our searching we found ourselves there the most often, hoping to find two to three acres. One day about three in the afternoon (after supposedly just going to Publix) Kathy came bursting in the door, the picture of excitement. "Roger, Roger! You're not going to believe it; exactly what we've been looking for. Everything! I found it! Wait till you see it!" I was pretty sure I knew what she meant.

"Wow Hon, you sound pretty excited. If you want, we can take a ride tomorrow and you can show me."

"No sweetheart, I want you to see it now! It's not that far; right near where we were looking. You're going to love it!" To make sure I got the point she rushed over and gave me a big hug—the likes of which I had only gotten from June years ago. Oh, if you want to know why any man would love Kathy: a couple months ago June passed away in England, and my loving wife—having spoken to June on several occasions and known the length and depth of our mutual affection, encouraged me to attend the memorial service. (I will admit, after June's passing there was a "hole" in the world, just knowing she wasn't somewhere in it.)

Using a hand-drawn map from the realtor, after a couple wrong turns, and forty-five minutes later we were there. It wasn't on a main road—not by a long shot; two turns off Route 76 and then about a half-mile down a hard-packed dirt road (with only two houses and one mobile home on it). Kinda what we wanted. Viewing the property from the street I could see why Kathy was so excited. We wandered the property from corner to corner, taking our time—not anxious to leave. Kathy showed me numbers on the bottom of the note: *3.25 acres!* There was a large flat grassy area in the center (*perfect* for a home) with groves of tall pines on both sides and extending indefinitely behind it; and most of these pines were the revered Long Leaf pines—a credit on any property. It was beautiful and respectfully silent, except the whisper of the breeze through the pine needles. I was happy that Kathy had picked it, because it was exactly what I was envisioning. Returning to the car I had a scary thought: While this remote location was perfect for our desired solitude, *how long is it going to take Kathy to drive to a Walgreens, or for me to get to the nearest Home*

Depot? Overcome by the perfection of the site we put off those practical questions. The closing went smoothly except something was amiss with the old survey and as the buyer I had to pay for new one. It cost more than I expected, especially since two guys did it in about an hour. To make me feel better the head guy told me "You'll be glad you have it—you'll have occasion to use it many times." It would turn out he'd be right. About ten days later we were the proud owners!

An Idea

That night, although I'd never done any RV-ing, I mentioned it might be a neat adventure if we leased a trailer, parked it on the property and lived in it while I was building the house. That way there'd be no driving back and forth; more time to spend on the house and keep an eye on the sub-contractors. If we did that and hired reliable subs we might only be in it a few months. And guess what? *Surprise!* I didn't even have to coax her. As the wonderful wife she was, when I suggested it she jumped up and ran around the table to me.

"Oh Roger, what a great idea. It'll be so much fun. Oh, thank you for thinking of that."

I told her I was glad she thought so, but it won't be a big trailer so *she may be ready to divorce me by the time the house is done.* Hearing this she acted like she was going to punch me, then gave me another one of those hugs. We found several RV sales lots and checked their (huge) inventory. Maybe just because I'm a shiny-metal kind of guy, but after I saw one of those polished aluminum Airstreams, that's what I wanted. A week later we closed the deal on a 24 ft. long, 1974 Argosy Airstream. I couldn't tow it with my car. A truck-owning friend of mine (for just a steak dinner) towed it to the property. Finally there, the Airstream unhooked, he commented that I could be in trouble since the electric poles stopped about 500 feet short of our property. I'd actually noticed that. Not a deal breaker, but for sure it was going to cost us. Kathy's sweeter than me. I'll assign her to sweet-talk the county on extending the line and hooking it up to the Airstream.

Selling the Oceanfront Home

I put a "For Sale" sign in front of our oceanfront home. One good thing about selling an oceanfront home: you don't really need a realtor. Anyone who wants to live on the ocean in Florida just gets in their car and drives up and down A1A (the closest road to the beach), until they see an oceanfront house with a For Sale sign. I probably did more sprucing-up work than necessary—at least everybody said I did. I replaced all the sinks and faucets in the house with new ones. And in the bathroom walls, behind the toilet—that shutoff valve in the line up to the tank; well they always corrode—turn a bluish-green color; so I replaced all of them with shiny new ones. Knowing how dirty, crowded garages can make a home look old, I took every single thing out of the garage and off its walls (no shelves, no hooks—nothing) and spackled every single hole. I then painted the walls a satin aqua green and the floor a glossy tan epoxy (that you could see your face in)! I do have to admit, I did do one expensive project: I installed a driveway of those four-inch thick ceramic pavers. The house was a verdigris color, so I picked green and gray pavers, matching the colors of the house.

It sold quick, but not to the first person that looked at it—she wanted the master bedroom on the ocean side. I didn't tell her, *that's just what you think now*. (After a couple hurricanes pound the dunes and blow 50 mph rain against the windows, they would realize that's not a great place for the bedroom.) However, whether it was because I had done all the fixing up or not, we did sell it to the second person that looked at it. Only when emptying it for their occupancy did I realize how big of a storage unit we needed.

Moving Into Our New Digs

Kathy did a good job arranging for electricity. Florida Power and Light installed two poles to extend the electric to our property; something they did in one day and cost $1200! They ran the wire to the Airstream for nothing (even though it was a little more than 100 feet from the road). At first I was surprised at having adequate closet space, and really—enough pantry and kitchen cabinet space. Besides a bunch of clothes, Kathy had brought some linens, some household cleaning stuff, the packaged foods, and everything that was in the refrigerator (after which the Argosy did get looking smaller). And as you might imagine we had a TV dish installed on the roof. Our first night in Kathy did up a steak and baked potatoes with sour cream. (I washed it down with a Heineken, while Kathy did the same with a good Merlot.) After dinner, both of us with smug smiles, my impression was that we could do three months in the Airstream, no sweat. Kathy agreed, flopped down beside me and grasped my hand in both of hers. I got the message; later that night we christened our new dwelling with one of our most successful intimacies.

May 1st, Beginning Construction

If getting the proper permits were any indication of how quickly this project was going to progress, I was in big trouble; four different offices, including both county and state. And acting as the General Contractor—when you are not a certified GC, did not make things easy. Not only did I have to show the zoning board a copy of the deed, that surveyor guy was right; only one week into the project and I had needed his survey twice! Finally—we had all the permits we needed (and posted in the conspicuous places required). To celebrate that first accomplishment, that night Kathy whipped up bratwurst, potato cakes, and red beet plate (once again washed down with a cold Heineken). The first week in our Airstream we found ourselves not at all minding the restricted space; in fact, genuinely enjoying the new existence; kidding and roughhousing in our own little comfy cave. We got hooked on the *Seinfeld* re-runs, spending many a fun night laughing at Elaine and Kramer! It was early on, but it looked like three months were going to be easy—real easy.

The surveyor had staked out the corners of the property so we could plan where and on what angle the house would be located. He told me to remember that the well had to be no less than 150 feet from the sceptic tank and drain field. With that in mind, having stood at various spots on the site, getting a feel for a location (both in the morning sun and the late afternoon sun) we came up with an exact location and orientation for the house. With a 50-ft metal tape and a laser penlight, together we were bold enough to drive in the corner stakes of the chosen location. Since there would be all kinds of scrap accumulating, I contacted a dumpster supplier and got a three-month rental on their biggest one. A few days later it was on the property—a sure sign something was going to happen.

The first step would be digging the trench for the footer; the depth of which I learned, depended on the soil "bulk density." To save money, knowing the dimensions of the trench I leased a back hoe and set about it myself, doing one whole side. At the end of the day I was beat. My back hurt and I had blisters, but thought it looked pretty good. (Kathy wasn't so sure.) I gave in and hired a professional to do it. He completed it—all four sides and an indent straight as an arrow, in a day and a half (choosing to re-do some of what I had dug). His guys also built the form and poured the footer. After a week of settling and drying, the foundation guys arrived and built the concrete block foundation upon the footer. That evening—alone, Kathy and I stood in admiration of the now raised outline of our new home.

Before the slab could be poured, we had to have the plumbing and electrical contractors dig their trenches and lay their conduits. Both these contractors informed us that the free plans we got from our friend in Riyadh were not sufficiently precise to do what they had to do. This resulted in a week delay and $450 for a more precise plan. I got a good price by physically working alongside the electric and plumbing guys, mainly digging the trenches or running back and forth to get things out of their trucks. This work was completed in four or five days, and an approval given by the inspector several days later. The following week the plywood footer forms were taken away and the slab was poured, which first required a layer of gravel and a vapor barrier. That evening—the sun reflecting off the slick slab, Kathy and I again stood in front of the new construction, holding hands and looking at the floor of what would be our new retirement home. After a pleasant time surveying it, we decided to go out to dinner.

Body and Mind. The Good and the Bad

That night when we got back to our trailer, the closeness we were feeling as our new dwelling and future seemed to be coming together, I sensed that Kathy was in a happy, grateful mood, maybe even one of her (thankfully rare) *physically* loving moods. As soon as she was in bed I knew by the nearness she sought that this would be a night for one of our infrequent encounters. Thanks to the gods of love-making I was just firm enough to enter her and she appeared satisfied, no matter how unspectacular I carried out my duties. I was of course thankful it happened at all, knowing it was due, and a proper intimacy for us at this satisfying time in our project. Unfortunately it caused me to compare my performance here to the euphoria of my success with Mireille and her tearfully thankful response that first night in Dakar, and every time thereafter. But worse, it brought to mind my transgression on that last chance-visit to her in France just before we left Saudi, *and reflect with bitter remorse on the only infidelity I had or would ever have while married to Kathy.*

June 1st

After showing our plans to a couple of local contractors, they advised us that for this home, especially having an unroofed interior patio with the four side wall arches, we should go with a concrete block ground floor;

we could frame the second floor over the rear part of the house. I got some bids and we had the first floor done concrete block. I saved them hiring a third guy by delivering the blocks and buckets of mortar to them, and a handful of other tasks that saved them time. It was completed in less than a week. Once again, at sunset the day it was completed, Kathy and I stood arm in arm, full of anticipation, viewing an undeniable sign of progress.

The next step was to have the ceiling joists installed over the living area. Once they were laid I ordered the plywood sheathing (rough flooring) to go on top of them, and am proud to say I did it all myself, which stepping across the gap between the separated joists was not a safe job. The next job would be the largest task I'd yet personally undertaken: framing the second floor! I was pretty sure I could do it; having helped my father on two houses, and after reading a book on framing I got from Home Depot. I did do it—eight hours a day for a week, but it wore me out, surprisingly more than I thought it should; to the extent I gave myself a couple day's rest afterwards. I then had the roof trusses installed on the garage and the second floor. The view from the street now boldly stated, that it was definitely going to be a house!

July 1st

The next steps I did myself, but probably shouldn't have: sheathing the outside of the second floor and the two roofs. It was physically demanding, hefting 4x8 sheets of half-inch-thick plywood up onto the second floor and worse—the roof. I started with a ladder but soon realized renting and using a scaffold was the only way. It was so hot I couldn't work on the roof between noon and 3 pm, but still got the whole thing done in three weeks, and I have to admit I was real tired by the end of each day, dozed before supper, and certainly didn't make it a late TV night. Kathy was real supportive of all I was getting done, but continued to insist that me doing so much work was taking its toll. And if I wanted to admit it she may well have been right, because I was surprised that after all my years of exercising, these daily activities were taking more out of me than I anticipated—more fatigue, more muscle and joint aches than I would have expected. If I was going to do a project like this, I should have done it twenty years ago, when I was younger. And on the real hot days when I would enter the air-conditioned trailer—all sweaty and overheated, I'd get the chills. Kathy (as the good wife she was) joked that it was good my semi-annual physical was coming up soon. During the next couple weeks

I installed all the doors and the windows; placing the windows into the "rough openings, which although built exactly to specs—surprisingly to me, still left ¾ of an inch of space on each side of the window frame. (I was told this was normal.)

When the day of my doctor's appointment came, to make Kathy happy I promised her I'd tell him about my fatigued state. Dr. "Jay" (a shortened version of a long Indian name) had been my primary care physician for years before we went to Saudi—so he knew I was a health nut; jogging, lifting weights, and playing tennis any chance I got. We even worked out at the same local gym. He gave me a thorough physical and said I was in "ship shape." I said maybe so, but I sure feel rundown and have even lost a few pounds. He responded "Well no shit Rog, look what you're doing at your age and in the middle of the summer! Your lungs are clear and your heart sounds like you're going to live to be a hundred. Let's see—you did lose six pounds, but what do you expect, sweating all day. Just take it easier from here on out, and drink more water!" When I told him how much water I *wasn't* drinking, he said (after an expletive): "All the complaints you've been voicing, are the classic—textbook symptoms of dehydration! I'd be willing to bet you've been chronically dehydrated for three straight months."

Kathy met me pulling onto the property, with a look that said *well what did he say?* Of course I was pleased to relate his evaluation; especially about the water, which come to think of it, I wasn't drinking *near* enough of—in fact, hardly any during the day. Kathy was pleased to hear the doctor had given me a clean bill of health. Having missed most the day I still had time to get on the phone and confirm a "go ahead" with the roofers. They were there in two days, put down the underlayment (a neat kind of stretchy rubber sheeting with adhesive on the underside), and laid the red barrel tile that Kathy had picked out. I was able to save a fair amount of money making two significant contributions to the roofers: First—for some reason two pallets of tiles had not been craned up onto the roof. So, I had to carry about a hundred armfuls over to the base of the ladder. Second, having mastered the masonry saw, they'd mark a tile, throw it down to me, and I'd cut it and throw it back up. So while it wasn't exactly a back-breaking job, I *was* out there all day every day. The house was now completely "dried in." Late in the day, when the guys had left the property, Kathy and I did our ritual walk out to the street and viewed our new home, barely holding the tears back. Looking at me standing there—exhausted, Kathy remarked that we probably should have just contracted to have the house built, and stayed in the oceanfront home while some general contractor did the whole thing. I had to admit she was probably right. I shouldn't have tackled this home-building thing alone—especially at my now 62 years of age. I never felt this exhausted in all my life! Thank God we were this far along and could truthfully say: *Yeah, but just look—we're almost done!*

Next the plumbing and electrical contractors did their interior roughing in. I watched it being done, but did not offer myself as a "helper" this time. Kathy wanted lap-strack wood siding on the second floor, and as visible as any mistakes would be on those surfaces, I passed on that job and hired a siding company to do it. They covered it in a weather guard membrane, installed the exterior window casements and put on the boards themselves; and a good thing too because I would have been on a ladder all day or moving a scaffold ten times a day. Afterwards though, I did do all the priming and painting, which saved a couple hundred bucks (and by doing the west side in the morning and the east side in the afternoon, I could stay in the shade).

August 1ˢᵗ

I was anxious to start the interior work and almost felt guilty agreeing when Kathy came up with an idea: "Let's take a break and go to that old motel we went to just south of Key Largo. That'll really be different, and we haven't taken a long drive together since we've been back."

"Wow, that's going to be over three hours each way, and we don't have any reservations."

"No matter. If we can't get in there we'll get another one." *If that's what she wanted, that's what we were going to do.* The drive went smoothly and we joked the whole time. And Popp's Motel had an open kitchenette unit right on the beach. We spent each day sitting on the beach or lying in a shaded hammock. I had suspected I needed this rest, but surprisingly when the time came to leave I still felt tired. At my age to have undertaken this home-building project was something it was going to take me some time to bounce back from. But it was a worthwhile project and our living in the trailer did turn out to be the fun thing we hoped for.

The drive back was as much fun as the one down—maybe even more, as we both were looking forward to seeing our new home again. Our excitement rose as we turned onto the dirt road leading to our house, and we were not disappointed when it came into view. I'm not sure what

Kathy was thinking as we gazed at the house, but I was remembering the drywall would be delivered tomorrow, and the day after that, the drywall guy (I found through a clerk at Home Depot) would arrive and we'd start that job. Kathy used her mother's recipe to make a pierogi and golumpki dinner that was out of this world. We went to bed in a loving mood, she laid her head on my chest and held my hand till we fell asleep. What could be better? I was even able to almost forget Mireille. *How lucky I was.*

The Last Interior Work

The next day the drywall did arrive, and the day after that the drywall guy. Working side by side with him, I found out this is a much harder job than you might imagine. First it would help to be seven-feet-tall, and carrying the sheets—have forty-inch-long arms. And that "mudding" and "taping" of the joints is an art. I thought I was doing it just like Brian, but you could see where my sheets joined, much easier than his. (In fact you couldn't even see his.) We spent a week and a half on this part of the job (talk about aching shoulders). But it was a big step completed, and as soon as it was, Kathy spent most the next day walking through all the rooms holding up the color chips she'd picked up at Home Depot. Before tackling the painting we hired a guy to skip trowel all the ceilings—a finish sometimes referred to as a "Mediterranean" finish (but leaves a helluva mess on the floor)! Once I'd done the cleanup, Kathy and I spent the next two weeks painting. I didn't complain to Kathy, but I was glad the job was almost done, because I knew I was beat. It'd been something almost all day every day for more than three months, and it had definitely weakened me.

I had several times thought I had picked up some bug, but while I was debating it, Kathy did get it. The day we were going to Lowes to tell them we were ready to have the kitchen and bathroom cabinetry delivered, Kathy woke up with a slight fever and some chills. (We had chosen Lowes because they gave us a ten percent discount just for ordering a Lowes credit card and paying for it with that card!) I gave her the day off and took it off myself. She was only down for two days, and then ready to get with it and do what she could to help me finish the home. Once the cabinetry was in I tackled all the trim work, the inside door and window casings, and what must have been ten miles of baseboards. I did this while the plumber and the electrician did the final installations of their hardware and fixtures.

I knew we'd carpet the bedrooms upstairs, and guess I must have been thinking we'd carpet the ground floor as well. Wrong. Stupid me. This was a Spanish-style house and Kathy (being smarter than me) knew wood flooring was a must on the whole first floor. After our many trips checking out the variety of widths, colors, grains, etc., we ordered it from Lumber Liquidator. The salesman convinced Kathy that it would look every bit as good and have many advantages, if we used a laminate. You couldn't visually tell it wasn't real wood and it sounded the same when you walked on it. We chose *Cinnabar Oak*. I decided to lay the flooring myself—the whole ground floor, including the kitchen (before realizing what this would mean to my lower back and knees). Thank God I'd bought a table saw earlier on in the project, because I was using it every two minutes on this job. I was on my hands and knees the whole day, and—listen to this: being the cheap screw I was I didn't buy those $19 padded plastic knee guards. I just figured I could use a small pillow to kneel on. Of course the damned pillow never seemed to be in arm's reach and both my knee caps paid the price! And geez—just my luck, in the middle of doing this up again down again flooring job I caught a real ugly summer cold. Thank God I'm almost finished.

The plan worked out perfect; a couple days after I finished the flooring—just about the last piece of interior work, we had all our stuff in storage delivered. The next day, while we tried to arrange the furniture, the dumpster people picked up the dumpster. Once it was off the property Kathy and I looked at each other and smiled; for some reason, both feeling this event marked the "official end" to a long and tiring project. It was at last over. We were ready to move in! No more waking up at six, putting on steel-toed boots, strapping on a tool belt and walking around half the day carrying a skill saw, a 4x8 sheet of plywood, a half dozen 2x6's, or an eighty-pound bag of mortar! And I was glad the project was done, since I still had that mean summer cold hanging on. The night I finally threw it, I woke up drenched at 2 in the morning. No two ways about it, I should never have tackled this job alone! Thank God it was finished and the both of us could take a much-needed rest, and soak in the beauty of our labors.

Chapter Thirty-Two
FINISHED

Nirvana, at Last

Life in our new home could not have been better; it was everything we'd imagined and more. The newest and strangest thing to me, was—for the first time in my life "doing nothing" was just fine. We had built the home with the kitchen facing due east, so each breakfast the room was filled with the beautiful morning sun filtering through the backyard pine boughs. It was a time in the day that excluded any thoughts other than the most cheerful and optimistic. I went from a one-cup coffee guy to a two-cupper; and could sit there with Kathy till ten. We'd take turns making breakfast. I had a healthy (and delicious) pancake recipe; one that included whole wheat flour, wheat germ, and oatmeal—and always eaten with "Pure Vermont" maple syrup.

I tried going back to the gym, but was so embarrassed at my lack of endurance and the light weights I had to use at this age, I gave it up for a daily two mile walk, which—on trails out in this wooded area, may have been even better for my temperament. (Plus the closest gym was a thirty minute drive.) Kathy joined a Zumba class and loved it. Man! I didn't think such an existence was even possible. And we had not yet exhausted the *Seinfeld* re-runs! For the first time in my life, no worries about money and completely in love with my wife. A wife incidentally, who said now that everything was done, she'd feel better if I got another clean bill of health, even though I had gotten over the flu, and at least imagined I was gaining strength. But to make her happy I said "*Sure,*" and a couple days later called for an appointment.

Kathy may have been right; the project may have taken a toll on me,

I GUESS I JUST WASN'T THINKING

because shortly after sitting down with Dr. Jay he commented that I didn't look as sturdy as he remembered me from the last visit, about which I had to agree. He asked me a series of what I thought were good questions; about my recent activities, diet, sleep pattern, how I was feeling at differing times during the day, and even if I had any personal problems that might be weighing me down. (Fact was: in my whole life I'd never had less problems!) After referring to the form the nurse completed on my arrival, he said I was running a low grade temperature right now; that he would give me a thorough physical and order a full blood workup. About a week later his office phoned and said I needed to come in for another blood test. I did have the flu—and a weird strain of it evidently. The second test Dr. Jay told me was called a nucleic acid test, first used in Germany about six months ago, and would surely nail down what I had.

It was two weeks before they got the results and when they did— something a little worrisome; *they called me to come right in.* When I saw Dr. Jay, his face was drawn. "Rog, not sure how to tell you this, but the fact is, you've got HIV, and worse—stage 3! That's full blown AIDS. You've either contracted this from your wife, or if—and no dispersions, if it was you who had it, unfortunately, you've certainly given it to her by now." Seated, slumped, and stunned, his answer to my next question was: "Well if you'd come in a few months ago, who knows. A company called Gilead Science came out with a new cocktail for Stage 1 HIV. But now, with the pathogen density you have... to answer your question: One year, maybe two."

Mireille. Had to be. My sole infidelity since I'd met Kathy.

CPSIA information can be obtained
at www.ICGtesting.com
Printed in the USA
LVHW081414021121
702248LV00021B/124